WHERE THE LOCALS GO

Celebrating Songkran in Chiangmai, Thailand

WHERE THE
LOCALS GO

MORE THAN 300 PLACES AROUND THE WORLD TO
EAT, PLAY, SHOP, CELEBRATE, AND RELAX

COMPILED BY THE NATIONAL GEOGRAPHIC TRAVELER TEAM

NATIONAL GEOGRAPHIC

WASHINGTON, D.C.

Raising a glass
outside a bar
in Venice

CONTENTS

Dancing in
the streets at
Seville's Feria
de Abril

INTRODUCTION

Throughout more than a half century of traveling I count as one of my great pleasures the happy accident. And when I set out to discover somewhere new I try to increase the likelihood of having one. Because predictability is the bane of truly enriching travel, I try to avoid attractions and services designed to engage tourists.

I want what the locals have.

That doesn't mean I avoid the icons—the Louvre, the Statue of Liberty, the Sydney Opera House. Those sorts of wonders are part of the main course. But the condiments are all the other discoveries a place has to offer.

So I gravitate to where the locals go. Places and attractions that came about organically, not in response to the siren call of tourism. The restaurant locals *know* has clam chowder beyond compare and is true to the roots of its seaside community. Open-air markets that were established to meet the needs of its nearby inhabitants. An event that celebrates the spirit and culture of its environment.

These are the stumbled-upon little epiphanies that become the stuff of traveler's tales. I collect these places like charms on a bracelet.

The London ale house that exhibits its true pubness in a city that has virtually lost such cultural legacies to wine bars and franchise operations. The pocket park in New York's East Village that offers a front-row people-watcher's perch on the day-glow eccentricity that is the city's specialty. The tidy little market in Quito, Ecuador, that clearly caters to nearby dwellers who bring their kids to the adjacent playground—and where I bought a clay iguana for three dollars (a fraction of what it would command at a more touristy venue). The same day—based on the recommendation of, yes, a local—our family of four dined at a seafood restaurant in an old monastery where there were only four tables, and our sublimely Ecuadorian meal came to $28.

This book is a sparkling, surprising collection of off-the-beaten-track finds, ah-hahs, neighborhood secrets, and the pleasures of those who live in a place 24/7. So before you ask the concierge where to go or what to do, dive in and enjoy *Where the Locals Go.*

Keith Bellows
Editor in Chief,
National Geographic Travel Media

Vancouver's lights from the nearby ski slopes

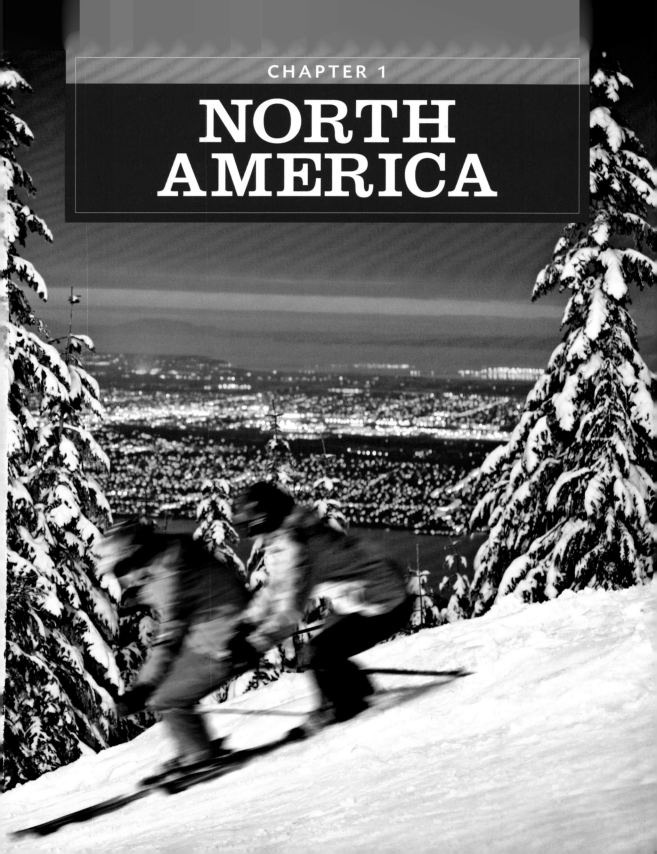

CHAPTER 1

NORTH AMERICA

HONOLULU, HAWAII
HULA SHAKEDOWN

Adorned with leis—floral garlands usually made of fragrant plumeria—hula dancers aged from 14 to 60 and above vie for supremacy in the King Kamehameha Hula Competition, part of the weeklong festivities to celebrate the founder of Hawaii's birthday.

Says *kumuhula* (hula teacher) Lilinoe Lindsey, "It's about more than competition. It's about knowing our culture and continuing the traditions." Just being there is exciting. Everything from the sight and smell—all the flowers are fresh, nothing fake—to the language, which must be spoken clearly and correctly, comes together on stage.

IN THE KNOW: Dancers perform the two basic styles of hula. The more traditional *kahiko* is performed to chants (*oli*); *aunana,* which is accompanied by song (*mele*), takes a more fluid, contemporary form. Because Hawaii had no written language, "Our stories, journeys, and history are marked in the chant and mele used in hula," says B. J. Allen, executive director of the State Council on Hawaiian Heritage. "Hula contributes to Hawaii's cultural heritage in preserving those stories and takes us back to times of simplicity, hardship, and joy." Participants come from other islands and even Japan. Lindsey continues, "Hula is our way of spreading *aloha* around the world."

WHERE TO GO: The two-day competition is held in the Neal Blaisdell Center around June 20, a few days after Kamehameha Day (June 11), commemorating King Kamehameha, unifier of the Hawaiian Islands in 1810.

JOINING IN: For Lindsey, "A *halau* (hula school) is family, so if you know a performer, you go along and cheer for them." Pick your favorite halau and get shouting.

■ *Essentials:* Neal Blaisdell Center (777 Ward Ave., tel 808/768-5400 or 808/536-6540, hulacomp.webstarts.com)

MORE: Hula Costumes

Aloha Fabrics: This store on Sand Island access road sells Hawaiian print fabrics—most costumes are painstakingly made by hand—as well as ready-made palaka skirts, pantaloons, puff-sleeved tops, grass skirts, rattles, and leis. alohafabrics.com

Hula Supply Center: As well as hula costumes and Aloha shirts, this store on South King Street sells music, books, and ukeleles. hulasupplycenter.com

King Kamehameha is celebrated with hula demonstrations and competitions.

THIRD STREET FASHION

According to L.A. stylist Bridgette Bugay, there is a relaxed playfulness to Angelenos' style. "It ranges from simple elegance in a linen shift on the beaches of Santa Monica to full-blown glamour in a gorgeous gown on Hollywood's red carpets."

Whether for hipster style or megawatt movie-star glamour, some of the most exclusive stores representing the L.A.-look exist on one little stretch of road—the section of Third Street between South Edinburgh Avenue and La Cienega Boulevard.

WHERE TO SHOP: Moving east from Edinburgh to La Cienega, the first store of note is Trina Turk. A longtime resident of Silver Lake in Los Angeles, Trina's California surfer and sun-inspired bright patterns are now world famous. A few blocks down on your left, enter Satine. Elegant but edgy, this store prides itself on carrying hard-to-find items—Isabel Marant Runway, exclusive Vanessa Bruno dresses, celeb-favored A.L.C., vintage Chanel bags, and Dior jewelry. For men, a similar fashion-haven exists a few blocks farther east, on the left side of the street: Douglas Fir. And don't miss their affiliated shoe store located directly opposite, where you can find L.A.-only designers and some of the most beautifully crafted men's shoes you will ever see.

LOCAL KNOWLEDGE: Stop in bright and early, on the way to Third Street, at one of the U.S.A.'s few branches of the sassy Brit chain Topshop, located just a few minutes away in The Grove shopping zone.

MORE: L.A. Style

SoBev: Trendy locals head here instead of Rodeo Drive. S. Beverly Dr., Beverly Hills

Santee Alley: In L.A.'s Fashion District, Santee Alley buzzes with shoppers looking for bargain clothing, shoes, perfume, and toys. Between Santee St. and Maple Ave., from Olympic Blvd. to 12th St.

Westfield Santa Anita: This upscale mall caters to all retail needs but especially luxury. 400 S. Baldwin Ave., Arcadia, westfield.com/santaanita

WHERE TO EAT: If you're feeling glamorous and in the mood for a little snack, Fonuts is the perfect choice. These gluten-free, diet-friendly "fake-donuts" taste better than the real thing. The banana chocolate chip and maple bacon flavors are particularly good. With stunning clothes and diet donuts, it's no wonder celebrities have such an easy time looking red-carpet ready.

■ *Essentials:* Trina Turk (8008 W. 3rd St., tel 323/651-1382); Satine (8134 W. 3rd St., tel 323/655-2142, satineboutique.com); Douglas Fir (8311 W. 3rd St., tel 323/651-5445); Fonuts (104 W. 3rd St., tel 323/592-3075, fonuts.com); Topshop (189 The Grove Dr., tel 323/900-8080, thegrovela.com)

"Los Angeles is ground zero for boho chic—the ultimate expression of California cool." —BRIDGETTE BUGAY, STYLIST WITH CAMPDEN HILL IMPORTS

Browsing Third Street—home to recherché labels and boho chic. Opposite: A bird's-eye view down Third Street

Enjoy a mass ride through San Francisco.

SAN FRANCISCO, CALIFORNIA
CYCLING WITH CRITICAL MASS

On the last Friday of each month, local cyclists converge for Critical Mass, a good-natured, if sometimes noisy, two-wheeled takeover of the city's streets. For Critical Masser Eric Anderson, the event is a true epiphany: "This movement has given me my career, many lifelong friends, my health, my sanity, hope, joy, and damn near my life."

WHERE TO GO: There are no leaders of Critical Mass—the movement represents participatory democracy in its purest form. Just show up (usually at Justin Herman Plaza at the foot of Market Street) and ride.

JOINING IN: You'll need a sturdy, reliable bike; a helmet (although these aren't required by California law); and appropriate clothing. Dress for the weather: Summers can be downright chilly in San Francisco, while September and October are usually the warmest months.

LOCAL KNOWLEDGE: Critical Massers may loathe authority, but they do acknowledge a few unwritten rules. Stay close to the general body of cyclists. Obey all traffic lights and road signs. Some motorists are dismayed by the event and take umbrage when faced with large numbers

MORE: Critical Mass Cities

Critical Mass, Berlin, Germany: Bike-riding Berliners reclaim the streets on the last Friday of each month. The routes are spontaneous to avoid the need to inform the police in advance. cmberlin.blogsport.de

Velorution, Paris, France: Paris's *masse critique* takes place on Saturday afternoons, avoiding the rush-hour gridlock some cyclists delight in provoking. Place de la Bastille, first Sat. of the month, 2 p.m. velorution.org

of cyclists; don't confront them, and don't respond to provocation. What can you expect from a Critical Mass ride? At the very least, an invigorating tour of San Francisco unimpeded by all that pesky traffic.

■ *Essentials:* Last Fri. of the month, late afternoon. Routes and other details vary. sfcriticalmass.org

TEA AND RELAXATION

Providing a respite from San Francisco's frenetic pace, the Japanese Tea Garden in Golden Gate Park is where locals go to unwind, meditate, and celebrate special occasions. Says Bay Area publisher of yoga books, Linda Cogozzo, "I have loved coming here since I was a child. Then the pagoda and arching drum bridge provided a place of wonder. Now the cherry trees and Japanese maples give this city dweller a place of tranquillity." Paths curve past reflecting pools teeming with colorful koi to the historic Tea House and centuries-old bronze statue of the Buddha. Turn a corner to discover the peaceful Zen Garden, and another to find the Sunken Garden. Adorned with stone lanterns, it is located where the home of Makoto Hagiwara, the creator of this 5-acre (2 ha) garden, once stood.

WHEN TO GO: Cherry trees put on a show in March and April, while the maples are most colorful in the fall.

TAKING A BREAK: Relax at the Tea House, where you can sample *sencha* or *genmaicha* green tea with a plate

MORE: Garden Tea

Samovar Tea Lounge: Experiment with oolongs, whites, blossoming, and other specialty teas at this chilled modern tea house while drinking in the views of the Yerba Buena Gardens in which it sits. 730 Howard St., San Francisco, tel 415/227-9400, samovarlife.com

of *kuzumochi* (sweet rice cakes) or a fortune cookie. Legend has it that Makoto Hagiwara's baker sweetened the traditional Japanese cookie recipe to appeal to American tastes, and the cookies spread throughout the world.

■ *Essentials:* Tea House (75 Hagiwara Tea Gdn. Dr., tel 415/752-4227, japaneseteagardensf.com)

Japanese garden designers strive after balance and human scale.

DIGGING DEEPER

Make a reservation at the Tea House to attend *chanoyu*, the formal tea ceremony. Once reserved for nobility, it celebrates the preparation, serving, and drinking of *matcha* (powdered green tea).

OFF-STRIP POKER

Out-of-towners stick to the flamboyant Strip, but Vegas residents with a penchant for betting hang out at the smaller, less flashy, local casinos. The old gambling houses along downtown's Fremont Street, such as the Golden Nugget and Pioneer Club, have had their day and today's local faves are scattered all around town.

WHERE TO GO: Tucked away at the bottom end of the Strip, Southpoint Casino combines gambling and dining with an equestrian center and an arena for special events, from gun shows to craft expos. Meanwhile, old-timers swear by Sam's Town on Boulder Highway, opened in the late 1970s to attract Vegas residents who spurned the Strip. Sam's offers a popular race and sports book, penny slots, and locally dominated blackjack tournaments.

FARTHER AFIELD: At Red Rock Casino on the west side of town, you can join local insomniacs for "moonlight poker" (2–6 a.m.) or enjoy a meal at the casino's Feast Buffet (voted best in Vegas by readers of the city's daily newspaper). Red Rock also has a luxury spa, 16-screen cinema complex, bowling alley, and childcare. If you can tear yourself away from these indoor attractions, you're near the incredible desert scenery of Red Rock Canyon National Conservation Area, where you might spot a wild burro or two.

SPECIAL ATTRACTIONS: These local casinos offer low-stakes gaming, busy bingo rooms, and special promotions, such as the "Young at Heart" program at Sam's Town for over-50 gamblers. Some locals even risk cashing their paychecks at the casino to have a chance at winning free drinks or other prizes (the "paycheck bonanza").

■ *Essentials:* Southpoint Casino (9777 Las Vegas Blvd. S., tel 702/796-7111, southpointcasino.com); Sam's Town (5111 Boulder Hwy., tel 702/456-7777, samstownlv.com); Red Rock Casino Resort Spa (11011 West Charleston Blvd., tel 702/797-7777, redrock.sclv.com), Red Rock Canyon National Conservation Area (Scenic Loop Dr., tel 702/515-5350, blm.gov)

"Locals have all their gaming needs met in the suburbs."
—BILL "AINTNOLIMIT" HUBBARD, POKER COACH

Punters play blackjack at the Red Rock Casino.

PORTLAND, OREGON
CRAFT BREWPUBS

Microbreweries are the antidote to every anemic, unsatisfying generic beer you've ever tasted. With a focus on quality and flavor, craft beer makers keep brewing traditions alive while constantly innovating and experimenting in their quest for the perfect taste.

Portland, Oregon, is the epicenter of an American craft beer revolution, which began to take off in the 1980s. It has more than 50 microbreweries, many of them started by families or groups of friends who shared a love of beer, a passion for brewing, and a desire to prove that beer, when made right, can be just as sophisticated on the palate as wine. "Portland has more breweries than any other city in the world because of our great water, close access to ingredients, and consumers who really support local products," says Alan Sprints, brewmaster of the town's Hair of the Dog Brewing Company.

WHAT TO EXPECT: Craft beers are usually subtle and complex. These handcrafted brews tend to have a richer flavor and higher alcohol content than their mass-market counterparts They are perfect for pairing with food and nibbles, or just drinking on their own. Most brewpubs pour sample-size servings so you can try a wide range of beers, which sometimes number in the hundreds.

LOCAL FAVORITES: The BridgePort Brewery and Brewpub based in Portland's Pearl District crafts a wide range of beers and sells them directly to the public to enjoy on site. Start with the rich, malty Blue Heron pale ale before moving on to a seasonal beer such as Ebenezer Ale, or one of their India Pale Ales, such as Hop Czar, which have a hoppier, more bitter flavor. Upright Brewing takes inspiration from classic European beers. Try their Engelberg Pilsener: It's the equal of anything served at a Bavarian bierhaus. Hair of the Dog specializes in high-alcohol beers. Its 10 percent ABV "Adam" (a dark, rich brew with notes of chocolate)—packs a punch.

■ *Essentials:* BridgePort Brewery and Brewpub (1313 NW. Marshall St., tel 503/241-7179, bridgeportbrew.com); Upright Brewing (240 N. Broadway, Suite 2, tel 503/735-5337, uprightbrewing.com); Hair of the Dog Brewing Company (61 SE. Yamhill St., tel 503/232-6585, hairofthedog.com)

BUYING COWBOY BOOTS

Savvy San Antonio residents make a beeline to Lucchese (pronounced *lou-casey*) when they need a new pair of cowboy boots. Why? Because of the fit and the quality. As Carlos, a Lucchese salesman, tells customers: "You're looking for a snug fit across the instep, but some slippage in the heel."

WHAT TO BUY: Decisions, decisions. The boots come in a rainbow of colors: purple, red, midnight blue, metallic, and every shade of brown from palest tan to deepest chocolate. Should you get something practical in brown calf leather? Something whimsical in turquoise and cherry red? An exotic leather such as caiman, ostrich, or python? And then there's the tooling. The options are almost endless—you can have a pair custom made, but this will take two to three months and the sky's the limit on price.

HOW TO WEAR COWBOY BOOTS: In Texas, men's pant legs go over the boots, hiding the fancy tooling. When a customer asked what good the tooling was if no one could see it, the fitter replied: "You'll know it's there." Women show off tooled boots by wearing them with skirts, skinny jeans, or shorts.

WHERE TO WEAR THEM: While eating a monster breakfast taco at local hot spot Café Salsita; when taking a mosey along the Riverwalk; or for eating steak San Antonio style at Myron's Prime Steakhouse. As local boot wearer Bill Dupont says, "Cowboy boots feel comfortable all day."

■ *Essentials:* Lucchese (255 E. Basse Rd., tel 210/828-9419, lucchese.com); Café Salsita (555 E. Basse Rd., tel 210/826-6661); Myron's Prime Steakhouse (10003 NW. Military Hwy., tel 210/493-3031)

Jeans can be worn tucked in or out, though Texans usually opt for "out."

"Like anything worth wearing, you'll need more than one pair."
—BILL DUPONT, SAN ANTONIO ARCHITECTURE PROFESSOR

Hey Cupcake!'s airstream trailer sparkles.

MOVABLE FEAST

Social media is the best way to follow most of these meals on wheels.

■ Hey Cupcake!, Austin, TX

It's hard to miss the location—a trailer topped with a revolving cupcake with pink frosting and sprinkles. To get your cupcake with a free injection of whipped cream, Austiner Katie Kanzler advises, "Say 'Make it a whipper snapper.'"
heycupcake.com

■ Roxy's Gourmet Grilled Cheese, Boston, MA

With more than 60 food trucks roaming the city, how do Bostonians choose a lunch spot? "Ask your bartender," says James Sabatino of Roxy's Gourmet Grilled Cheese, one of the first trucks on the streets. "They always know the best places." Chances are one of them will send you to Roxy's for the popular Green Munster Melt, made with munster cheese, bacon, and guacamole.
roxysgrilledcheese.com

■ Bite into Maine, Portland, ME

The Maine-style lobster roll is a Downeast classic: Chunks of sweet lobster, a light touch with the mayo, and a sprinkling of chives on a toasted hot dog roll. But, say owners Karl and Sarah Sutton, "Locals order a 'picnic style' lobster roll"—the classic improved with coleslaw, celery salt, and butter—"and a local Maine soda," Karl says. Sarah suggests Moxie, the bitter and beloved official soft drink of Vacationland.
biteintomaine.com

■ Whitecross Street Market, London, U.K.

Paella, carnitas, falafel, fish tacos, even gourmet scotch eggs, Whitecross Street Market can satisfy any lunch craving. Thursday and Friday lunch boast the largest selection, with more than 30 street food vendors—and the largest crowd of in-the-know office workers. After you brave the lines, head to nearby Fortune Street park for an urban picnic.
inlondonguide.co.uk

■ Herring Stands, The Hague, Holland

The first barrel of *Hollandse nieuwe haring* to arrive each June is a celebration, but herring is an everyday tradition—"the Dutch hamburger"—in the Hague. The raw, salted herring filets are dipped in chopped onion, dangled overhead, and eaten in one gulp—or sandwiched in a white bun, for the less coordinated.
denhaag.nl

■ Tripe Carts, Florence, Italy

Although these carts have wheels, most are stationed permanently at busy intersections. The better to return for another taste of a certain *panino con il lampredotto* (a sandwich made from the cow's tender fourth stomach). Order this working man's lunch with *salsa verde* (parsley, capers, and garlic) or *piccante* (chili oil)—and lots of napkins.
firenzeturismo.it

■ Puchka Wallas, Kolkata, India

A pile of crisp semolina shells towers over each puchka stall, waiting to be cracked, stuffed with spiced potato and chickpeas, and dipped in a pot of tangy tamarind sauce. Kolkata's idea of heaven on a plate.
westbengaltourism.gov.in

SANTA FE, NEW MEXICO
GALLERY-HOPPING

The hip Railyard Arts District is Santa Fe's answer to New York's Soho. Living in the town with the fourth largest art market in the U.S. gives locals an advantage when it comes to buying art: The city's artists are not only their neighbors but often become friends. Says longtime resident Malcolm McFarlane: "No person or creative act is too weird to be accepted here, which makes it a fertile space for artists. Plus there's a mix of cultures: Native American tribes, a long Spanish influence, and the live and let live of the wide-open West." His wife, Megan, chimes in: "I love that the city incorporates art at bus shelters, overpasses, and sculptures on traffic circles."

WHERE TO GO: The art district runs along Guadalupe Street between Agua Fria and Paseo de Peralta. Drop in to the William Siegal Gallery where works of Mexican-born Carlos Estrada-Vega vie with Diego Rivera drawings on the white and terracotta walls. Then visit Zane Bennett Gallery whose historic exterior conceals an ultramodern interior, or head over to Sante Fe Clay, home to 20 ceramic artists, an art supply store, and gallery.

LOCAL KNOWLEDGE: On the last Friday of the month, you can join an art walk from 5 to 7 p.m. One local artist recommends visiting at Christmastime: "Don't miss the *farolitos* [paper bags weighed down with sand in which a candle flickers]. If you're lucky, the adobe walls will be dusted with snow, and dozens of farolitos will flicker along walls, fences, sidewalks, and roofs. Magical."

■ *Essentials:* William Siegal Gallery (540 S. Guadalupe St., tel 505/820-3300, williamsiegal.com); Zane Bennett Gallery (435 S. Guadalupe St., tel 505/982-8111, zanebennettgallery.com); Santa Fe Clay (545 Camino de la Familia, tel 505/984-1122, santafeclay.com)

Railyard Eats

The Railyard District is home to an artisan market on Sundays and a farmers' market on Saturdays and Tuesdays. In August and September, the air sings with the smell of roasting chilies. Eat on the hoof at the market, grab a burrito at **Zia's Diner** (326 S. Guadalupe St., ziadiner.com), or stop at **Second Street Brewery** (1607 Paseo de Peralta #10, secondstreetbrewery.com).

Arizona's Canyon de Chelly in the heart of the Navajo Nation

NAVAJO NATION, ARIZONA
HOGAN HOMESTAY

There's no more local experience than actually living with someone. In the heart of the Navajo Nation, some locals open their hogans and their hearths to visitors for a night, offering a rare insight into Navajo culture.

A WAY OF LIFE: The Navajo still use the traditional one-room hogan as a home and a place for sacred ceremonies. Built in harmony with nature, the windowless, domed structure plucks its resources from Mother Earth. Juniper logs form walls that are generously insulated with juniper bark and plastered with red desert dirt on the outside, keeping the interiors cool in summer and warm in winter. A fire in the center of a tamped-earth or flagstone floor provides warmth, the smoke curling upward to a square opening in the roof that also lets in a ray of light. A single door faces east, toward the rising sun.

JOINING IN: On a clear starry night, you might find yourself sitting round the campfire with your hosts as they talk you through everything from the role of corn in every-day Navajo life to the rites of passage for young Navajo women. "It's really relaxing here," says Howard Smith, who rents out his hogans at Spider Rock Campground. All around spread the sheer-sided mesas, thick forests, lofty plateaus, arid deserts, and 10,000-foot-high (3,000 m) mountains of the reservation which covers more than 27,000 square miles (70 million ha) in northeast Arizona, New Mexico, and Utah.

WHAT TO EXPECT: The accommodation is not luxurious: There is no electricity or running water, and bathroom facilities are shared. Heat is provided by a stove in the center of the hogan. But it may turn out to be the best night's sleep you've ever had. Smith says that his guests report "sleeping like babies. There's no noise, nothing at all outside but the night and the stars."

ANOTHER FAVORITE: In Monument Valley, FireTree Inn provides bed and breakfast in hogans with a few home comforts, including evaporative coolers.

◼ *Essentials:* Spider Rock Campground (Canyon de Chelly National Monument, tel 928/674-8261, spiderrockcamp ground.com); FireTree Bed & Breakfast (Monument Valley, firetreeinn.com)

MEMPHIS BARBECUE JOINTS

"No sir, barbecue ain't barbecue unless it's Memphis barbecue," declared a character in the TV cop show *Memphis Beat*. That's how residents think in this hardboiled city on the Mississippi River. Pitmasters slow-cook their meat over a low hickory wood fire in aboveground brick or cinderblock "pits." Of the two styles, wet (with sauce) and dry (without sauce), Memphis goes for the dry method—a rub of paprika, salt, and a few secret ingredients applied before the pork goes into the pit. While ribs are the prevailing cut, pork shoulders and pulled-pork sandwiches are other local hits. Shrimp, chicken, and beef also receive the Memphis treatment.

WHERE TO GO: Residents and visitors alike scope out the city's World Championship Barbecue Cooking Contest each May. But locals have the advantage of eating barbecue year-round at joints like Payne's Bar-B-Q. Difficult as it might be, skip the ribs in favor of the signature chopped pork sandwich (topped with coleslaw). At the Bar-B-Q Shop order the dry-rub rib and pulled pork combo (with spaghetti) and you may not have to eat again for days. One of the city's older barbecue joints is Charles Vergos' Rendezvous, opened in 1948 in a

MORE: Memphis Blues

The Blue Worm: On Friday and Saturday, this no-frills neighborhood club on Airways Boulevard showcases the true veterans of the Memphis juke joint scene. Also has a great house band. 1405 Airways Blvd., tel 901/327-7947
Mr Handy's Blueshall: If you just have to listen to blues on Beale Street, this is the one real deal left. memphisbluessociety.com

downtown alley. The eclectic menu includes offbeat treats like barbecued shrimp and pork nachos.

■ *Essentials:* Payne's Bar-B-Q (1762 Lamar Ave., tel 901/272-1523, closed Sun.–Mon.); Bar-B-Q Shop (1782 Madison Ave., tel 901/272-1277, dancingpigs.com, closed Sun.); Charles Vergos' Rendezvous, 52 S. 2nd St., tel 901/523-2746, hogsfly.com, closed Sun.–Mon.)

Barbecue ribs Charles Vergos' style

Kicking up a storm at the Spotted Cat

NEW ORLEANS, LOUISIANA
JAZZ ON FRENCHMEN STREET

The locals' Bourbon Street, they call it, where jazz plays late into the night, and crawfish po-boys and fried oysters sate hungry crowds. This is Frenchmen Street, a two-block enclave steps from the French Quarter where some of the best live music venues mix with busy restaurants, trendy shops, and über-talented street artists. Any night of the week music is on tap, and you never know what amazing experience to expect. "One Tuesday at d.b.a.," says Scott Emile Simon of iheartnola .com, "a band announced it would be their last gig ever. Classic after classic vibrated on this magical night. The band was on an emotional high and all of us were chasing its dragon." Just another run-of-the-mill Tuesday on Frenchmen Street.

WHERE TO GO: The Maison for jazz and good eats; Snug Harbor for regional cooking and modern jazz; The Spotted Cat for good local jazz bands; and Blue Nile for free salsa lessons preceding Jamaican music and dining.

FITTING IN: Tip the band generously. Tips are often the only money these talented musicians will make.

MORE: Live Music

Maple Leaf Bar: Tucked away on Oak Street in Uptown New Orleans, the Leaf has live music every night. Local music legends like Rebirth Brass Band and Papa Grows Funk like to play here. mapleleafbar.com

Tipitina's: Stop by this storied juke joint on a Sunday evening for *fais do-do*, a celebration of Cajun music and dance. tipitinas.com

■ *Essentials:* frenchmenstreetlive.com; d.b.a. (618 Frenchmen St., tel 504/942-3731, dbaneworleans.com); The Maison (508 Frenchmen St., tel 504/371-5543); Snug Harbor (626 Frenchmen St., tel 504/949-0696, snugjazz.com); The Spotted Cat Music Club (623 Frenchmen St., tel 504/943-3887, spottedcatmusic club.com) Blue Nile (532 Frenchmen St., tel 504/948-2583, bluenilelive.com)

SOUTHERN FEASTS

The cooking of the southern United States evolved from French, German, Native American, and African-American cultures. Chicken, corn, greens, rice, and pork provide the mainstays, while leftovers become stew or gumbo, all flawlessly seasoned with spices.

WHERE TO GO: In 1943, local resident Selma Wilkes opened a boardinghouse in Savannah. Although it hasn't been a boardinghouse for years, and Mrs. Wilkes died in 2002, lunch at the boardinghouse's restaurant remains a Savannah tradition. Each weekday lines form an hour before the doors open at 11 a.m. Once inside, friends and strangers sit around tables of ten while servers bring platters and bowls heaped with beef stew, snap beans, mashed sweet potatoes, okra gumbo, black-eyed peas, collard greens, banana pudding, and fried chicken. Customers help themselves family style. And just like at home, everyone clears their own place.

ANOTHER LOCAL FAVORITE: Five miles (8 km) outside town, Sweet Potatoes Kitchen rustles up delicious home-cooking at inexpensive prices. Try pecan-crusted trout with roasted Brussels sprouts and okra and tomatoes followed by peach cobbler.

■ *Essentials:* Mrs. Wilkes' Dining Room (107 West Jones St., tel 912/232-5997, lunch only, closed Sat.–Sun.); Sweet Potatoes Kitchen (6825 Waters Ave., tel 912/352-3434)

Southern hospitality at Mrs. Wilkes' Dining Room

"It is the satisfaction of seeing people from every walk of life sit down and enjoy my family-style meals that has kept me going." — SELMA WILKES

KEY BISCAYNE, FLORIDA
BY THE WATER'S EDGE

"This is totally different from the glitzy, tony scene of Miami Beach," says Miami-Dade Parks supervisor and native Miamian Ernie Lynk, surveying the dazzling white sands of Crandon Park. Overlooking the clear, shallow waters of the Atlantic Ocean, with 2 miles (3 km) of beaches dotted with majestic coconut palms swaying in the ocean breeze, their smooth, gray trunks topped with feather-shape fronds, Crandon Park on Key Biscayne never feels crowded even though it's just 20 minutes from downtown Miami. Remarking on the number of music videos, commercials, and magazine and catalog shoots happening here, Lynk asked a director why they film here instead of on Miami Beach. "The palm trees, man, the palm trees," the man replied, looking wistful. "You've got them in the sand."

WHERE TO GO: Local families gravitate toward winding nature trails snaking through the park's dunes and mangrove swamps, head to shaded picnic tables and grills on the beach under the palm trees, or seek out the concession stands at the south end of the beach for a quick snack. The more energetic head for the north end to rent cabanas, kayaks, stand-up paddleboards, and kiteboards.

LOCAL KNOWLEDGE: Snorkeling is best at high tide, which brings out all the tiny creatures living in the sea-grass beds off the beach. For turtle-lovers it doesn't get any better than watching hatchlings get their first taste of the ocean. At the height of the turtle-hatching season in late summer, the Miami-Dade Parks Sea Turtle Nesting and Relocation Progam holds evening release sessions on Crandon Park's beaches aimed at getting local kids interested in turtle conservation (reservations required). The nests are cordoned off to protect them from humans and other critters, but you might get a chance to guide a hatchling gently into the sea.

■ *Essentials:* Crandon Park (6747 Crandon Blvd., tel 305/361-5421, miamidade.gov)

....

"This is definitely a place to chill." —ERNIE LYNK, PARKS SUPERVISOR

Crandon Park, Miami's quiet twin

TAILGATING AT THE UNIVERSITY OF FLORIDA

If football is one of America's favorite pastimes, then tailgating (and all the revelry that comes with it) is a close second—particularly at large state schools. And at the University of Florida, it may as well be a sport all on its own. The tradition of tailgating—a term coined to describe sports enthusiasts who cheered on teams from the backs of wagons—has evolved considerably since its start in the 1860s. Today's tailgators can be seen pulling up outside the U.F.'s Ben Hill Griffin Stadium (also known as the Swamp) in cars, trucks, and even RVs by the thousands to socialize and cheer on their players long before, during, and after the game. But that's not the only thing that keeps these party caravans going: Fans feast on burgers, debate stats and strategy, play rock or country music, sing fight songs, and maybe even toss the old pigskin around with friends and people in neighboring cars. Besides a spot to park and a ticket to the game, all you'll really need for a U.F. football tailgating party is a set of wheels, some foldable chairs, friends, family, and food.

WHAT TO WEAR: The team's colors, of course. That way, when you walk into the towering stands, you'll feel right at home in the roaring sea of orange and blue. The student fans (or "rowdy reptiles," as they're sometimes called) tend to gear up in bright combinations of both colors, donning everything from flashy pants, bedazzled shoes, and funky hats to decorative swirls of paint and lettering on their faces (or emblazoned on their chests). But you don't need to be a super-fan to have a good time: A T-shirt and a foam finger from local shops or the Gator website is all you need to get into the spirit. And don't forget that you're likely to get a lot of sun during a three- or four-hour day-game (not including the hours you'll spend grilling and gabbing outside of the stands) so bring a hat and sunblock, alongside the chow and beverages in your cooler.

LOCAL KNOWLEDGE: The designated parking lots are first come first served and fill up hours before the game. "The town really comes alive, with camper vans lining up at dawn," says Bunky Mastin of the Wine and Cheese Gallery, a deli on Gainesville's Main Street. "You can't normally drink on campus, but when there's a Gator game on, they turn a blind eye. Fill up your cool box at one of the local delis or takeouts, or bring one ready packed. We try to raise the tone a little [from beers and bbq] with European cheeses, pâtés, salads, baguettes, and wine."

■ *Essentials:* Ben Hill Griffin Stadium (158 Gale Lemerand Dr., tel 352/375-4683, gatorzone.com); Wine and Cheese Gallery (113 N. Main St., Gainesville, tel 352/372-8446)

MORE: Tailgate Fodder

LL's Bar-B-Que: Former Pi Lambda Phi chef Louis Lee barbecues the old-fashioned way using only wood and a smoker. 3807 E. Univesity Ave., tel 352/672-6555

Hogan's: Owner Walt Spelman is on a mission to offer the biggest sandwiches in town. hogans83.com

DIGGING DEEPER

If you're tailgating for the day, do as the rowdy reptiles do: Play a common tailgating game, like Cornhole, to pass the time. Two teams of players throw beanbags at a raised board with a hole in one end as they attempt to throw the bags through the hole.

A home team
crowd cheers
on the Gators.
Opposite: Grilling
Gator style

Live music draws the crowds to the seafront.

LAUDERDALE-BY-THE-SEA, FLORIDA
CONCERTS BY THE OCEAN

On Friday and Saturday evenings, the center of Lauderdale-by-the-Sea on Florida's Atlantic coast buzzes with activity as everyone in town gathers for live music sponsored by a few local restaurants. The bands and music may change nightly, but the camaraderie remains a constant.

WHERE TO GO: Mere yards away from the pier, restaurant teams from The Village Grille (for sushi), Athena By The Sea (for Greek food, naturally), and 101 Ocean (for pizzas and flatbreads) set up tables and chairs in the street facing a makeshift stage.

After a stroll through the hamlet, drinkers and diners scope out the best seats in the house. If you want to eat, settle down at one of the tables around the edge of the square; or you can perch with a drink in the central area. As if on cue, the band du jour will strike up and harmonize on rock, jazz, or blues. Fingers strum, hands

pat, and toes tap to the beat. Pretty soon swaying to the music segues into dancing in the street. Tracy King from 101 Ocean says, "It's a real neighborhood thing. Just a time to kick back and relax at the weekend." Locals never tire of the view—a fireball sun inching below the horizon as a soft ocean mist hovers over the buff-colored sandy beach.

BY DAY: Fishing, snorkeling, and miles of sandy beaches make Lauderdale-by-the-Sea a great place to hang out, soak up the sun, or sleep off the night before.

■ *Essentials:* Anglin Beach Village (Commercial Blvd. at El Mar Dr., lauderdalebythesea-fl.gov); The Village Grille (4404 El Mar Dr., tel 954/776-5092, villagegrille.com); Athena By The Sea (4400 N. Ocean Dr., tel 954/771-2900, athenabythesea.net); 101 Ocean (101 E. Commercial Blvd., tel 954/776-8101, 101oceanlbts.com)

GAULEY RIVER, WEST VIRGINIA
RIDING THE RAPIDS

The raft steadies for what seems like a nanosecond before the crest of a wave hooks the thick rubber inflatable and propels it through the broiling water. With names like Heaven Help You and Pure Screaming Hell, the rapids on West Virginia's Gauley River are not for the fainthearted, especially in fall, when large releases of water from Summersville Dam turn the Upper Gauley into a churning mass of water.

WHERE TO GO: Stick with the locals, who favor the Gauley River rather than the busier New River. Upper and Lower Gauley offer 28 miles (45 km) of nonstop action through 150 rapids ranging from Class III (medium difficulty) to Class V, combining big wave trains and spectacular scenery.

WHEN TO GO: During the Gauley season (September–October), the Class V (difficult) rapids are the big draw. Try the Upper Gauley's Big 5: Insignificant—a misnomer—Pillow Rock, Lost Paddle, Iron Ring, and Sweet Falls. In spring and summer, water levels vary and outfitters adjust their routes to give the best ride possible.

WHAT TO WEAR: During spring and fall, when the water is chilly, wear wool or synthetics such as polypropylene. When it's downright teeth chattering, you'll need to wear a wetsuit. In summer, wear a swimsuit and/or nylon shorts, T-shirt, a lightweight rain jacket, and sneakers. Cotton is an absolute no-no—it is guaranteed to make you cold—so leave your favorite sweatshirt at home or save it for snuggling into after your trip when you're trying to purge the adrenalin. A helmet and life jacket go without saying.

■ *Essentials:* Trips on the Upper Gauley River start at the base of Summersville Dam; professional river outfitters provide the safest entry and exit points. wvaraft.com, class-vi.com

"The Gauley is an animal unlike any other. There's nothing like feeling your stomach drop as you crash through a Class V rapid, wondering if you'll make it out alive." —JUSTIN CANTERBURY, GAULEY ENTHUSIAST

A rough ride on the Gauley River

A potential buyer inspects a plow before the auction.

GORDONVILLE, PENNSYLVANIA
AMISH MUD SALE

Handcrafted wooden furniture, farm tools, intricately sewn quilts, black buggies, livestock—people donate all manner of items to Pennsylvania Amish mud sales to raise funds for local fire departments. The ground underfoot is muddy—these auctions are named for the large, usually sodden early springtime fields they're held in—but pull on your boots and join the search for the perfect oak cabinet or cast-iron coffee-grinder.

WHERE TO GO: One of the largest mud sales takes place every March (usually on the first or second Saturday) in the town of Gordonville. In their straw hats and cotton bonnets, Amish auction-goers dominate a crowd that runs into the thousands. Some are there to buy, others to watch and mingle, at one of the region's biggest annual social gatherings.

LOCAL FAVORITE: Horse-trading is the highlight of any mud sale. Gordonville's horse auction usually takes place at the southern end of the grounds. Sturdy mules, giant draft horses, buggy-pullers, and fine riding horses parade around the ring as the auctioneer belts out bids in a melodic tenor from his wooden lean-to. To get a close-up view, you'll need to compete with the throngs of Amish boys for a spot at the ringside. Better yet, position yourself among the spectators on the hill between the auction arena and Old Leacock Road—a perfect perch for watching the action unfold while munching on a slice of homemade coconut cream pie.

■ *Essentials:* Gordonville Mud Sale (Old Leacock Rd., tel 717/768-3869, gordonvillefc.com, padutch.com)

DIGGING DEEPER

Search out a game of cornerball *(eck balle)*, the ultimate plain game of the Pennsylvania Amish. Played between teams of Amish and Mennonites, or teams of Amish married and single men, this fast and spirited take on dodgeball can get very competitive.

PARTY ON THE PARKWAY

One day a year, a living mosaic of red, white, and blue covers the ground outside Philadelphia's Independence Hall and flows out onto the nearby streets and lawns. The crowd listens to excerpts from the Declaration of Independence, and a sea of miniature American flags waves in cheerful reply. This is the spot where the Founding Fathers signed the Declaration of Independence in 1776 and where, a year later, the first organized Fourth of July celebration took place.

JOINING IN: During the day, Philadelphians head for Benjamin Franklin Parkway and the Party on the Parkway: Seven blocks cordoned off for food vendors and live acts. While adults fill up on Philly cheesesteaks, kids can skip to the Go 4th & Learn interactive area. At twilight, join the locals on Lemon Hill or picnicking along the Schuylkill River to listen to the free concert and enjoy the fireworks. Says Philly native Rob Harting, "Seeing the fireworks from the steps of the Philly Museum of Art is a big thing. The Museum is at the end of the Parkway and has a great view."

Philly's Favorite Sandwich

Philly is famous for its cheesesteak, but you'll find locals picnicking on roast pork sandwiches—thin-sliced pork, broccoli rabe, and extra-sharp provolone, served on a crusty roll. Find them at Tommy DiNic's (tommy-dinics.com) and John's Roast Pork (johnsroastpork.com).

WHEN TO GO: At dawn's early light for a good view of the parade, which starts at 11 a.m. That's when enthusiasts and history buffs stake out their spots on the Parkway. Position yourself here to watch a cast dressed in 1770s garb lead a procession of colorful floats, marching bands, and tributes to the U.S. military right past your lawn chairs.

■ *Essentials:* General information: visitphilly.com

The Quaker City String Band performs in Philadelphia's Fourth of July parade.

THE POLISH TRIANGLE

Next to Warsaw, Chicago has the world's second largest Polish population. The Polish Triangle, center of the city's original Polish Downtown, is its oldest, most prominent Polish settlement, full of local Polish shops and restaurants. Although the years have taken their toll, the area has recently undergone a renaissance and is once again becoming a thriving business district, full of nightclubs, restaurants, and cafés.

WHERE TO GO: What Podhalanka, a hole-in-the-wall former tavern, lacks in atmosphere, it makes up for in Polish comfort food. For the past 27 years, Krakow-born Helena Madej and her family have run this homey, no-frills establishment. "Dining here is like eating in your grandmother's kitchen, complete with pink vinyl tablecloths, plastic flower centerpieces, and Polish soap operas playing in the background," says local writer Barbara Sanford. Polish knickknacks share the shelves behind the bar with a poster of Pope John Paul II.

HOW TO ORDER: Start your meal with a bowl of cabbage soup or the white borscht, a creamy sausage-filled soup with fresh dill. No Polish meal is complete without *pierogi* (potato and cheese, meat, or cabbage dumplings) with sour cream and caramelized onions—hearty enough for a main dish or try a small plate as an appetizer. For your main course, order crispy potato pancakes with applesauce and sour cream or go for the *golabki* (stuffed cabbage) with meat filling and mashed potatoes. Then loosen your belt and keep the calories coming with sweet cheese blintzes sprinkled with confectioners sugar and served with sour cream. A glass of *kompot* (fruit juice) complements the meal, or bring your own bottle (there's no corkage fee).

OTHER LOCAL FAVORITES: Since 1978, Staropolska has served good Polish-American cuisine in a warm, Old Poland atmosphere with chandeliers, brick walls, a mural, fireplace, and beamed ceiling. Bring a large appetite to Red Apple's (Czerwone Jabluszko's) extensive all-you-can-eat buffet of fresh, homemade Polish specialties and dishes from around the world, including entrées, salads, and desserts. Polish beer is on tap at the bar.

■ *Essentials:* Podhalanka (1549 W. Division St., tel 773/486-6655); Staropolska (3030 N. Milwaukee Ave., tel 773/342-0779, staropolskarestaurant.com); Red Apple (3121 N. Milwaukee Ave., tel 773/588-5781, redapplebuffet.com)

MORE: Polish Delis and Markets

Endy's Deli: Polish sausages line the wall of this Polish deli known for sausage, ham, cheeses, pickles, kraut, and sandwiches. 3055 N. Milwaukee Ave., tel 773/486-8160

Kurowski's Sausage Shop: A long line of Polish-speaking customers waits patiently to buy fresh, homemade sausage, ham, cheeses, and other Polish specialties. 2976 N. Milwaukee Ave., tel 773/645-1692

Polish Triangle Marketplace: Head to this summer farmer's market for fresh goods (including vegetables, pastries, teas, artisanal cheeses, fresh herbs) and live entertainment. Division St. and Ashland and Milwaukee Ave., 3-7 p.m. Thurs., June through Sept.

"If you crave your Polish mother or grandmother's recipes—in my case my mother- and grandmother-in-law's recipes—Podhalanka is the place to go." —DAN LAMBERT, CHICAGO-BASED VIDEO EDITOR

Starapolska's rustic interior. Opposite: Red Apple's bar is stocked with Polish beer.

BOSTON, MASSACHUSETTS
HOME OF CHOWDER

If there's one thing Bostonians cherish more than their beloved Red Sox, it's clam chowder—the white, thick version, of course, because New Englanders consider tomato-based chowder from Manhattan to be sacrilegious. The *Boston Evening-Post* published the oldest known New England clam chowder recipe in 1751, and the rich, thick soup has now become as much a part of the Boston culinary scene as baked beans and Sam Adams beer.

LOCAL KNOWLEDGE: New England clam chowder includes three basic components—clams, potatoes, and cream or milk. Salt pork, onions, and celery are also common ingredients. Various herbs and spices add depth, while parsley provides a garnish. You can crumble oyster crackers into your soup to thicken it even more.

LOCAL FAVORITES: Local chowder fans like to rub shoulders with longshoremen at Belle Isle Seafood, a working-class café in Winthrop, over the bridge from Boston. At the other end of the spectrum is the upscale Neptune Oyster restaurant in the North End. Don't be dissuaded by the fact that Legal Sea Foods is a chain—it's a longtime local favorite, especially its flagship branch at Liberty Wharf. "I have been going to Legal Sea Foods since I was a child and it first started at Inman Square in Cambridge," says Susan Clarke, a Boston native. "Now I love Liberty Wharf Legal. You can't beat the views over Boston Harbor on a hot sunny day."

■ *Essentials:* Belle Isle Seafood (1 Main St., Winthrop, tel 617/567-1619, belleisleseafood.com); Neptune Oyster (63 Salem St., tel 617/442-3471, neptuneoyster.com); Legal Sea Foods (270 Northern Ave., Liberty Wharf, tel 617/477-2900, legalseafoods.com)

Rich and creamy
New England
chowder

"I love the creaminess with the salty sea taste of the clams. Add some toasted or grilled bread for dipping and I'm set." —STEPHANIE LE, FOOD WRITER

Brant Point Lighthouse overlooks Nantucket Harbor.

A BREAK FROM THE BIG CITY

When it's just too darn hot, these are the go-to getaways.

■ Nantucket, MA
Once a whaling community, now a summer home to wilting professionals lured from Boston and New York by the sea breezes, unspoiled beaches, and quaint clapboard houses. "You want to feel it with your feet: the dunes, the cobblestones," says summer resident Brian Hurley.
nantucket.net

■ Point Reyes, CA
The wild peninsula of Point Reyes is only an hour from San Francisco. "I love walking in the Pierce Point area as you're almost guaranteed a glimpse of Point Reyes' famed Tule Elk," says local graphic designer Camilla Saufley-Mitchell.
nps.gov/pore

■ Brighton, U.K.
A population of relaxed bohemians and energetic

art students is swelled by daytrippers from London. Says Londoner Sam Kennedy, "I love that tacky retro charm. Not to mention the fish and chips."
visitbrighton.com

■ Île de Ré, France
Wealthy Parisians escape to Île de Ré, an island off France's Atlantic coast, in summer. Get away from it all as you bike past oyster farms, vineyards, and salt pans to the pretty village of La Flotte.
holidays-iledere.co.uk

■ Sitges, Spain
If many Med resorts are uptight and high-rolling, the freewheeling democratic spirit of Sitges near Barcelona is the antidote. Rub shoulders with the Catalan intelligentsia who live in the town's famed modernist apartments; hang out with relaxed young

Europeans squeezing in one last drink before the sun sets, and it's time for dinner and more wine.
visitsitges.com

■ Viareggio, Italy
Spend long enough in Viareggio and you might find yourself adopted by one of the many Italian families that descend on the town's beach to escape steamy Florence or Pisa. As night falls, join the promenade along the city's beachfront under the gaze of gently decaying grand hotels.
aboutversilia.com

■ Chengde, China
In days gone by the palace of the Manchu emperors, today Chengde is the playground of Beijing's newly wealthy. The resort's 120 palaces offer great views of artificially landscaped beauty spots.
cnto.info

■ Kashid, India
Kashid's 2 miles (3 km) of soft white sand offer a prospect more often associated with the tropical south of India than nearby Mumbai. The beach, whose high waves are perfect for surfing, beckons. For a truly authentic experience stay in one of the local villagers' cottages. They're the best places to taste rich Kashidi curry.
kashidresort.com

■ Blue Mountains, Australia
Reaching into the air above the city's western flank, the Blue Mountains are a haven for sweltering Sydneysiders. "I think of the mountains as a place that's both wild and tame at the same time," says Becca Grey, who has been visiting since her childhood.
bluemts.com.au

VANCOUVER, CANADA
GROUSE MOUNTAIN

L eaving their offices in downtown Vancouver on dark winter evenings, outdoorsy Vancouverites don't dare glance to the north or they face being very late home. "The lure," according to local author Peter Neville-Hadley, "is Grouse Mountain. Its brightly lit slopes hang over the city like a giant Christmas decoration and are only 15 minutes' drive away." The strings of lights illuminate 14 ski runs that remain open until 10 p.m. each evening.

LOCAL FAVORITES: Grouse can also be reached by a regular city bus service, and a sudden impulse sees many Vancouverites at 4,100 feet (1,250 m) before they know it, choosing between the Cut, a broad, runway-like piste for beginners, and narrower, winding runs, such as Dogleg and Buckthorn, that take more experienced skiers slaloming swiftly down through thick forest. Floodlights gleam on snow-laden branches; far below, sodium-yellow lights outline the grid of Vancouver streets while the navigation lights of vast, oceangoing vessels twinkle in English Bay. "Once you're down, a muscle-relaxing bath at home is only a short journey away," adds Neville-Hadley.

JOINING IN: Take a taxi, or the seabus ferry from Waterfront Station across the harbor to Lonsdale Quay, and then the 236 bus to Grouse Mountain. You can rent skis, snowboards, boots, and poles on-site. A free smartphone app provides up-to-date snow conditions and tracks you on the slopes, so you can show fellow skiers where you've been over hot chocolate in the Peak Chalet.

FARTHER AFIELD: Vancouverites' nearest major ski area is Olympics-hosting Whistler, 1.5 hours away.

■ *Essentials:* Grouse Mountain (6400 Nancy Greene Way, tel 604/980-9311, grousemountain.com)

Glide with a View

Winter wouldn't be complete without a glide around an outdoor skating rink, and Grouse Mountain, with its fresh air and panoramic views, boasts one of the prettiest. Go during the day with the kids, or on a romantic evening for two. During the holiday period, Santa and his reindeer set up shop alongside the rink. grousemountain.com

Grouse Mountain's ski slopes are a nightly draw for locals and visitors.

OTTAWA, CANADA
WINTERLUDE

Local crowds gather to watch pond hockey matches, figure skating, triathlon competitions, and hospital-bed races. Excited kids shimmy through ice tunnels and mazes and line up for turns barreling down giant ice slides; adults brave the cold to dance, skate, attend concerts, and watch fireworks well into the night. Ottawans don't just embrace winter, they wrap up warmly and celebrate it with Winterlude, a three-week, citywide party each February when the locals get outside and play. "Winterlude is a special place," says Ottawa resident and ice-carver Kenny Hayden. "I have the opportunity to demonstrate my passion for ice carving and see the pleasure it brings to people of all ages."

JOINING IN: Just about everyone skates on the Rideau Canal Skateway, which snakes through the city center. You can rent skates at several locations along the route, and pros are available to give lessons. In Gatineau's Jacques-Cartier Park, the kids can frolic in Snowflake Kingdom, a giant snow playground filled with local families on the weekends. The lines for the ice slides may be long but they move quickly. In the evenings, festival-goers head to Confederation Park to eat beavertails and see the ice sculptures in the Crystal Garden or dance to music spun by local DJs in the Rogers Crystal Globe.

■ *Essentials:* General information: canadascapital.gc.ca

Kiosks tempt skaters with hot chocolate and pastries on the Rideau Canal Skateway.

An indoor Eden in downtown Calgary

CALGARY, CANADA
INDOOR PARADISE

A lush green oasis perched high above a busy downtown shopping mall, Devonian Gardens is a favorite refuge and chill-out destination for Calgarians. "Bottom line? If you need a green fix in the heart of winter or you want to take a nature break during your lunch hour, this is a great spot for relaxing," according to local resident Denise Kitagawa.

LOCAL KNOWLEDGE: After four years of refurbishment, the gardens reopened in 2012 with a contemporary new design and the addition of a living wall. "We went down to take a look at the brand new gardens and the kids loved it!" enthuses Melissa Vroon, a local mom. "The gardens feature gorgeous skylights to let in a ton of natural light, unique plants, and a brand new playground. The ponds are stocked with koi, which my kids could probably watch forever. I had to pry them away."

WHAT TO DO: In this light-filled haven in the sky, you can walk among exotic plantings of palm-like *Pandanus*, spindly-leaved *Beaucarnea*, spiky-flowered *Strelitzia* (Bird of Paradise), and hundreds of other plants; eat lunch under a tree; read in a quiet corner; or just escape the winter cold.

■ **Essentials:** 4th Level, Core Shopping Centre (317 7th Ave. SW., tel 403/268-2489, visitcalgary.com)

DIGGING DEEPER

The Devonian Dialogue Series—free, 30-minute, weekly lunchtime sessions held in winter—delves into gardening, bird-watching, and other horticulture-related topics. Mums and Sprouts, twice weekly, features interactive activities to teach kids about plants and the natural world.

CALGARY, CANADA
RODEO DAYS

The chute swings open and horse and rider gallop into the arena. To roars from the crowd, the rider guides his horse on a zigzagging course around three barrels in a race where speed and agility count within an average 14- to 16-second window. It's the Calgary Stampede—parade, rodeo competitions, evening music-and-dance show, plus a citywide bonanza of beer gardens, free pancake breakfasts, and parties—that takes place for ten days each July. "When we pull on the cowboy boots and dust off our old hats, some strange spirit comes over us all. We drink, we drawl, we swagger and swing. It's summer and we go Stampeding, like a herd of wild horses," enthuses Calgarian Cinda Chavich.

LOCAL FAVORITES: Rodeo events are at the heart of the Stampede and the most popular are bull riding—competitors attempt to cling on for a tense eight seconds as their rides try to unseat them—and the chuck wagon races. Standing tickets, at ground level by the rails, put you in the thick of the action and you may get the chance to chat with competitors and their teams. Around 11 p.m., a red warning flare above the grandstand signals the start of the fireworks—if you're not in the stadium, find a spot, such as on the midway, with a clear view of the sky. End the evening at the Nashville North country-and-western marquee for a can of Bud and some top country acts.

WHAT TO WEAR: Stampeders don Western attire from head to toe—plaid or denim shirt, jeans, boots, and hat. Cowboys and girls strut their individualism with their belt buckles—the bigger the better. Generally made from silver, pewter, or leather, the buckles are engraved with horseshoes, cowboy boots, or a cowboy's favorite animal.

■ *Essentials:* Stampede Park (1410 Olympic Way SE., tel 403/261-0101, calgarystampede.com)

Stampede-wear

Calgary's favorite cowboy boutiques for the rodeo look:
Lammle's: Lammle's stocks top brands of all things western. lammles.com
Riley & McCormick: Calgary's oldest western store. realcowboys.com
Smithbilt Hats: Home of Calgary's white cowboy hat. smithbilthats.com

A competitor hangs on tight in the saddle bronc riding event.

Underground art installations draw shoppers and restaurant-goers.

MONTREAL, CANADA
UNDERGROUND CITY

Ask "Which way to the underground city?" and Montrealers will point to the nearest ground-level access point (there are more than 120, indicated by RÉSO signs) or just motion you to follow as they descend into a subterranean complex hidden deep beneath downtown Montreal. Sheltered from the vagaries of the weather, the Ville Souterrain—a vast web of pedestrian tunnels (20 miles/32 km in all) lined with nearly 2,000 stores and 200 restaurants—is where Montrealers go to shop, play, and eat year-round. Says Montreal-based illustrator Sam Montesano, "Rain or shine, I love wandering Montreal's underground city. I can shop, visit a museum, have lunch, and shop again without ever stepping outside."

LOCAL FAVORITES: L'Art des Artisans du Québec sells one-of-a-kind home accessories. Le Parchemin is good for French-language literature and guidebooks. Three Monkeys specializes in designer clothing—the in-house-designed T-shirts featuring Montreal landmarks are good buys.

■ *Essentials:* L'Art des Artisans du Québec (150 rue Ste.-Catherine Est, tel 514/288-5379, artdesartisansduquebec.com); Le Parchemin (505 rue Ste.-Catherine Est, tel 514/845-5243, parchemin.ca); Three Monkeys (1455 rue Peel, tel 514/284-1333, threemonkeys.ca)

Underground Art

In late winter, contemporary artists from dozens of countries fill public spaces along 4 miles (6.5 km) of passageways in the **Ville Souterrain** with installations and performance art. This annual festival, known as **Art Souterrain,** kicks off its two-week run on Montreal's **Nuit Blanche,** a citywide, all-night bonanza of cultural and culinary events. montrealenlumiere.com

PRINCE EDWARD ISLAND, CANADA
LOBSTER SUPPERS

May through October is lobster season on Prince Edward Island, when islanders enjoy nothing more than tucking into a lobster supper. These no-frills, eat-'til-you're-stuffed affairs are held in venues that open specially for the season.

WHERE TO GO: St. Ann's Church in Hope River began staging lobster suppers in 1964 to help pay off its mortgage. The tradition continues today with meals served six days a week in summer.

WHAT TO EXPECT: Don't expect a private setting. You'll be seated at long communal tables in a low-slung church basement. But that's part of the charm of these evenings, as is the chance to swap stories with the regulars. Supper starts with a hearty chowder, warm-from-the-oven rolls, and green salad. Your server brings heaped platters of steamed blue mussels next, followed by the main course of lobster served either cold, as generally preferred, or hot with potato salad, coleslaw, and sautéed vegetables. The

MORE: Lobster Suppers

Other island churches run lobster suppers to fund-raise on an ad hoc basis. Look for hand-painted signs.

For a lobster supper in a restaurant, locals recommend **Cardigan Lobster Suppers** (peicardiganlobster suppers.com) or **New Glasgow Lobster Suppers** (peilobstersuppers.com).

meal finishes with a choice of desserts—a wedge of lemon meringue pie, tart rhubarb crisp, or strawberry shortcake.

■ *Essentials:* St. Ann's Church (Rte. 224 between Stanley Bridge and New Glasgow, tel 902/621-0635, lobster suppers.com, closed late Sept.–mid-June and Sun.)

Prince Edward Island's lobsters are fresh off the boat.

MEXICO CITY, MEXICO
SPIRIT CITY

Dancing skeletons, death-themed candies, altars lining the streets: The Day of the Dead—when people honor and celebrate the departed—takes place on November 1–2 and is a turbulent affair in Mexico City. Families gather to remember their deceased loved ones with processions and vigils. At night, cemeteries light up with flickering candles as families arrange *ofrendas* (decorated altars) beside family graves, and the scent of *cempazuchitls* (marigolds) fills the air to beckon the spirits to return.

JOINING IN: Public ofrendas spring up all over the city. The Zócalo (plaza) hosts the largest display, while museums such as Museo Dolores Olmeda in Xochimilco and the Diego Rivera–designed Museo Anahuacalli in Coyoacán, both in the south of the city, create elaborate ofrendas each year. You can attend a vigil at the Rotunda of Illustrious Persons in the Panteón de Dolores, Chapultepec Park, as Mexicans pay their respects at the tombs of famous Mexicans. After dark, many people join local residents in the cemeteries of San Andrés Apostol in Mixquic, a pre-Hispanic village on the city outskirts, or San Gregorio in Xochimilco for all-night vigils. Some families are lost in private contemplation; for others, this is a happy time and people admire one another's exquisitely decorated graves.

WHAT TO EAT: "Try the traditional *pan de muerto* (bread of the dead)—delicious pastries decorated with sugar bones," says Iván Salgado, a local university teacher. "As a child I was terrified of them, as my grandmother convinced me the red icing was the blood of the dead! But now I eat them with hot chocolate."

■ *Essentials:* dayofthedead.com; Museo Dolores Olmedo (Ave. México 5843, tel 52 (1) 55 5555 0891, museodolores olmedo.org.mx, closed Mon.); Museo Anahuacalli (Museo 50, San Pablo Tepetlapa, tel 52 (1) 55 5617 3797); Panteón de Dolores (Ave. Constituyentes)

Finding the Best Pan de Muerto

Café Tacuba: The colonial-style surroundings will take you back to the Viceroy era. cafedetacuba.com.mx
Pastelería Ideal: Enjoy delicious pan de muerto in a setting resembling a 1920s movie. pasteleriaideal.com.mx
Pastelería Suiza: Try a traditional pan de muerto or the one stuffed with custard. pasteleriasuiza.com.mx

Catrina dolls are part of the Day of the Dead observances.

I ♥ My City

Miriam Martínez
*Editor, NG Traveler,
Mexico*

We all have our dead. And in November they come to join us, so we don't miss them so much. On November 1 the children arrive, and on the second the party is for real. The living wait with altars on which we place photos of the dead, and their favorite food and drinks. We decorate the altars with *cempazuchitl* flowers, their orange color brightening the spirits of the living and the dead. But this is not all: We like to laugh. The absence of our dead is heavy, and to combat sadness we sweeten our visits to the cemetery with candies in the shape of skulls with our names written on them. The party also invades the media: Newspapers often publish *calaveritas* (skulls)—rhyming poems that caricature the living as if they were dead.

MEXICO CITY, MEXICO
JACARANDA DAYS

When jacaranda trees fill the streets of Mexico City in March and early April with clouds of lavender-blue flowers, *chilangos* (as the locals call themselves) know that summer days are on their way. Like cherry blossoms in Japan and turning leaves in the United States, jacaranda flowers are celebrated by locals as the symbol of a new season. "Jacaranda trees remind me of my childhood, finally wearing sandals," muses Fernanda Gonzales Vilchis, editorial director of *National Geographic Traveler Latin America*.

WHERE TO GO: You'll find jacarandas blooming throughout the city, on avenues and side streets, parks and gardens. The shady Parque México in Colonia Condesa is famed for its jacarandas, as are the peacock-filled gardens of the Museo Dolores Olmedo in Xochimilco. The former home of a socialite patron of the arts, the Museo displays paintings by Frida Kahlo and Diego Rivera among other national heroes. The roof terrace of the Hotel Condesa DF, the ideal place for an alfresco cocktail, overlooks the jacaranda-lined Avenida Veracruz.

JOINING IN: "Jacaranda time is the perfect moment to indulge in a venerable Mexican tradition: Lunch that turns into dinner," advises Vilchis. "With lots of heated discussion, we fix the world, hug our friends, and stay until night settles in." Begin your meal in local style with a tamarind margarita and appetizers—perhaps tuna *tostadas* and *salpicón de jaiba* (shredded crab). A *carajillo* is the perfect cap to the meal, involving equal measures of espresso and liqueur.

■ *Essentials:* Parque México (Ave. México, mexicocity-guide .com); Museo Dolores Olmedo (Ave. México 5843, tel 52 (1) 55 5555 0891, museodoloresolmedo.org); Hotel Condesa DF Hotel (Ave. Veracruz 102, tel 52 (1) 55 5241 2600, condesadf.com)

Long, Lazy Lunch Spots

Casa Bell: A traditional family restaurant. Praga 14, tel 52 (1) 55 5208 4290

El Cardenal: Try the appetizers: escamoles, tuna tostadas, and salpicón de jaiba. restauranteelcardenal.com

San Ángel Inn: Watch multigenerational Mexican families eat in tribe-like fashion. sanangelinn.com

A vivid display of jacaranda blossom beside the boating lake in Chapultepec Park

Vanilla's rich aroma develops during the drying process.

PAPANTLA, MEXICO
A TASTE OF VANILLA

Vanilla stars in all kinds of local dishes, even chicken and seafood. Hotel Tajin's Restaurant Totonaca serves cocktails flavored with vanilla, while *Camarones xanath* (vanilla shrimp) is a delicious regional specialty at Sorrento, an open-air restaurant that is often packed with locals watching the big TV screen.

LOCAL FAVORITES: Look for pure, high-quality vanilla extract in the Mercado Hidalgo (Hidalgo Market) off the *zócalo* (main square) or buy the finest gourmet vanilla from the Gaya Family shop. Gaya also makes and sells a deep chocolate-colored, heady vanilla liqueur called Xanath, which is served over ice. Booths in the zócalo sell aromatic animal and flower figures woven from cured vanilla pods for seasoning food or for their fragrance alone.

IN THE KNOW: The Totonac people of Papantla, in eastern Veracruz, were the first people on Earth to produce vanilla when they found that curing the pod of the Mexican *planifolia* orchid in the sun released an intense flavor.

■ *Essentials:* Mercado Hidalgo (Ave. 20 de Noviembre); Gaya Family (Ave. Hidalgo 56, Gutiérrez Zamora, tel 52 22 33 24 604); Hotel Tajin (José J. Nuñez y Domínguez 104, tel 52 (1) 784 842 1268); Sorrento (Enriquez 105, Col Centro, tel 52 (1) 784 842 0067)

DIGGING DEEPER

Papantla celebrates its valuable crop at the annual Vanilla Festival, held on the Feast of Corpus Christi (60 days after Easter). All kinds of vanilla products tempt the crowds, and the town's famous *voladores* (dancing flyers) perform from the top of a 98-foot-high (30 m) pole.

OAXACA, MEXICO
SHOPPERS' PARADISE

Join Oaxaca's housewives as they shop, bargain hunt, and greet friends at the city's original market. Enter Mercado Benito Juarez through one of the archways and head into the main hall. It's a burst of color right at the heart of town, alive with merchants and local residents, who have been shopping here for generations. "I remember coming here with my grandmother," says a native Oaxaqueño. "She would shop for dried chilies by touching to make sure they were still soft. Their smoky aroma and deep red color made her *mole* so special. I still love the place today."

WHAT TO BUY: As you squeeze along the narrow alleys you'll be met by a rainbow assortment of colored bags, scarves, and traditional Mexican shawls festooning the rows of small stalls. Everyone buys the vibrantly colored market totes (some with iconic Mexican logos), which are perfect for carrying purchases. Or choose a lightweight, flexible basket from one of the weaver's stands at the north entrance. Woven from narrow palm fronds in colorful geometric patterns, the lidded baskets make great storage containers and the smaller ones are good gift packaging. Then ask vendors to point the way to the beautifully crafted paper-mâché animal masks. These little-known treasures produced for carnival celebrations make unique wall decorations.

Locals use the market for all manner of clothes and domestic items: blouses, scarves, shawls, cotton placemats, and tablecloths. If you're interested in the local liquor, be sure to check out the hand-carved *jícaras*, or gourds, used for drinking mezcal.

FITTING IN: Don't try to barter—prices here are usually fixed. Oaxaqueños are proud of their crafts and cuisine and eager to answer questions about their products, and basic Spanish will go a long way toward establishing a good rapport with vendors.

■ *Essentials:* Benito Juarez Market (corner of Flores Magón and Colón)

The market's basket weavers work quickly, producing intricately patterned containers.

The surf rolls in at Jamaica's Boston Bay.

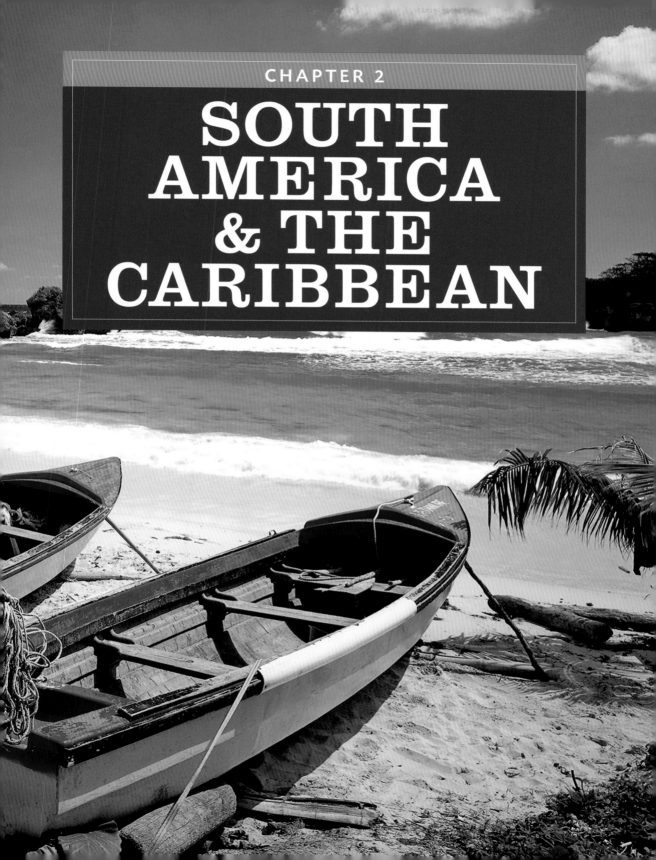

CHAPTER 2

SOUTH AMERICA & THE CARIBBEAN

NASSAU, THE BAHAMAS
JUNKANOO PARADE

The distant roar of brass horns, rhythm sticks, cowbells, whistles, and pounding goatskin drums grows louder, and the crowd cheers in anticipation as the parade approaches. Standing on their seats, Bahamians crane their necks for the first sighting of the dancers. Soon Bay Street is a kaleidoscope of color: Groups of up to 1,000 dancers gyrate through the streets of Nassau, one troupe following another as the crowds and musicians spur them on. Onlookers dance on their chairs, and the sidewalks, balconies, and even rooftops appear to sway to the beat, with everyone grooving to the music.

WHEN TO GO: Junkanoo parades are held annually on Boxing Day (December 26) and New Year's Day throughout the Bahamas—the festival's origins likely date back to the 1700s, when slaves had a few days off for the holidays—with the largest parade in Nassau, the capital city.

Groups dance through the night, from 2 a.m. till dawn, refueling as they go.

JOINING IN: "If you arrive early enough, you can speak to a group leader and join their troupe for the parade," says Adrian Kelly, a Nassau resident. "Choose a smaller group so you don't feel overwhelmed. You'll soon pick up the moves—I've seen it done."

There are prizes for the best dressed, and performers spend months crafting elaborate paper costumes. Look out for the Valley Boys and Saxon Superstars, who are sure to put on a show.

WHAT TO EAT: Food vendors on side streets cook Bahamian favorites: conch fritters, conch stew, cracked conch, conch salad, and johnny cakes (pan-cooked bread).

■ *Essentials:* General information: bahamas.co.uk

Costumed performers parade, or "rush," through the streets of Nassau.

Getting down low at a road tennis match.

BARBADOS

TENNIS HITS THE ROAD

Children pioneered this fast and furious cross between lawn tennis and table tennis in Barbados in the 1930s, chalking out tennis courts in the street. "Normal tennis was too expensive for locals, but it looked fun, so they came up with road tennis," explains Dale Clark, who has been playing since he was a boy.

Since then, road tennis has evolved into an adult sport with tournaments throughout the West Indies. It is a sport you can play almost anywhere. Courts are painted in blue and yellow—the Bajan national colors—and measure 20 by 10 feet (6 by 3 m). They are marked out on any hard, flat surface from parking lots and playgrounds to roads. The plywood net stands just 8 inches (20 cm) tall. Standard tennis balls are the orb of choice, stripped of their felt covering and deflated to diminish their bounce. Rackets are similar to those used for Ping-Pong, without the rubber coating. The first player to reach 21 points (by a 2-point advantage) is the victor.

JOINING IN: Head for St. Michael's Parish and the city of Bridgetown. If you see kids or grown-ups playing road tennis stop and ask if you can try it. Bajans are proud of their homegrown game and will almost always say yes.

WHERE TO WATCH: Amateur and professional events include the Racquets of Fire national championship in November and the National Inter-Parish Road Tennis Tournament in January. Locations change from year to year, but venues include the BIDC car park off Princess Alice Highway in Bridgetown, the courts in Road View area in St. Peter, the Belfield courts in Black Rock, Bridgetown, and the Dover courts in Christ Church.

■ *Essentials:* Professional Road Tennis Association (Clevedale Development, Black Rock, St. Michael, tel 11 246 233 8268 or 11 246 245 3953, proroadtennis.com); for private lessons or information on events, contact Dale Clarke, Barbados Pro Road Tennis (tel 11 246 245 3953)

GRAND CAYMAN, CAYMAN ISLANDS
FISH FRY

Despite its tiny size, the Cayman Islands has developed a considerable culinary reputation. To get the good stuff—the traditional Caymanian food—seek out modest restaurants and beachside huts frequented by Caymanians. Stewed turtle (the green sea turtle) is the iconic dish, these days prepared only with meat from the government's sustainable turtle farm on Grand Cayman. Other local favorites are fish and fritters, chicken with dumplings, and sweet and spicy heavy cake.

WHERE TO GO: At lunchtime, local workers pile into Mango Tree in George Town, which has a long list of Caymanian dishes, including stewed turtle, conch fritters, tripe beans, and cow foot. On weekends, locals head for Vivine's Kitchen, overlooking the beach at East End. "Sundays are real busy," says owner-chef Vivine Watler. "That's when we do seafood and conch stew, as well as the usual barbecued chicken, curried pork, and fish."

LOCAL KNOWLEDGE: On Saturday morning (from 7 a.m.), mingle with locals at Market at The Grounds, at Savannah on Grand Cayman, to sample cooked stews and baked goods (try plaintain tart) as well as fresh fruit and vegetables, juices, jams, and pepper jellies. Everything is home-produced and sold directly to the public. You can eat your hand-picked feast at one of the picnic tables.

■ *Essentials:* Mango Tree (518 Shedden Rd., George Town, Grand Cayman, tel 11 345 949 0732); Vivine's Kitchen (Austin Dr., East End, Grand Cayman, tel 11 345 947 7435, closed some Mons.); Market at The Grounds (Savannah, Grand Cayman, thegroundscayman.ky)

Heavy Cake

An island favorite, "heavy cake" is a dark and deliciously moist dessert made from grated cassava, coconut milk, dark sugar, and spices. **Vivine's Kitchen** bakes the gold standard, but you can also buy it by the slice at farmers' markets, including the Wednesday (afternoon only) **Camana Bay Farmers' Market,** on the corner of Market Street and Forum Lane.

It's hard to beat locally owned beachside restaurants for fresh fish.

El Chanchullero serves simple food in a lively atmosphere.

HAVANA, CUBA
HABANERO HANGOUTS

Adele singing on the iPod, smartphones at the ready, and mint Audis cruising the Malecón—welcome to the "new" Cuba, where economic reforms are sparking an explosion of entrepreneurial spirit and consumer capitalism. *Paladares* (private restaurants) lead the way in small business start-ups, with everything from porch-front pizza parlors to haute cuisine hideouts competing for Cuba's new money. Despite the changes, old habits die hard: Service can be spotty; certain menu items—mushrooms, feta cheese, vegetarian anything—are pure fiction; and napkins continue to be an endangered species. Still, Cubans hunger for something new, different, and modern, and they love to celebrate with food—even if it means spending their last cent to do so.

LOCAL FAVORITES: The laid-back (almost) seaside eatery La Chuchería is "all the rage right now," according to Habanero Daniel Sánchez; don't be surprised if you have to wait for a coveted terrace table. Avoid the crowds by going in the morning and having a rare real bacon, eggs, and toast breakfast. In a sweet, still ragged-around-the-edges pocket of Old Havana, El Chanchullero jumps with young

Cubans noshing and gossiping around rough-hewn tables. The upstairs lounge is a cozy, secret spot where those in the know take liquid dinner or a date. There's no sign here; look for the sidewalk chalkboard menu. A prime Old Havana location pairs with a fresh, modern menu at Ivan Chef Justo. Chef Ivan rolls out pasta and shaves chocolate onto Havana's best dessert in the tiny, open kitchen, giving this upscale eatery a homey feel. Bollywood, Cuba's first and only Indian restaurant, is packing in diners in droves. They come for their first taste of tandoori, curries, and roti.

LOCAL KNOWLEDGE: A burger and beer cost half a month's salary for most Cubans (the monthly pay is about US$20); for them, eating at a private restaurant is out of reach. For monied locals and visitors looking for a taste of Cuba, paladares hit the spot.

■ *Essentials:* La Chuchería (1era Ave., corner Calle C, tel 53 (0) 7 830 0708); El Chanchullero (Teniente Rey #457A, between Bernaza and El Cristo, tel 53 (0) 7 872 8227); Ivan Chef Justo (Calle Aguacate #9, corner Calle Chacón, tel 53 (0) 7 863 9697); Bollywood (Calle 35 at #1361, tel 53 (0) 7 883 1216)

ISLAND JERK JOINTS

You can jerk just about anything—beef, goat, fish, or shrimp, though pork and chicken are mainly used in Jamaica's spicy barbecue. What makes it jerk is the slathering of zesty sauce and the slow-cooking over a pimento-wood fire. The sauce normally contains allspice (known as pimento in Jamaica), scotch bonnet peppers, scallions, and thyme, although many chefs toss their own "secret ingredients" into the mix. According to legend, the jungle-shrouded John Crow Mountain range behind Boston Bay on the island's east coast is the cradle of jerk cooking—escaped slaves known as Maroons pioneered the technique by roasting wild boar over pimento wood.

WHERE TO GO: "Ya, mon. We jerk the original way," says Devon Atkinson, chief cook and saucier at Mickey's Jerk Centre, one of more than a dozen barbecue stalls clustered on the coastal highway at Boston Bay. For something different, try Mickey's jerk fish smoked in aluminum foil. The original Scotchies jerk stall east of Montego Bay is a Jamaican institution—people drive two hours across the island for the jerked pork and chicken. Scotchies has expanded to new outlets in central Kingston and Drax Hall west of Ocho Rios. The latest in-place for jerk is Buccaneers at Llanrumney, a small town between Port Maria and Annotto Bay on the north coast.

■ *Essentials:* Mickey's Jerk Centre (A4 Coast Hwy., Boston Bay); Scotchies (A4 Coast Hwy., Coral Gardens, Rose Hall, tel 11 876 953 3301); Scotchies Drax Hall (St. Ann's Bay, tel 11 876 794 9457); Buccaneers Jerk & Juice (Llanrumney Sq., Llanrumney, St. Mary's, tel 11 876 992 5094)

Boston Bay, the birthplace of Jamaican jerk

"Jamaicans are choosy about their jerk—some like a little more ginger or garlic, some a little more heat." —ROSIE DODD, RESIDENT OF MONTEGO BAY

West Indies fast bowler Jerome Taylor takes aim. Opposite: Beach cricket is played and watched everywhere.

ANTIGUA AND BARBUDA, WEST INDIES
BATTING AND BOWLING

More than any other Caribbean island, Antigua is obsessed by cricket. Whether it's kids playing on the beach or in a vacant lot, adults participating in a local after-work league, or the professionals who hit for six and take wickets in international Test Matches, there's bound to be some kind of cricket taking place in Antigua on any given day.

LOCAL HERO: Batsman Viv Richards, voted one of the five top cricketers of the 20th century, is the island's most famous son and captained the West Indies team in the 1980s. In 1986, at the old Antigua Recreation Ground in St. John's, he batted the fastest Test-Match century (100 runs scored) ever. His bat is in the island museum and the new state-of-the-art stadium in North Sound, built for the 2007 World Cup and home to international matches, is named after him.

WHERE TO GO: Take a tip from the locals and see cricket up close and personal at one of the pitches that dot the island. The village green in John Hughes and the primary school field in Pigotts are both charming, but for an oceanside pitch with a cooling sea breeze, you can't beat the Falmouth Cricket Pitch on the south shore. Here you can munch on homemade fried chicken as you watch a game. Says Cee Cee Williams, who works at the Catamaran Hotel just up the road, "We go there every Sunday with all the family to sit and watch the game and talk cricket. It's got a really laid-back atmosphere." But don't be fooled by the relaxed vibe—the standard of play is high.

■ *Essentials:* Sir Vivian Richards Stadium (Sir Sydney Walling Hwy., North Sound, St. John's); Stanford Cricket Ground (Pavilion Dr., Osbourn, St. George); Falmouth Cricket Pitch (center of Falmouth). To find upcoming inter-island and Test Matches in Antigua, check the West Indies Cricket Board website at windiescricket.com/fixtures

"Cricket is the big thing in the islands. Everybody loves it."
—Cee Cee Williams, St. John's native

ISLA MARGARITA, VENEZUELA
DANCING WITH THE COWBOYS

The western half of Venezuela's Isla Margarita is cowboy country—all cactus-studded desert dotted with haciendas raising horses and cattle. On weekends, the island's *caballeros* head for their local bodegas to eat, drink, and dance to live *joropo* music.

While the dance known as joropo developed out of the waltzes that were popular throughout Latin America in the 19th century, the music derives mainly from the folk tunes of the *llaneros* (cowboys) of Venezuela and Colombia. Bands play such instruments as guitars and *cuatros*, drums, maracas, and small harps called *arpa llanera*. The lyrics are mostly about lost or unrequited love, bygone memories, or lovable cowpokes who don't seem to have a lick of sense.

WHERE TO GO: The best joropo joints have a Wild West vibe—look for pickup trucks parked outside adobe bars with thatched-roof dancing areas. El Caney de Lencha in the dusty village of El Espinal, in the middle of the island, attracts a steady stream of top joropo acts and local aficionados. Order a thick steak from the barbecue man, wash it down with an ice-cold Cerveza Polar, then take to the dance floor. Don't be surprised if some of the other patrons are packing Colt revolvers and other firearms—this side of Margarita is still the Wild West.

WHAT TO WEAR: You might have brought a bikini or shorts for the rest of your stay, but beachwear won't do for joropo. Skintight jeans and cowboy boots are de rigueur. This is the place to brush down the suede and put on the Stetson.

■ *Essentials:* Restaurante El Caney de Lencha (Ave. Simplicio Rodriguez, El Espinal, tel 58 295 297 3361, closed Mon.)

Local kids are always happy to demonstrate.

Girls at Trinidad's carnival

CARNIVAL!

These parties-to-end-all-parties happen just once a year in the days before Lent.

■ **Trinidad**
In the early hours of pre-Lent Monday morning, J'Ouvert (from the French "Day is Open") explodes onto the streets. People smeared with mud, oil, and paint play the part of devilish folkloric figures. Over the next days, people pack the streets, dancing to the costumed "Mas bands."
gotrinidadandtobago.com

■ **Veracruz, Mexico**
The nine-day-long bash begins with a ceremony called the *quema del mal humor*, or "burning of the bad mood," in which an effigy of an unpopular figure is gleefully set alight. Then, it's parades, floats, and nonstop music and dancing.
veracruz.travel

■ **Ororo, Bolivia**
Join the locals to watch the battle between good and evil at the Diablada, or "Dance of the Devils." Participants wear fearsome masks and elaborate headdresses and parade to the cathedral, where homage is paid to the Virgin of Candelaria, patron saint of miners. Chicha, a powerful maize-based spirit, fuels the after-party in the plaza.
ladiabladadeoruro.com

■ **Cologne, Germany**
The carnival lasts a week, but the locals won't miss Rosenmontag, "Rose Monday procession," when characters on lavish floats throw candy and flowers to the crowds. The next day, those in the know head to the burbs, where the party goes on until midnight and the "Nubbel" (a life-size straw figure) is ceremonially burned.
cologne-tourism.com

■ **Basel, Switzerland**
At 4 a.m. on the Monday before Ash Wednesday, the carnival cliques (Cliquen) in outlandish costumes, accompanied by pipers and drummers, carry huge transparent lanterns through the dark streets. Within are depictions of topical events.
fasnachts-comite.ch

■ **Binche, Belgium**
Insiders come out on Shrove Tuesday to see the Gilles of Binche, local men and boys wearing wax masks and snowy ostrich feather headdresses. Bells jangling on the waists of their colorful straw-stuffed costumes, they carry sticks to ward off devils and baskets of oranges to throw to the crowd.
carnavaldebinche.be

■ **Nice, France**
Carnival in Nice lasts two weeks, but the local favorite is the flower battles. Costumed characters on the huge floats rolling along the promenade des Anglais hurl a barrage of flowers at the crowds, filling the street with perfume. Buy your ticket early.
nicecarnaval.com

■ **Cadiz, Spain**
Gaditanos, as local people are known, would never go to one of the big processions without wearing a costume. The big draws are the Gran Cabalgata on the first Sunday and the Cabalgata del Humor on the last weekend of Carnival.
andalucia.org

■ **Ivrea, Italy**
At the Ivrea orange battle, said to date from a 12th-century insurrection, groups of villagers in medieval dress pelt each other with oranges. To signal that you are not an orange-thrower, wear one of the red hats, *berretto frigio*, sold on the street.
italia.it

OLINDA, BRAZIL
THE BEAT GOES ON

A throwback to the celebrations of old, carnival in the seaside city of Olinda, in northeastern Brazil, is freeform and spontaneous. There are no pricey entrance fees, cordons, or guards—everyone joins in—and there is none of the orchestrated glitz of Rio's equivalent. Performers simply dance their way through the historic city's narrow cobblestone streets.

WHEN TO GO: The carnival gets off to a rousing start in February, finishing in time for Lent. On the Sunday before the official opening, the Virgens do Bairro Novo—hundreds of men dressed in drag vying to become the latest carnival "queen"—parade through the streets. As the week heats up, everyone joins in the fun—school and church groups, residents of all ages, and anyone from out of town who feels the urge to samba till dawn.

Traditional *troças*—carnival groups—organize *blocos* (parades and street parties) and some, such as Pitombeira dos Quatro Cantos, invite the public to watch their rehearsals before carnival starts. Processions include giant papier-mâché puppets of world leaders, celebrities, and traditional favorites such as Homem da Meia-Noite (Midnight Man).

WHERE TO GO: The Cidade Alta, the historic center, becomes a hub of music, costume, and dancing, its small squares and side streets filling with revelers. "The secret to enjoying Carnival in Olinda is not to plan anything," advises José Teixeira, a local language teacher. "Just go there and get lost in the spirit and joy of carnival, not to mention the beer and *caipirinhas* [the Brazilian national drink made with rum and limes]. I love the feeling of total freedom—there's nothing like it."

LOCAL FAVORITES: Dancers entertain the crowds with the *Maracatú*, based on African rhythms and steps, *Caboclinhos*, inspired by Brazil's Amerindian heritage, and *Frevo*, an acrobatic dance often performed with a miniature umbrella to brass band music.

■ *Essentials:* Pitombeira dos Quatro Cantos (Rua 27 de Janeiro 128, Carmo); off2brazil.com, carnivalbookers.com

> *"The crowd goes wild when the frevo dancers go by."*
> —JOSÉ TEIXEIRA, LOCAL TEACHER

Maracatú lance-carriers get into the spirit with energetic warrior dances.

A priest gives his blessing to a car before the owner douses it in beer.

COPACABANA, BOLIVIA
TOASTING THE VIRGIN MARY

The small lakeside town of Copacabana may be the sleepy gateway to Lake Titicaca for most of the year, but arrive there during the first week of February and you are engulfed by a raucous local festival of music and dancing, eating and drinking—especially drinking. The excuse is to celebrate the Dark Virgin of the Lake, whose carved, dark wood statue rests in the white, Moorish-style Basilica de la Virgen de la Candelaria.

The local tipple is Pilsener La Paz. Fresh Titicaca trout, eaten with rice and fries, dominates food from lakeside vendors, but it is the beer (and nothing stronger) that is central to the annual festival, which is very much a local event and can change dates on a whim.

LOCAL FAVORITES: In front of the church at 10 a.m. each day, people gather to watch a baseball-capped priest conduct the *benedición de movilidades*, the blessing of cars, adorned with garlands and flags for the ceremony. Owners then baptize the vehicles with champagne or beer to the tat-tat-tat of firecrackers.

At nonstop street parties women in traditional bowler hats and brightly colored dresses dance while their husbands drink until they drop, and then wake to drink some more. The alcoholic haze is penetrated on day three by a rough-and-ready version of "running of the bulls," when local bravados dodge cantankerous bulls in a grassy makeshift arena on the Yampupata road.

JOINING IN: You can segue smoothly into the dancing of the troupes and their bands. The whole enchilada begins with the parade of the Dark Virgin. This is not the real one: Legend says that if the Virgin is moved from the church, Lake Titicaca will flood Copacabana, so a substitute statue does the honors instead.

■ *Essentials:* General information: tourismoboliviaperu.com

PATAGONIA, CHILE
GAUCHO COOKOUT

The *asado*, or barbecue, is part of gaucho culture in Chile, especially on the vast estancias (ranches) of Patagonia at the country's southern end. With bodegas few and far between and towns widely scattered, asados are often the only venues where gauchos and other ranch workers can socialize. The affair normally stretches out for two or three hours as the meat is salted, fixed onto long metal poles (*asadones*), and slow-cooked over a campfire, brick hearth, or frontier barbecue made from a steel drum.

WHAT TO ORDER: Sheep is the meat of choice in southern Chile, although beef, pork, and venison can round out the spread. Common side dishes include boiled potatoes, tomato and onion salad, and fresh bread, plus copious amounts of Chilean red wine.

JOINING IN: Cordial sorts, gauchos are apt to invite total strangers to their asados. You can join in by signing up for a horseback trail ride or overnight stay on the handful of working estancias that take guests. The *asador* (grill master) might even let you join in the cooking.

WHERE TO GO: Sprawling across 250,000 acres (100,000 ha), Estancia Cerro Guido is one of the oldest and largest sheep and cattle spreads in Chilean Patagonia. The heart of the ranch is a red-roofed villa with an enclosed asado hearth, adjacent bar, and dining room with picture windows that look out over the Torres del Paine mountain range. Overlooking the Strait of Magellan, Estancia Rio de Los Ciervos lies on the outskirts of Punta Arenas at the very southern end of mainland Chile. Sixty miles (97 km) north of Punta Arenas is 19th-century Estancia Rio Verde, part working cattle farm and part hotel, on the shores of Skyring Sound, where you can join in the work of the ranch, or just enjoy your choice of meat barbecued in front of the big hearth in the dining room.

■ *Essentials:* Estancia Cerro Guido (Torres del Paine, tel 56 (0) 61 360 305, cerroguido.cl); Estancia Rio de Los Ciervos (Km. 5.5 Ruta 9 Sur, Punta Arenas, tel 56 (0) 61 710 219, estanciariode losciervos.com); Estancia Rio Verde (Km. 97 Ruta I-50, Rio Verde, tel 56 (0) 61 311 131 or 56 (0) 9 8392 8132, estanciarioverde.cl)

The Torres del Paine rise up from the flat pampas.

Santiago's trendy
Vitacura district.
Opposite: A sparkling
first course

NOUVEAU CHILEAN DINING

The overthrow of the military junta in 1990 liberated more than Chile's human rights—it also set the stage for a revolution in Santiago's food scene. Young Chileno gourmands began to travel overseas and study under the master chefs of Europe and North America. Equipped with world-class culinary skills, many returned to open their own restaurants, transforming the Chilean dining experience into one of the most savory in South America and delighting local foodies.

Santiago's new-wave restaurants are known for both their food and their stunning locations in plazas, parks, and historic mansions. "In the last five years it has changed so much," says Carolina Bazán, the Parisian-trained chef who runs Ambrosía restaurant with her father. "It's a new generation, new attitude. People go out to eat so much more now than during the military years."

WHERE TO GO: Recently relocated from downtown to trendy Vitacura in northern Santiago, Ambrosía fuses international and Chilean trends. Try the *pulpo grillado* (grilled octopus) or the *ciervo con puré de zanahoria* (fillet of venison with carrot puree). Housed in a low-slung, modern structure that could have been designed by Frank Lloyd Wright, Mestizo is one of those rare restaurants that's both a hip hangout and a fine-dining hub. Grab an outdoor table overlooking the park, order a bottle of wine, and dig into the Magallanica king crab with candied razor clams.

WHAT TO ORDER: Ceviche, marinated raw seafood, is Chile's national dish, served at what seems like nearly every restaurant. Santiago's restaurants offer interesting variations on ceviche using different types of fish, herbs, or spices. These eateries also offer offbeat versions of pisco sour, a cocktail made with grape brandy (pisco), citrus juice, and bitters.

The nouvelle Chileno treatment extends to other traditional dishes, such as *lomo saltado* (stir-fried beef) and *pernil crocante* (pork loin). Wash it down with a fabulous cabernet sauvignon or sauvignon blanc white from Chile's Central Valley.

MORE FAVORITES: Hot bread served in a small brown bag, sea urchin sprayed with pisco, rock fish chicharrón served on hot lava rocks? Culinary inhibitions are left behind at Boragó, where Santiago-born chef Rodolfo Guzmán specializes in innovative food using Chilean ingredients. Fashionable diners looking for new experiences choose from an array of artistically "designed" dishes.

■ *Essentials*: Ambrosía (Calle Pamplona 78, Vitacura, tel 56 (0) 2 217 3075, closed Sun.); Mestizo (Ave. Bicentenario 4050, Vitacura, tel 56 (0) 7 477 6093); Boragó (Ave. Nueva Costanera 3467, Vitacura, tel 56 (0) 2 953 8893, borago.cl)

MORE: Santiago Seafood

For simply prepared very fresh seafood—say, fried shrimp followed by seabass with avocado and salsa on the side—go to Santiago's old fish market in the atmospheric **Mercado Central,** on the corner of Calle 21 and Calle San Pablo. Here, amid the vast banks of fresh fish and shellfish, restaurants do a roaring lunchtime trade. Do as many of the Chileans do and climb the spiral staircase to the balcony level. Afterward join marketeers for a refreshing beverage called *cola de mono* (monkey's tail) in the **Quinto Patio,** a typical working-class bar.

"The Mercado Central, I love it! You can mingle with the people and sample fabulous fresh seafood." —CAROLINA BAZÁN, CHEF

BUENOS AIRES, ARGENTINA
ANYONE FOR POLO?

Horses go with polo like gauchos with pampas, so it's no surprise that when the sport was introduced into Argentina by British settlers in the 1870s, the country was soon turning out some of the world's best players. The sport has an exclusive image, but that doesn't mean stuffy. Professional polo player Charlie Wood, who has worked on an estancia, says, "It's a total polo culture in Argentina. Polo is just a normal part of people's lives on the ranches; no one dresses up. A typical game day starts slowly, with people getting to the club after lunch. We play in the late afternoon, have a swim at the club pool, a drink, and then head off to someone's estancia [ranch] for a barbecue. Dinner's not till 11 p.m. It's just very relaxed."

JOINING IN: Polo is especially strong on the estancias of Buenos Aires Province and the pampas spreading west to Mendoza. Fans flock to the Estancia Grande Polo Club near San Luis for tournaments throughout the year at all levels, including youth and women's events. The Argentine Open Tournament—"the best tournament in the world," says polo player Santiago Boudou—takes place at Campo Argentino de Polo in the Palermo district of Buenos Aires between late November and early December.

FITTING IN: What to wear depends on the match. Mostly it's smart-casual—sports jacket, jeans, and cowboy boots for men; summer dresses and sun hats for women. Between chukkas at Campo Argentino de Polo, locals like to grab a cold beer, cocktail, or maté tea at the Alpi Chico: The Polo Pub, where profits go to a local charity.

■ *Essentials:* Estancia Grande Polo Club (Autopista Ruta 9, San Luis, estanciagrandepoloclub.com); Campo Argentino de Polo (Ave. del Libertador, Buenos Aires, tel 54 (0) 11 4777 8005, aapolo.com)

Tea Time

Maté tea is drunk from a calabash gourd through a silver straw that filters out the leafy particles. With the gourd passed from hand to hand, it's more social activity than thirst-quencher. "Yerba [tea leaves] and hot water, that's it!" says Santi Boudou. "We drink it morning, noon, and night—with each other while talking horses, with the grooms, and with the vet."

Daredevil riding skills pump up the excitement at the Campo Argentino de Polo.

BUENOS AIRES, ARGENTINA
FLORIDA STREET

In the Argentine capital, Calle Florida draws crowds of shoppers, including financial district workers from nearby offices. This mile-long (1.6 km), elegant pedestrian walkway sells everything from upscale clothing to Argentine-themed memorabilia. And with scores of cafés and restaurants, street musicians and tango dancers, it's a great place to soak up the local atmosphere.

WHAT TO BUY: Argentine wool and leather products—sweaters and scarves, leather jackets, shoes, gloves, and purses—are good buys. Several stores sell fine lingerie at inviting prices, others silver and jewelry set with precious stones sourced in South America.

WHERE TO GO: The street's pedestrianized section runs between Avenida Rivadavia and Plaza San Martín. You can order custom-made leather goods at Ashanti Leather Factory. For trendy women's leather fashions, try Blaquè in the Galerías Pacífico mall, a glorious beaux arts building with a fresco-decorated cupola, on the corner of Calle Florida and Avenida Córdoba. El Boyero in the mall is good for silver crafts, including jewelry and gaucho belt buckles.

TAKING A BREAK: Relax and connect with the impeccably dressed *porteños*, the city's residents, over a cup of *café con leche* and a *medialuna* (croissant), at one of Calle Florida's numerous cafés. Strike up a conversation with one of the locals and you will probably get some good tips as to where to find the best bargains.

■ *Essentials:* Ashanti Leather Factory (Calle Florida 585, tel 54 (0) 11 4394 1310); Blaquè (Galerías Pacífico, Calle Florida 725, blaque.com.ar, tel 54 (0) 11 5555 5100, galeriaspacifico .com.ar); El Boyero (Calle Florida 953, tel 54 (0) 11 4312 3564 or 3565, elboyero.com, closed Sun.)

MORE: Shopping Chic

Cool young porteños comb the cobblestoned streets of **Palermo** in northwest Buenos Aires for independent designers and one-off stores. Key streets are Gurruchaga, El Salvador, Nicaragua, Thames, and Gorriti, though the whole area is full of interesting retail nooks, characterful buildings, great little bars, cafés, and art spaces.

Barmen mix Pisco sours at a Lima festival.

LIMA, PERU
PISCO SOUR HAPPY HOURS

The afternoon customers fill every table and prop their elbows on the bar's marble top. Conversation, gesticulation, the smell of roasted pork, and the rattle of ice in a cocktail shaker create an ambience that can't have changed much in Antigua Taberna Queirolo's 120-year history. "Entering is like going back half a century," says financial analyst Alfredo Calle of this taverna in the Pueblo Libre district of Lima. "Locals of all ages come here in search of delicious traditional food and to kill their thirst with drinks blessed with the spirit of pisco." As they talk about work, politics, and football they tuck into pork sandwiches, beef tripe, and mussels.

LOCAL KNOWLEDGE: A fresh, briefly-aged grape brandy—Antigua Taberna Queirolo makes its own—pisco is the principal ingredient in the country's most famous drink, pisco sour, mixed with egg whites, lemon juice, syrup, and ice to create a tart, textured, firecracker of a cocktail.

ANOTHER FAVORITE: Mayta, in Miraflores, specializes in *macerados*—pisco infusions—made from local plants and herbs (including guava, yucca, tamarind, and eucalyptus).

■ *Essentials:* Antigua Taberna Queirolo (1090 Ave. San Martín, tel 51 (0) 1 460 1441); Mayta (Ave. 28 de Julio 1290, San Antonio, tel 51 (0) 1 243 0121)

DIGGING DEEPER

To while away an increasingly rowdy Saturday evening in Antigua Taberna Queirolo, do as the locals do and order a *res:* A waiter brings a bottle of house pisco to the table along with a mixer (usually 7-Up or Canada Dry), a plate of limes, some cane syrup, and a bucket of ice.

The best bars take their drinks seriously.

BARTENDERS' FAVORITES

The city's best bar is the one its bartenders hang out in when they're not mixing drinks.

■ Huaringas, Lima, Peru

Pisco aficionados will tell you that the best of South America's grape brandies are meant to be sipped straight—until they taste Huaringas's infusions, flavored with maracuyá (passion fruit), uva (tropical grape) and coca leaves, and its frothy, ice-cold pisco sour. No less than Lima's star chef Gastón Acurio is a fan.
brujasdecachiche.com.pe

■ Smuggler's Cove, San Francisco, CA

Is this Prohibition-era Havana? Your rumrunner is Smuggler's Cove owner Martin Cate, the man behind the resurgence of the Tiki bar. You'll find dozens of exotic drink options on the tiny bar's menu—but no food. Where to eat before imbibing? "Locals never eat clam chowder from sourdough bread bowls," Cate says. "Get a burrito in the Mission to complete your visit."
smugglerscovesf.com

■ Bar Tonique, New Orleans, LA

Beyond sugary Hurricanes in souvenir glasses, New Orleans hides a serious cocktail scene. You've found it when you spot the small chalkboard advertising the French Quarter's Bar Tonique, a favorite of NOLA's restaurant industry folks and anyone who appreciates carefully crafted classic drinks with a side of cocktail wonkery.
bartonique.com

■ Hop Sing Laundromat, Philadelphia, PA

There's a lot of buildup to a drink at Hop Sing Laundromat: Find the unmarked Chinatown door, meet the unwritten-but-enforced dress code, and greet the eccentric owner Lêe. But the cocktails deliver—top-shelf alcohol, fresh-squeezed juices, and a story with every drink—making Hop Sing a gathering spot for food critics, bartenders, and chefs.
hopsinglaundromat.com

■ Ruby, Copenhagen, Denmark

The unmarked door to Ruby's chandeliered rooms opens at 4 p.m., perhaps the only time you'll find the popular canal-side bar quiet enough for a chat with the knowledgeable staff. Order a seasonal cocktail: Celebrate the short Danish strawberry season with a champagne cocktail and warm the long winter with cognac and caramelized fig.
rby.dk

■ Pivovarský Klub, Prague, Czech Republic

Choose from hundreds of beers, including local craft brews that can be hard to find in this Pilsner Urquell–dominated city. Upstairs, the neighborhood bar and bottle shop doubles as a beer lover's souvenir shop; downstairs, try the hearty Czech dishes.
pivovarskyklub.com

■ Quinary, Hong Kong, China

Many Hong Kong cocktail bars are helmed by celebrated expat bartenders. Not so at Quinary, where homegrown talent Antonio Lai mixes it up. His signature is the Earl Grey Caviar Martini with tea-infused "caviar" (froth) in place of olives. Lai calls it "multisensory mixology." Regulars at the laid-back bar just call it "wow."
quinary.hk

You can see Highland dancing competitions at events all over Scotland.

ES €15 PER SQ.FT.
01 6185500

Whatever you
wear, make sure
it's green.

DUBLIN, IRELAND
PAINTING THE TOWN GREEN

Dublin's River Liffey dyed bright green, children with their faces painted the green, white, and orange of the Irish flag—the time to be in the Irish capital is mid-March, for St. Patrick's Day, when the city remembers Ireland's patron saint. For four days, the locals celebrate Irish culture and history and enjoy the best Irish music, dance, art, street theater, and folklore.

JOINING IN: The main event is the parade on St. Patrick's Day itself, March 17. This outpouring of floats and dance troupes begins at Parnell Square around noon and winds along O'Connell Street, past Trinity College, and finishes at St. Patrick's Cathedral. To get a good vantage point with 500,000 people on the streets, stake your place early.

POST PARADE: Later on, retreat to a pub with the crowds; Long Hall in the St. George's area is good for an afternoon of storytelling with the regulars over a few pints of the black stuff. Trendy tipplers drink at South William.

■ *Essentials:* stpatricksfestival.ie; Long Hall (51 S. Great George's St., tel 353 (0) 1 475 1590, pubsdirect.ie); South William (52 S. William St., tel 353 (0) 1 672 5946, southwilliam.ie); O'Neill's (2 Suffolk St., tel 353 (0) 1 679 3656, oneillsbar.com)

"When I've had enough of the hullabaloo, the greenery, and the marching bands, I slip into O'Neill's on Suffolk Street and sip a pint in the snug." —GARY MCKEONE, LOCAL ARTS ADMINISTRATOR

DUBLIN, IRELAND
FISH AND CHIPS

Dubliners rarely agree on anything as unanimously as they do on Leo Burdock's fish and chips emporium on Werburgh Street. This cozy little slot, unchanged for the better part of a century, is a Dublin must. A board lists the names of celebrities who have darkened this simple door, but it's the line of locals waiting for their piping hot hit of fish and chips that is the real proof. "On a summer evening, I like to collect my bag from Burdock's, hop in the car, and set off for Sandymount Strand [on Dublin Bay's south shore]," enthuses Derry-man Ian Doherty, a regular business visitor to Dublin. "During the ten-minute drive, the salt and vinegar suffuses the fish and chips, and the first waft of steam when you open the bag is heaven."

WHAT TO ORDER: Choose lightly battered cod fried to a golden crisp, with a dash of malt vinegar for acidity. Ask for some extra crispy pieces of fried potato and the server will throw in a few caramelized crunchies filled with taste.

HOW TO EAT: The only remaining question is where to devour this simple yet supremely satisfying communion with the North Atlantic and the supreme Irish tuber, cut

MORE: Dublin Seafood

At the other end of the scale from Dublin's "chippers" are restaurants serving Dublin Bay lobster and prawns (shrimp). **Restaurant Patrick Guilbaud:** A two-Michelin-star restaurant revered for its locally sourced, seasonal menus. restaurantpatrickguilbaud.ie
Lobster Pot: This family-run restaurant is famed for its seafood and extensive wine list. thelobsterpot.ie

into perfect-sized chunks and fried to al dente perfection. You can sit and dig into your bag of happiness in the courtyards of Christ Church or around St. Patrick's Cathedral, and along the back of Dublin Castle. In the rain, stick with the indoor benches at Burdock's.

■ *Essentials:* Leo Burdock (2 Werburgh St., Christchurch, tel 353 (0) 1 454 0306, leoburdock.com)

Dublin's lively Temple Bar district includes a branch of Leo Burdock.

JOIN IN THE JIG

From outside the barn at Vaughan's Pub in the small village of Kilfenora, County Clare, you can hear the squeeze box setting the pace of a wild reel. Inside the rustic, stone-walled space, locals are dancing up a storm. The infectious rhythm moves them in figures of eight, feet stomping the floor. This is one invitation to the dance you won't be able to resist.

LOCAL CULTURE: Long before the advent of discos or online dating, singles in rural Ireland would meet and mingle at *céilís*—social gatherings with music, dancing, and, perhaps, matchmakers to help you find the perfect mate. The tradition has undergone something of a renaissance in the early 21st century as the Irish rediscover their roots.

JOINING IN: Accordions, fiddles, flutes, and *bodhráns* (drums) provide the rhythm for lively set dances with everyone taking part. Some you do "line" style or in circles; others are more like square dancing, performed with locked arms and alternating partners.

WHEN TO GO: Highlight of the town's annual music festival in April is an open-air céilí in Kilfenora's village

MORE: County Clare Céilís

You can usually find céilís at large public events.
Roadside Tavern, Lisdoonvarna: Public céilís take place here during the town's annual Matchmaking Festival each September. roadsidetavern.ie
Town square, Kilrush: Several public céilí sessions take place in the town square during the Music and Set Dancing Weekend each August. kilrush.ie

square. But on just about any weekend you can find céilí music and dance in Vaughan's Pub. "It's a really really good night. It's in our barn. Even if you don't know the steps, the locals will show you what to do," explains Kay Vaughan, owner of Vaughan's Pub.

■ *Essentials:* kilfenoraclare.com; Vaughan's Pub (Main St., tel 353 (0) 65 708 8004, vaughanspub.ie)

Céilís are informal events.

St. Mary's church in Wedmore is a typical Come and Sing venue.

ENGLAND

COME AND SING HANDEL

Spot an advertisement reading "Come and Sing Handel's *Messiah*" outside a village church, large city church, or concert hall and the temptation to join in can be irresistible. Come and Sing events, which are open to all, consist of a temporary choir coming together for a day or afternoon of rehearsals culminating in a public performance in the evening.

LOCAL FAVORITE: At the beautiful parish church of St. Mary's, next to The George, an old coaching inn, in the Somerset village of Wedmore, the chorus for the *Messiah* comprises all manner of locals—farmers, teachers, retired people—as well as visitors. "We're encouraged to study the score beforehand—but it's not essential," says Wedmore resident Ian Armitage. Four trained singers take the solo parts, and the church organ substitutes for the orchestra. At the evening performance anything can happen, from a bat flitting around the rafters to a missing soloist.

FARTHER AFIELD: Performances from scratch occur all over the country; and not just of the *Messiah,* although that is probably the most popular classical piece. London's Royal Albert Hall puts on several such events each year. At other venues, Come and Sing events take place on an ad hoc basis and are advertised on the internet.

■ *Essentials:* Come and Sing concerts around the U.K.: choirs .org.uk/comeandsing.htm or search under come and sing; Royal Albert Hall (Kensington Gore, London, tel 44 (0) 845 401 5045, royalalberthall.com)

York Theatre Royal's Robin Hood and his Merry Mam (mother)

YORK, ENGLAND

SHOWTIME, CHRISTMAS

Raucous and ribald, the Christmas pantomime—at heart, a form of musical comedy based loosely on well-known fairy tales—is a uniquely British part of celebrating Christmas. Expect cross-dressing, audience participation, plenty of songs, and slapstick humor (plus a hefty dose of sexual innuendo sailing over the children's heads). "Like most British children, my first visit to the theater was at Christmas to see the local pantomime. I was instantly enthralled by the comedy, the songs, the costume changes, and spectacular scenery," says playwright Mark Ravenhill. "I still go to one every year."

JOINING IN: Forget theatrical innovation, a "panto" is all about fun. Everyone—actors hamming it up, children squealing in delighted terror, parents suppressing giggles, even the ushers doling out ice cream—is having the time of their life. As much enthusiasm is expected of the audience as the actors. If you aren't roaring "He's behind you!" with everyone else as the villain tiptoes up on the hero, you really aren't pulling your weight. "I enjoy joining in the songs and calling out 'Behind you' whenever the need arises," adds Ravenhill.

WHERE TO GO: The city of York's Theatre Royal is the center of the pantomime world. Its annual production is a labor of love from Berwick Kaler, Britain's longest-serving pantomime dame, who writes a new play each year. Unlike the identikit sets seen elsewhere, every item on stage at York is handcrafted for the production.

■ *Essentials:* York Theatre Royal (St. Leonard's Pl., tel 44 (0) 1904 623568, yorktheatreroyal.co.uk)

DIGGING DEEPER

For a truly unique experience, find an amateur production local to where you are (noda.org). These performances are so bundled with manic energy, and packed with well-wishers, that when the performance is over you'll feel intimately acquainted with the entire cast and half the audience.

COTSWOLDS, ENGLAND
QUIZ NIGHT AT THE PUB

With roughly 22,000 pub quizzes held weekly all over Britain, the Cotswolds in Gloucestershire isn't the only place where you can tease your brain over a pint. However, this region of picturesque villages and rolling farmland is probably one of the prettiest. Players clustered around the tables in the snug, stone-walled bars are not there for cash prizes, but simply for the warmth and camaraderie—and, of course, the tipple.

HOW TO PLAY: Whether you're sipping on beer, cider, or wine, the quiz format rarely varies: Teams of up to eight people confront questions divided into categories that range from art and literature to television soaps and the occasional local legend. "Between rounds, teams swap answer sheets for grading—which can cause good-natured squabbles between even the best of neighbors" according to local quiz regular Tony Allan. At the end, the quizmaster

tallies up the scores and the winning team celebrates with a complimentary bottle of wine—or just a round of applause.

JOINING IN: Visitors are welcome and can usually be slotted into a local team short on numbers. Quiz locations tend to be advertised only locally and then sometimes just by word of mouth. So before you head out to show off your barley-fueled brain power, give your chosen pub a quick call to check the details.

LOCAL FAVORITES: The Tite Inn in Chadlington, the Churchill Arms in Paxford, and the Ram Inn in Old Bussage near Stroud hold lively, popular quiz nights.

Essentials: The Tite Inn (Mill End, Chadlington, tel 44 (0) 1608 676910, thetiteinn.co.uk); Churchill Arms (Paxford, tel 44 (0) 1386 594000, thechurchillarms.com); Ram Inn (Old Bussage, tel 44 (0) 1453 883163, the-ram-inn.co.uk)

A typical Cotswold scene in the village of Paxford

"I ask the questions, you answer. It's an old-fashioned tradition."
—QUIZMASTER TO UNRULY PARTICIPANT, THE TITE INN, CHADLINGTON

ALL VOICES BRIGHT AND BEAUTIFUL

The sound of a choir of heavenly voices soaring beneath a vast 15th-century fan-vaulted ceiling is enough to uncoil the most tightly wound heartstrings. And this is the effect when you listen to the choir of King's College Cambridge as they perform a choral version of the evening service known as Evensong.

Henry VI established the King's College choir of men and boys at Cambridge in 1441 to provide sung accompaniment to the daily chapel services. Today's choir does much the same, albeit with a far wider repertoire. And they are well known for the Festival of Nine Lessons and Carols, which is broadcast live on Christmas Eve around the world and which for many Brits marks the start of Christmas.

WHAT TO EXPECT: Seeing the choir perform on their home ground in the King's College chapel is a heady blend of sacred and profane pleasures. Says Cambridge graduate David Hatt, "Listening to the choir can be a spiritual experience. It's also a total steal—where else would you hear such voices for free?" The Evensong service lasts about an hour and includes two readings. Unlike in most parish churches, only the clergy and choir sing: The congregation listens.

WHEN TO GO: Choose your evening carefully. The full choir of men and boys sings during term time on

Tuesday, Thursday, Friday, Saturday, and Sunday, with the weekend services being by far the busiest. To get a more intimate experience, attend Evensong on Monday to hear the King's Voices, the college's mixed-sex choir, or Wednesday when the boys have their night off and only the men sing. On either of these days you're more likely to share the chapel with college dons seeking a moment of quiet reflection or students hoping for divine inspiration to see them through that impending essay crisis. No matter what day you go, you will have to stand in line, so it's worth arriving at the chapel about 45 minutes before the service begins to get a good seat with a view of the choir.

LOCAL KNOWLEDGE: While the fan vaulting—the largest in the world—is an architectural highlight, no fewer than four master masons have left their mark on the chapel, each intent on outdoing the others with his architectural details and flourishes.

Though Cambridge students and townsfolk might not like to admit it, some of the chapel's most striking features were plundered from the Low Countries. The stained glass in every window except the west one was produced in Flanders, and above the altar hangs "The Adoration of the Magi" by the Flemish painter Peter Paul Rubens.

■ *Essentials:* King's College (King's Parade, tel 44 (0) 1223 331100, kings.cam.ac.uk)

MORE: Cambridge Evensong

Clare College: The Chapel Choir is made up of male and female students—most of them Choral Scholars, supplemented by volunteers. clare.cam.ac.uk

St. John's College: The bright energy of its boy choristers and the resonant tones of the male Choral Scholars fill the chapel, the tallest in Cambridge. joh.cam.ac.uk

Trinity College: Trinity's Chapel Choir is modern by Cambridge standards, consisting of undergraduate male and female singers on choral scholarships. They bring an unfettered passion to Evensong in the 500-year-old wood-paneled chapel. trin.cam.ac.uk

"The synthesis of angelic voices and sublime surroundings provided an ideal respite from studying." —ELISABETH BANFIELD, ALUMNA OF KING'S COLLEGE

The choirmaster puts the King's choir through its paces. Opposite: The chapel's gothic exterior

Members of the town's Bonfire Societies on parade

LEWES, ENGLAND
BONFIRE NIGHT

Torch flames light up Lewes's steep, cobbled streets as processions of men and women in historic costumes, their faces streaked with paint, march through town. The cold November air is thick with smoke, a heady, anarchic excitement, and the deafening racket of firecrackers. Says local student Giacomo Luke, "There's lots going on. The procession is really fun. But brace yourself for the explosives and fire on the streets."

WHEN TO GO: Each November 5, the U.K. remembers the Gunpowder Plot of 1605, when a group of English Catholics, including soldier Guy Fawkes, tried and failed to blow up King James I at the Houses of Parliament. While much of the country attends firework displays, this usually sleepy Sussex town stages dramatic parades through the streets, complete with effigies of Guy and unpopular public figures.

WHAT TO EXPECT: Lewes's six Bonfire Societies, each with its own procession, costumes, and route through town,

organize the night's events. "I march for Southover Bonfire Society," says Luke. "There's rivalry between the societies to see who has the biggest bonfire and fireworks at the end of the night." The parades meet in the town center, where they're joined by a procession of blazing crosses commemorating 17 Protestant martyrs who were burned at the stake in Lewes during the reign of Catholic Queen Mary in the 16th century. The evening culminates with the effigies disappearing on bonfires amid a fanfare of fireworks.

JOINING IN: Make straight for the Western Road/High Street, where the processions come together, then choose a society bonfire to watch. Pubs will be packed to the rafters (or closed), but street vendors sell warming food and drink. Wrap up warm, prepare for revelry, and be on the lookout for people tossing firecrackers onto the sidewalk.

■ *Essentials:* lewesbonfirecouncil.org.uk

WHITSTABLE, ENGLAND
SHELL OUT FOR OYSTERS

The Romans were so fond of Whitstable oysters that they shipped them home to Italy in sacks of snow. King George III granted them a Royal title. In the mid-1900s pollution, storms, and overfishing almost killed them off, but the Natives—as Whitstable's indigenous oysters are called—are now back, prized by locals and visitors alike.

WHEN TO GO: Summer is the Natives' breeding season and they are off the menu. They really come into their own from October onward, and on sunny weekends in the fall, folks from nearby descend on Whitstable to eat oysters and stroll the seafront.

HOW TO ORDER: They are usually sold by the half dozen or dozen, often raw, grilled, or battered. Forget champagne or a dry white to wash down the delectable bivalves, and go for Whitstable Oyster Stout, brewed in the town's own brewery.

LOCAL FAVORITES: The Crab and Winkle on the harbor serves seafood fresh from the boats. The Royal Native Oyster Store has views of its own oyster beds. Wheelers Oyster Bar (BYO wine) is a cozy place to eat oysters in batter or *forestière* (with mushrooms).

■ *Essentials:* Crab and Winkle (South Quay, The Harbour, tel 44 (0) 1227 779377, crabandwinklerestaurant.co.uk, closed Mon. July–Sept., and Sun.); Royal Native Oyster Stores, (Horsebridge Rd., tel 44 (0) 1227 276856); Wheelers Oyster Bar (8 High St., 44 (0) 1227 273311, wheelersoysterbar.com)

Whitstable is famous for its homegrown oysters and colorful beach huts.

"Don't chew, don't gulp. Crush the oyster gently between tongue and palate. Savor our Natives like strawberries."—MARK STUBBS, HEAD CHEF, WHEELERS OYSTER BAR

GET REELING

Not Scottish? Don't know the steps? Don't worry, you'll soon be twirling and whirling to the infectious rhythms of such dances as Speed the Plough, Mairi's Wedding, or the oddly named Machine without Horses. The lingo—policeman's halt grip, Tulloch hold, teapot, and cartwheel—may be unfamiliar, but the steps are easy to pick up in the infectiously friendly atmosphere of the dance floor.

WHERE TO GO: On long, light summer evenings local enthusiasts gather at the Ross Bandstand on Princes Street Gardens for sessions of Scottish country dancing that are open to everyone. Set beneath the ramparts of Edinburgh Castle and the spiky skyline of the Old Town, the gardens make an atmospheric venue. A band provides the accompaniment for energetic programs of toe-tapping reels and jigs, and slow and stately strathspeys. Each program also features a performance by a demonstration team from one of the many Scottish Country Dance clubs active in the city and beyond.

JOINING IN: Anyone—including absolute beginners—is welcome to join local enthusiasts on the dance floor. Every session includes some easy dances that need little or no instruction. Others, more complicated, give experienced dancers a chance to show off their skills. Scottish country dancing is surprisingly vigorous and out-of-breath

newcomers are likely to welcome the opportunity to enjoy a much needed break as they watch the experts.

TAKE YOUR PARTNERS: Dancers line up in sets, and as you dance, you change partners, meeting new people as you swing your way around the floor. Be sure not to stand nearest the band—this spot is reserved for the top couple that leads the dancing and knows what to do. Some advice: If you lose your place, sway in time for a moment, then join in with what everyone else is doing. Gentlemen shouldn't spin their partners around too vigorously and ladies should remember to curtsy, not bow, at the start and end of each dance.

WHEN TO GO: Weekly dance sessions at the Ross Bandstand take place—usually on Monday evenings from 7:30 to 9:30—throughout June, July, and August. To check exact dates and planned programs see the website below. This is also the place to go for last-minute updates on cancellations due to bad weather, with decisions made after 3 p.m. on the day.

WHAT TO WEAR: Although some men wear kilts, people turn up in anything from jeans to formal Highland dress. Spike heels, capable of delivering a painful stab, are the only no-no. Because the bandstand is an outdoor dance floor with a hard surface, many participants prefer to wear sneakers rather than traditional dancing shoes.

■ *Essentials:* Ross Bandstand (Princes St. Gdns. West, princes streetgardensdancing.org.uk)

Dancing Shoes

Scottish dancing shoes are available in specialist stores, although you don't need them to join in.

Dancewear: This Edinburgh store sells flat dancing pumps and lace-up brogues for Scottish dancing. dancewear-edinburgh.co.uk

Dancia: This specialist shop on the south side of the city stocks shoes suitable for Scottish country dancing. According to Ellen Kelly, a local Scottish Country Dance enthusiast, "The shop staff are extremely helpful to anyone seeking the right dance shoe in the right size." dancia.co.uk

"It's a great way to meet other dancers and join in the local Scottish country dance scene." —TIM BOLTON-MAGGS, EDINBURGH DANCE TEACHER

REYKJAVIK, ICELAND
HOT DOG HEAVEN

There's something about Iceland that brings the colder parts of North America to mind, and the capital Reykjavik feels like a curious hybrid of Scandinavian cool, London hip, and Alaskan outback. The city—and indeed the whole country—has a long-standing addiction to hot dogs *(pylsur),* which are best enjoyed after you have been out partying all night and are waiting in the early morning chill for your bus home.

WHAT TO EXPECT: These are no ordinary sausage-meets-bun ensembles. Reykjavik's hot dogs are special. In fact, they have been widely acclaimed as the finest in the world. The sausage, braised in beer and various secret ingredients, is made with lamb mixed with smaller quantities of pork and beef, enclosed in a light and fluffy bun. Then there are the condiments: Ask for *eina með öllu* (one with everything) in order to experience the marvelous combination of ketchup, super-tangy mustard, a notably fine remoulade (a sweet pickle and caper-flecked mayonnaise), and raw and caramelized onions.

LOCAL FAVORITE: Reykjavik's most famous stand (established in 1937) is the utterly unprepossessing red-and-white

MORE: Fast-food To Go

Ning's: Reykjavik's best Chinese takeaway, Ning's has a good MSG-free menu featuring noodles and stir-fries. Situated east of the main tourist area. Suðurlandsbraut 6
Nonnabiti: Locals flock here for generous sandwiches stuffed with hot and cold fillings. Try the lamb sub. Branches at Kopavogur 14–16 and Hafnastraeti 11
Noodle Station: The menu is simple: Noodle soup with beef, chicken, or vegetables. Skólavörðustígur 21a
Vitabar: This is the place to come for the best burgers in town. Bergthorugata 21

Bæjarins beztu pylsur (literally, the best hot dog in town) down by the harbor. The only downside is that lines can be long—but it's worth the wait.

■ *Essentials:* Bæjarins beztu pylsur (Tryggvagata 1)

Whatever the weather, there's always a line at Bæjarins beztu pylsur.

Reykjavikers relax and play in one of Laugardalslaug's hot-pots.

REYKJAVIK, ICELAND
TAKING THE PLUNGE

For generations Icelanders have socialized in the naturally occurring, geothermal hot springs that dot this volcanic island. But life moves on, and today they also convene at thermally heated neighborhood swimming pools, making the most of the water's health-giving benefits.

WHERE TO GO: Iceland's Blue Lagoon geothermal spa is justly famous, but why not go local at Reykjavik's Laugardalslaug thermal complex, where serious swimmers perfect their strokes in one of the two 165-foot (50 m) pools, kids challenge the two water slides, and exercisers hit the gym? The less athletically inclined lounge in the many outdoor *heitapottar*, or "hot-pots" (artificial versions of natural geothermal pools) and chin-wag over current events, the ever-changing weather, and local gossip. The temperatures in the hot-pots vary from a gently relaxing 95°F (35°C) to a so-hot-you'll-melt 113°F (45°C); at a mere 84°F (29°C), the swimming pool provides a refreshing between-soak cool down. A jacuzzi, steam bath, and optional massage therapies promise further bliss.

MORE: Reykjavik Pools

Reykjavik has many geothermally heated swimming pools and hot-pots. visitreykjavik.is

Árbaejarlaug: With pools, a slide, and fountains for kids, as well as a large outdoor swimming pool, this complex on the edge of town is known locally as the best family pool.

Sundhöllin: Reykjavik's oldest pool, Sundhöllin (meaning "the swimming palace") is perennially popular with residents. Located in the city center, it has an indoor swimming pool and outdoor hot-pots and jacuzzi.

JOINING IN: Everyone lathers before swimming. Even in winter, the locals forego pool shoes out of doors. Hot dogs (see p. 90) or ice cream are the go-to, after-swim treat.

■ *Essentials:* Laugardalslaug (Sundlaugarveg 104, tel 354 411 5100, swimminginiceland.com)

This page and opposite: Bars and cafés are a vital part of Grünerløkka's street life.

SHOPPING IN GRÜNERLØKKA

Shopping may not seem an obvious activity in one of the world's most expensive cities, but take some time to mix with the locals in the cool neighborhood of Grünerløkka and you'll have a good value day out and maybe pick up a vintage bargain. Originally a working-class district, modern Grünerløkka is a hipster paradise with a thriving mix of independently owned shops and bars alongside apartments and parks. The two main streets, Thorvald Meyers gate and Markveien, run north-to-south and are easy to reach from the city center by tram or on foot. Even if you don't plan to buy anything, Grünerløkka is an ideal area for browsing, window-shopping, or just passing some time with a walk.

WHERE TO GO: Make your first stop the Chillout Travel Centre for the very Norwegian *kaffe og kake* (coffee and cake) in the café while checking out their excellent selection of travel books and gear. Says Oslo resident David Nikel, "I spend many an hour in the Chillout Travel Café. Their *boller* (freshly baked buns) and coffee are the perfect accompaniment as I swap travel tips about far-flung destinations with total strangers."

Fans of vintage clothing find plenty to interest them in Grünerløkka. Trabant Vintage specializes in clothing from the 1950s to 1980s; fans of flares and platform shoes head here. Robot, a funky little store next to the Chillout Travel Centre beating out loud music to entice you inside, focuses on imported mod clothing. For more current styles, visit Mitt Lille Hjem or the Hunting Lodge, which celebrates the timeless T-shirt. Marita Butikken is a treasure trove of plates, mugs, retro furniture, old magazines and books, lampshades, and trinkets. It's the kind of store where, if you ask for something specific, they'll probably have it stored away at the back of the shop.

TAKING A BREAK: Stroll along the Akerselva River to see the old factory buildings, urban artwork, and waterfalls. Start by Blå nightclub and follow the river north. Inevitably for such a trendy area, there are plenty of watering holes. Oslo local and partygoer Amalie Victoria Kristoffersen says, "It's such a vibrant area, but my favorite bar is Aku-Aku. The barmen are highly skilled and offer some really interesting cocktails. Try their homemade chili rum, it's to die for!"

■ *Essentials:* Chillout Travel Café (Markveien 55, tel 47 22 35 42 00, stay.com/oslo); Trabant Vintage (Markveien 56, tel 47 22 38 55 55, trabantclothing.com); Robot (Korsgata 22, tel 47 22 71 99 00, trabantclothing.com); Mitt Lille Hjem (Markveien 56C, tel 47 22 35 01 50); Hunting Lodge (Markveien 58, huntinglodge.no); Marita Butikken (Markveien 67, tel 47 22 38 19 20, closed Sun.); Aku-Aku (Thorvold Meyers gate 32, tel 47 41 17 69 66, akuaku.no)

Grünerløkka Grub

Take a break in one of these popular eateries:

Havana Hotel: This delicatessen also sells hot food. Locals recommend the homemade paella. hotelhavana.no

Nighthawk Diner: American-style burgers and other U.S. classics in a retro setting. nighthawk.com

---

"Grünerløkka's regular market days [Sunday] draw out the locals in great numbers and stores spread onto the streets, all to the soundtrack of live music." —DAVID NIKEL, OSLO RESIDENT

Skiing the Peer Gynt Trail near the village of Gålå

PEER GYNTS RIKE, NORWAY
CROSS-COUNTRY SKI TRAILS

Vast networks of well-marked *skiløyper* (ski touring trails), freshly groomed each day, wend through Norway's birch and pine forests and slice across stunning expanses of unspoiled plateaus, the only sound you'll hear being the crunch of skis on sparkling snow. Many of the trails link traditional *hytter* (cabins), mountain lodges, and inns—each within a day's ski of the previous one—where locals often eat lunch or stay overnight.

WHERE TO GO: Norwegians consider Peer Gynts Rike (kingdom) north of Lillehammer, named for the legendary folk hero, to have some of the finest cross-country skiing terrain in the country. And of the region's nearly 400 miles (644 km) of ski routes, the Peer Gynt Trail's relatively level tracks make it popular with local families. The trail begins in Espedalen and passes through a handful of alpine communities on its 50-mile (80 km) route, including Fefor, Gålå, Kvitfjell, and Skeikampen. Along the way you'll probably pass family groups out together, some towing toddlers along on sleds. If you hear a shout of "*Løype*—Trail" from behind, a faster skier is asking you to make way so move to the side of the track. You'll find fellow skiers are happy to share notes on weather, wildlife sightings (elk, hares), and trail conditions, creating a convivial atmosphere, but don't expect much in the way of *après-ski* activities—after a little aquavit everyone goes to bed to rest up for the next day's trek.

WHEN TO GO: Although the snow base should be deep from late November through April, inn-to-inn treks are best undertaken during the warmer, longer days of spring. Accommodations may be difficult to find over the Easter period unless you make a reservation well ahead.

■ *Essentials:* General information: visitnorway.com; Peer Gynt Trail: peergyntsrike.com

LONGYEARBYEN, NORWAY
HERE COMES THE SUN

On March 8 or thereabouts each year, the 2,000 inhabitants of Longyearbyen, the most northerly town on the planet and the largest settlement in the Svalbard Archipelago, see direct sunlight for the first time since the previous October 26. Its appearance is cause for a week of celebrations—called Solfestuka, or Return of the Sun—for winter here is brutally cold and long, inhabitants enduring four months without direct sunlight.

LOCAL FAVORITES: Concerts, theater productions, and sled races fill the week. Toward the end, everybody rides snowmobiles to Hiorthhamn fiord for the annual sledding race *Ta Sjansen*—Take the Chance. Young hopefuls build sleds from whatever materials they can find and are cheered on by the crowds lining a steeply sloping course.

JOINING IN: At the beginning of the week, squeeze into the sunrise service at Svalbard church and then join the crowds on the steps of the old hospital, where everyone gathers to sing traditional songs and wait for the first glint of the sun to appear in the notch of a mountain pass. Even if clouds obscure the sun, spirits are not dampened; after all, it is Svalbard's first day of spring and the days grow longer more quickly here than at any settlement on Earth.

LOCAL KNOWLEDGE: When you enter buildings, remove your shoes. The tradition, which applies year-round, recalls the days when settlements were based around coal mines and prevented people from bringing coal dust indoors.

■ *Essentials:* General information: svalbard.net

Longyearbyen's residents dressed to welcome the sun

"After four months of polar night, we long for the sun. No wonder we have to celebrate for a week." —LINDA BAKKEN, SVALBARD RESIDENT

JOKKMOKK, SWEDEN
WINTER MARKET

I n nose-numbing temperatures—sometimes plunging to –31°F (–35°C) or lower—shoppers browse 500 stalls ranged along Jokkmokk's streets in search of warm socks, leather and wool gloves, fur hats, fox pelts, and whatever else they need to survive in northern Sweden's inhospitable climate. Meanwhile, scents of sausages and reindeer meat vie with the sweet smell of Swedish candy and donuts to attract customers to the food stalls. For more than 400 years, the Sámi—Lapland's indigenous reindeer herders—have gathered in this remote hamlet for the largest winter market and festival north of the Arctic Circle. "There are two markets a year in Jokkmokk, a small one in August and a much bigger one in winter—I go to them every year," says Jokkmokk native Victoria Emlünd.

WHAT TO BUY: "You'll find all kinds of special local foods—reindeer meat, cloudberries picked in the forests around Jokkmokk," explains Emlünd. "And craft items such as traditional Sámi knives with reindeer-horn handles, toys, clothes, art."

SPECIAL ATTRACTIONS: During the winter market everyone watches the daily reindeer parades, when Sámi

Reindeer Races

If you want a change from shopping, join the crowds at **Talvatis Lake,** a few minutes' walk from the market, to watch reindeer racing. The animals race two at a time, each pulling a sledge with passenger on board around the frozen lake. The drivers kneel—or lie on their stomachs— and have little control, the sledges sliding and banging into each other as they take the corners. Several helpers are needed to bring the reindeer to a halt at the finish.

families dressed in *gáktis*, their traditional costume of bright red or blue tunics with heavily embroidered collars, lead animals adorned with equally colorful headbands and girths through the streets. In the evenings, performances of Sámi folk-singing draw large audiences.

■ *Essentials:* General information: turism.jokkmokk.se

A Sámi man leads his reindeer through the market.

Treat yourself to a *semlor*—a light bun filled with marzipan and cream.

STOCKHOLM, SWEDEN
TIME OUT FOR CAKE

The national tradition of *fika* is almost a religion in Sweden. The closest English translation is to "meet up for coffee and cakes," but it is more than a kick of caffeine and sugar. Fika is time to relax, preferably with friends, while enjoying a to-die-for pastry or cake. It is even acceptable as a first date. "It allows you to treat yourself and spend time with your friends and work colleagues," says Helena Halme, author of *Coffee and Vodka*, a novel set in Stockholm. For many Swedish workers fika is virtually mandatory—not to partake makes you appear stand-offish. At 10 a.m. and 3 p.m. every day, they eat together on an equal footing, whatever their role.

WHERE TO GO: Fika cafés dot Stockholm and everyone has his or her favorite. The doll's house–like Sturekatten on Riddargatan, in the upmarket Östermalm district, has the best *semlor*—cardamom buns filled with marzipan and whipped cream. In Normalm, the main city-center district,

drop into Vete-Katten on Kungsgatan in the early afternoon, when they bring out the freshly baked scones with homemade jam and their specialty, *mjölnargårdsbullar*, a bun filled with vanilla custard.

JOINING IN: For the ultimate chilled-out fika, take a casual stroll on leafy Djurgården, one of Stockholm's 14 islands, and drop in at the Flickorna Helin Voltaire. You can warm up beside the fire in winter or catch some sun on the outdoor terrace in summer. Says office manager Ann-Sophie Ventura, "For me fika is a little oasis of calm in an otherwise extremely busy day—I don't know how people survive without it."

■ *Essentials:* General information; visitstockholm.com; Sturekatten (Riddargatan 4, tel 46 (0) 8 611 1612); Vete-Katten (Kungsgaten 56, tel 46 (0) 8 208 405); Flickorna Helin Voltaire (Djurgården, Rosendalsvägen 14, tel 46 (0) 8 664 5108)

EXPLORING THE ISLANDS BY BOAT

Stockholm's *skärgård* (archipelago) has thousands of islands, some large with cars, roads, and summer cabins, others small and uninhabited. You can take your own motorboat or yacht to almost any of them, for in Sweden you have the right, known as *Allemansrätten* (everyman's right), to go ashore anywhere that is not close to buildings: Plenty of choice here.

WHERE TO GO: Locals aim for the smaller uninhabited islands. Once landed, you'll likely have the island to yourself for the day (it is an unwritten rule that no other boats will moor nearby). Then it's time for a swim, and a picnic with Swedish coffee and cakes, especially *kanelbullar* (cinnamon buns). Keep your eyes peeled: You might see a deer swimming from one island to the next or a white-tailed eagle soaring overhead. You can fish—everybody does—the catch reflecting the brackish Baltic's mix of freshwater fish, such as perch, and sea fish, such as herring. Look for a gaggle of boats—that's where the herring are.

LOCAL KNOWLEDGE: A certain amount of sailing expertise is required. The islands and islets are obvious, but lurking just below the surface are legions of smooth rocks with no waves to give them away, so you'll need to watch your chart like a hawk. Also check the barometric pressure. There are no tides, but if high pressure dominates, the sea level in the Baltic drops, so the depth beneath your boat can be 18 inches (455 mm) less than that shown on the chart.

WHEN TO GO: Not in winter, when much of the sea is frozen. In summer, the region often has wall-to-wall sunshine with calm seas, but watch that wind. It can change direction in an instant, so the promise of a leisurely run home with the breeze blowing from astern could turn into frantic tacking all the way back to your *brygga* (dock).

■ *Essentials:* General information: visitskargarden.se; boat hire (including boats with skippers): sailmarine.com, midnightsun sailing.fi, rentaboat.se; safety training: srtc.se

"Fishing in the archipelago with a mother moose and her twins just yards away is pure magic." —SYLVE KARLSSON, STOCKHOLM PLUMBER

Mooring on Sandhamn
in the outer archipelago.
Opposite: Canoeing
through the islets
and islands

SEURASAARI, FINLAND
MIDSUMMER MADNESS

Two young newlyweds approach the island of Seurasaari, not far from downtown Helsinki. Selected from hundreds of applicants to lead the evening's festivities, the couple are dressed in old-style wedding clothes and walk beneath a canopy accompanied by musicians and dancers. It is June 21, the time of Finland's Midsummer Festival, when young people traditionally get married. Crossing a white wooden bridge, the chosen couple arrives on the island.

The rest of the year the Seurasaari Foundation keeps old customs alive with an open-air museum of traditional buildings and crafts and regular concerts of folk music and dance. But on Midsummer Eve local crowds come to watch the hoisting of the midsummer maypole; the *Lippulina* (procession of flags); the *Lasten Poloneesi*, a children's dance that winds around a clearing to the tune of fiddles and accordions; and the midsummer bonfires.

Built in all shapes and sizes, the fires include the tall, four-legged Karelian bonfire and the straw wheel of the Ingrian cogwheel bonfire, each representing one of Finland's former provinces. At around 10 p.m., when the onshore fires have all been lit, a team of rowers takes the bridal couple out in a long, narrow church boat to set alight a large floating bonfire. Its sparks, it is said, bring the couple good luck. This is followed by the Midsummer Night Dance in which everybody, no matter what their age or skill, can join in.

After that, people chat and party long into the night. "Even though it's Midsummer, the time of the midnight sun, it's cold at night, so we huddle by the fire with family and friends. We eat and talk till the fire goes out," says Helsinki resident Vanessa Barroso.

JOINING IN: Do as some locals do and take a boat or ferry to the island. You will avoid the evening crush on the bus from Helsinki (Bus 24) and have a good view of the string of fires along the island's shoreline.

WHERE TO EAT: Locals tend to take picnics with a plentiful supply of schnapps and beer. Alternatively, they book a table at Restaurant Seurasaari, a historic restaurant dating from 1890, which serves good Finnish food using locally sourced produce.

■ *Essentials:* Seurasaari Foundation: seurasaarisaatio.fi; bonfire evening cruises: stromma.fi; Restaurant Seurasaari (tel 358 (0) 9 626625, closed winter)

Helsinkians gather to watch the Midsummer bonfires.

STEAMED CLEAN

Finnish heaven is a log-built sauna, its seams caulked with moss for perfectly controlled ventilation, located beside a lake for that essential post-steam cold plunge. While this ideal isn't always attainable, most Helsinki apartments have their own small sauna, and the city's oldest wood-fired public facility, Kotiharjun Sauna, is always busy. You'll spot it by the row of men, and one or two women, sitting beneath its neon sign clad in nothing but towels, cooling off in the refrigerating breeze.

WHAT TO EXPECT: Inside, a basement locker room has the atmosphere of a library crossed with a hothouse, where towel-wrapped men (women have their own separate section) quietly play chess or read newspapers in the steamy warmth. Beyond the shower room, clients sit with bunches of birch twigs submerged in a bucket of lukewarm water, occasionally rising to disappear through a heavy wooden door into the sauna itself. Space is quietly made for newcomers on the tiered seating, and despite the nudity, the atmosphere is almost pious. Whistling and swearing are traditionally forbidden in the sauna, but someone may quietly remark, "It's not very hot in here, is it? The steam is too soft," producing lively if muted debate. This is a serious matter and the Finnish even have a word just for sauna steam—*löyly*.

■ *Essentials:* Kotiharjun Sauna (Harjutorinkatu 1, tel 358 (0) 9 753 1535, www.kotiharjunsauna.fi, closed Sun.)

MORE: Helsinki Saunas

Sauna Arla: In business since 1929, Arla has separate saunas for men and women (not all saunas do). Kaarlenkatu 15, Helsinki, arlansauna.net

Yrjönkadun UimahallI: This art-deco bathhouse has saunas and a pool. Swimsuits are frowned upon. Be sure to pick your day: Men swim on Tuesdays, Thursdays, Saturdays; women on Mondays, Wednesdays, Fridays, and Sundays. Yrjönkatu 21b, Helsinki.

Finland has more than two million saunas.

A Smørrebrød laden with shrimp

COPENHAGEN, DENMARK
THE ART OF SMØRREBRØD

Traditional Danish open sandwiches, *smørrebrød* (literally, buttered bread) consist of rye bread piled high with all manner of toppings, from swordfish to smoked duck breast.

LOCAL FAVORITE: At Ida Davidsen, in the Nyhavn area, the humble snack has been raised to an art form since Davidsen's great-grandfather founded the store in 1888. The phrase "as long as Ida Davidsen's menu" has entered the local lexicon to describe anything that is unfathomably long, and reflects the many choices on offer.

WHAT TO CHOOSE: The menu at Ida's lists 250 options, from *leverpostej* (duck-liver pâté) to complex combinations of crayfish and caviar. Smørrebrød can be treated like tapas: Order a variety to share depending on your appetite and finances—the plates range in price from DKK50 ($9) to an eye-watering DKK190 ($34) for *rødspættefilet luksus* (luxury fillet of plaice).

LOCAL KNOWLEDGE: Toppings are named after notable Danes and diners. Storyteller Hans Christian Andersen can be enjoyed in the form of pâté, bacon, tomato, and horseradish, while the clown prince of Denmark, comedian/pianist Victor Borge, lives on as an exotic topping of salmon, freshly marinated lumpfish caviar, crayfish tails, Greenland shrimp, lime, and dill mayonnaise. Even the former lord mayor of Copenhagen, Ritt Bjerregaard, is available as a slice of rye topped with smoked leg of lamb, scrambled eggs, and herbs.

■ *Essentials:* Ida Davidsen (Store Kongensgade 70, tel 45 (0) 33 91 36 55, closed after 4 p.m. and Sat.–Sun.)

"I love peeled shrimps on dark rye bread, usually with a beer, but for happy occasions we have schnapps." —SARA MICHAELSEN, SPEECH THERAPIST

MOSCOW, RUSSIA
BALLET MANIA

Ballet is to Russia what opera is to Italy, and on any given evening in Moscow there might be up to four ballets being performed. They'll probably all be sold out, but the jewel in ballet's crown is the Bolshoi. Says Muscovite Nadia Chernatolova, a product designer, "Even during Soviet times the Bolshoi was recognized as the best in the world. Not even a flawed political system could get in the way of Russian performing arts."

WHERE TO GO: Bolshoi means big in Russian, and the building lives up to the name. Be sure to get tickets for the Bolshoi Main Hall, which radiates show-stopping pizzazz, and not the smaller (and newer) New Hall. The huge columns of the Main Hall are visible at the front, facing the Kremlin. Inside, from the gilded woodwork to the magnificent chandelier in the lobby, the Bolshoi positively sparkles. (After a five-year restoration with a $1 billion price tag, it should.)

HOW TO GET TICKETS: Except for Moscow's nouveau riche, who will pay sky-high prices from scalpers, most people buy their tickets from little kiosks dotted all over Moscow, which offer instant availability for a small premium. For last-minute tickets for sold-out performances, a scalper may be the only option, but beware: Some tickets are fakes, and most are overpriced.

LOCAL KNOWLEDGE: At the Bolshoi refreshment stand, champagne and sandwiches for two might cost a staggering $200. It's best to eat before you go.

■ *Essentials:* Bolshoi Ballet (tel 7 (8) 495 455-5555, bolshoi.ru)

Pre-theater Eats

Rather than dine in one of the overpriced restaurants in the shadow of the Bolshoi, walk to **Scandinavia,** a fish and seafood restaurant near the entrance to the Tverskaya Metro, just a few blocks from the theater. Quiet, with great service, it is a favorite with everyone in the area. "I had one of the best tuna steaks I've ever had here," says literary agent Tatiana Vaniat. Afterward walk the few minutes to the Bolshoi or have the restaurant order you a taxi—no one ever hails down a taxi ad hoc in Moscow. scandinavia.ru

BUYING VINTAGE

Adore vintage? So do the young hipsters of Tallinn, Estonia's capital. The city's old town has some of Europe's best vintage stores, selling pre-owned garments that could grace the most fashionable closet, at very affordable prices. "Vintage clothing takes you back to a time full of romance and gives you a different look," says office worker and vintage collector Jurga Baranauskaite.

LOCAL FAVORITES: The store Oh So Retro Tallinn sums it all up. A classy and calm oasis, just up from busy Müürivahe Street, it makes every customer feel like a king or queen with quality clothes and good old-fashioned service. The assistants offer fashion knowledge and guidance. Go home with a tuxedo jacket, a designer dress, or an Italian-made purse. Fankadelik, in Vana-Viru, next to the old city walls, is a spacious trunk of funk with a century of clothing hanging alongside new designs from Estonian label Crystal Rabbit. Foxy Vintage packs everything from women's and men's clothing to toys to jewelry into its tiny shop space. It specializes in the 1970s but has stuff dating back to the '20s.

Vintage Fair

A one-day show, usually held twice a year (May and November) **Vintage Tallinn** features Estonia's best vintage outlets in one venue. It sets up shop in a different part of the city on each occasion, and people come from all over the country to buy and sell. It's a chance to pick up a complete new wardrobe for a song, and you'll also find furniture, lamps, jewelry, and records. vintagetallinn.weebly.com

LOCAL KNOWLEDGE: Keep an eye on the stores' Facebook pages to check out the latest new stock.

■ *Essentials:* Oh So Retro Tallinn (Suur Karja 13, closed Sun.–Mon. and daily a.m., tel 372 60 53584337); Fankadelik (Vana-Viru 6, tel 372 60 6455043, closed a.m.); Foxy Vintage (Pikk 9, tel 372 60 53483081, closed Sun.–Tues. and daily a.m.)

Fankadelik, a retro treasure trove

Jewelry and ornaments carved from "Baltic gold" in Gdańsk's Old Town

GDAŃSK, POLAND
IN SEARCH OF AMBER

When Polish violinist Hania Gmitruk was a child she collected amber from the beach. "Whenever there was a storm during the night, my sister and I would get up at 5 a.m. and go to gather the washed-up knobs of amber. Using an old dentist's drill, we would pierce the pieces and thread them into necklaces."

Gdańsk is the center of the Baltic amber trade. Amber fashioned into gold bands, looped onto necklaces, or set into pendants, rings, and brooches gleams in the shop windows of the cobbled streets. The value of individual nuggets of this fossil resin from the Baltic Sea region depends on its age (20 million years is young) and inclusions—trapped insects or organic matter that add to a piece's uniqueness.

LOCAL FAVORITES: High-end outlets include the S&A Gallery on Mariacka Street, known for twice-yearly jewelry collections, and Manufacture Michel on Długie Pobrzeże.

LOCAL KNOWLEDGE: Amber comes in shades of yellow, orange, and brown, but the rarest has a bluish tinge. Street stalls sell amber more cheaply than the stores. To find out if it is genuine, rub it in your hands; the real deal releases a woody scent. Take local currency with you as some vendors don't take credit cards or they may give a cash discount.

■ *Essentials:* S&A Gallery (Mariacka 36, tel 48 (0) 58 305 22 80, s-a.pl); Manufacture Michel (4 Długie Pobrzeże, tel 48 (0) 58 301 78 64, ambermanufacture.com.pl)

"Choose a light design inspired by current fashion trends."
—Anna Sado, journalist and amber specialist

WARSAW, POLAND
SWEET TREATS

The simplest things often turn out to be the best: *Rurki* are thin wafers rolled while warm to form a tube, which, when cold, are filled with sweet whipped cream. "I love the taste of the pure light sweetness hidden inside the crunchy wafer—I would never change it for *wuzetka* [a heavy cake with chocolate and cream that is also a specialty of Warsaw]," says local writer Kasia Boni, describing her number one treat.

LOCAL FAVORITES: For many people, the best rurki in Warsaw are at Cukiernia Robert Przewłocki, an insignificant booth near the bus station. They've been there for more than 50 years now, and the recipe hasn't changed since the first day. At the back, the mixer—nearly 6 feet (2 m) tall—beats the cream until it reaches the desired consistency. The ladies who fill the wafer with the cream tell about customers who remember this place from their childhood and now bring their own grandchildren. The owner laughs as he recalls the many mothers who come to buy rurki for their kids at home, only to end up eating them on the spot.

LOCAL KNOWLEDGE: There are different schools on how to eat your rurki. It seems so simple—just bite and eat. The real question is not "how" but "when." The longer the cream stays inside the wafer, the softer the wafer becomes. Your options are crunchy at one extreme and gooey at the other. Some say that the best consistency is reached after one hour. Buy another one and test this theory for yourself.

■ *Essentials:* Cukiernia Robert Przewłocki (210–212 Grochowska St., tel 48 (0) 22 621 15 18)

MORE: Rurki

Grycan: Although known for its ice cream, Grycan makes good rurki as well. Prepare to stand in line. Puławska 11, tel 48 (0) 22 849 89 38, grycan.pl

Rurki Lody: This rurki maker has been in business for almost 30 years. Some people claim it is even better than Przewłocki. Wolska 50, closed Sun.

Trou-Madame: The rurki are good, and the location is even better—inside Warsaw's most elegant park. Also good for ice cream in summer or mulled wine in winter. Łazienki Park, belvedere.com

A cream-filled rurki at Cukiernia Robert Przewłocki

Magda Szwedowska,
*Editor, NG Traveler,
Poland*

I love rurki but my favorite Polish pastries are *pączki*—deep-fried yeast doughnuts with a rose jam filling and sugar frosting, sometimes with candied orange peel on top. I practically lived on them when I was a child and if it weren't for the calories I'd eat them every day now. When I want to indulge myself, I head for the best pączki in Warsaw— Zagoździński shop *(15 Górczewska, tel 48 (0) 22 632 19 18, closed Sun. and July)*. The store was established in 1925 and is currently run by the great-granddaughter of the original owner. It opens from 9 a.m. and closes when the last pączek is sold, so get there early. I love to watch the ladies who work there wrap the doughnuts in paper and then tie a string around the package so that you can carry it. Yum!

Rynek Główny,
one of Europe's
finest squares

KRAKÓW, POLAND
CAFÉ CULTURE

Sitting in a café on the magnificent Rynek Główny, one of the largest and finest medieval squares in Europe—this is how Kraków's office workers and shoppers unwind after a hard day's grind. In the late afternoon, the clip-clop of horses' hooves echoes off the baroque and Renaissance facades, and the view of the medieval Cloth Hall and the splashes of brilliant color in the flower market create the ideal place to chill.

The former Polish capital, which spent centuries under Austrian control, out-pastries Vienna for café culture, serving espresso with attitude and heart-stoppingly rich cakes. Café-goers can sit inside or out on the square, depending on the season. Tunnel-like passages lead off flagstoned arteries to courtyards with ever more peaceful alternatives.

WHERE TO GO: Just off Rynek Główny, on Bracka, the low-ceilinged Nowa Prowincja sells rich and fluffy lemon meringue pie and Spanish-style hot chocolate so thick that it oozes very slowly from a tipped cup. A little north of the square, café Jama Michalika on Floriańska has art nouveau furniture and stained glass, with caricatures of actors, musicians, and writers lining the walls.

LOCAL FAVORITES: Polish writer Dorota Wasik says, "My favorite haunt is south of the square on Kanonicza. Bona serves coffee and cakes in a multilingual book store." In the bohemian Jewish quarter of Kazimierz, where Steven Spielberg shot *Schindler's List*, Singer Café—named for the sewing machines that double as tables—presents two aspects of Kraków: a quiet cappuccino in the daytime and then dancing on tables (sometimes) until 3 a.m.

■ *Essentials:* Nowa Prowincja (Bracka 3–5); Jama Michalika (Floriańska 45); Bona (Kanonicza 11); Singer Café (Estery 20)

Christmas on the Square

On the first Thursday in December, Rynek Główny is the setting for the **Kraków szopka** (Christmas crib contest), a tradition dating back to the 19th century. In a spirit of fierce competition, citizens present hand-crafted nativity scenes inspired by Kraków's buildings. Jesus's birth might be set in a model of the city's castle, the Cloth Hall, or any one of its many churches.

PRAGUE, CZECH REPUBLIC
CLASSICAL INTERLUDE

It's hard to picture a better musical backdrop than fairytale Prague. The city's Gothic spires, glittering domes, and opulent palaces could have sprung from the mind of an opera set-designer. A musical hub since the early 19th century, when it was a featured stop on the tours of Europe's top musicians, the city continues to draw orchestras from around the world to its concert halls. But for a more intimate musical experience, slip away from the crowds to join local music lovers in the churches, synagogues, and villas that host performances by Czech musicians in atmospheric settings. "My wife Irka and I particularly like the concerts at the Obecní Dům, Prague's former town hall," says Askold Krushelnycky, a journalist and long-term Prague resident. "During the interval we slip off to its stylish art nouveau American Bar."

LOCAL FAVORITES: The baroque church of St. Jilji, in the Old Town, regularly stages works by J. S. Bach, Franz Liszt, and Prague's most famous musical son, Antonín Dvořák. Its 350-year-old organ—one of the finest in the country—draws organists from far and wide. In the Jewish Quarter, the Spanish Synagogue's occasional concerts provide a unique way of experiencing the opulent setting while listening to anything from Jewish klezmer music to the hits of George Gershwin.

■ *Essentials:* Tickets for classical concerts: pragueticket office.com; Obecní Dům (Nám Republiky 5, tel 420 222 002 101, obecnidum.cz); Jilji's Church (Husova 8); Spanish Synagogue (Vězeňská 141, tel 420 222 749 211, jewishmuseum.cz)

Honoring Dvořák

Ask any Czech about classical music and it's difficult to get them to stop praising Antonín Dvořák. Visit the **Vila Amerika** (Ke Karlovu 462/20), an over-the-top baroque palace repurposed as the Dvořák Museum, where concerts are held in the music salon from May to October. Musicians in period costume recreate an imagined performance from 1904, as if Dvořák himself might step through the door at any minute and take up the conductor's baton.

The Berg Orchestra
performs in the
Spanish Synagogue.

Heiligendamm,
the grande
dame of German
coastal spas

BALTIC COAST, GERMANY
SPA REVIVAL

When the well-heeled from nearby Berlin and Hamburg need to recharge, they head for the Baltic Sea to max out their credit card at a spa. As well as bracing sea breezes, white-sand beaches, and seawater bathing, the historic spa resorts that line the coast offer serious pampering and TLC.

A day at a spa might begin with an invigorating dip in the sea, followed by a yoga session, and then a spa treatment or two—maybe exfoliation with sea salt and buckthorn (small orange berries rich in vitamin C) or a relaxing algae wrap. After a light but delicious lunch, you can curl up with a book on a *Strandkorb*—Germany's iconic hooded beach chair. "We get a lot of regular customers suffering from stress. They want to relax body and mind," says Kirsten Beckmann, a therapist at Grand Hotel Heiligendamm.

WHERE TO GO: The oldest resort, Heiligendamm centers on Hohenzollern Castle, the original home of Grand Duke Paul Friedrich and now part of the Grand. Here, guests can choose from detox and purifying packages or just pick from the à la carte spa menu.

MORE FAVORITES: Heringsdorf, on the island of Usedom, once hosted German royalty. A holder of the Premium Thalasso Europe award, the resort's facilities and treatments utilize the healing properties of the mineral-rich seawater, mud, and algae. On the Zingst peninsula you can get the circulation going with hiking and biking as well as sea mud and saltwater.

■ *Essentials:* Grand Hotel Heiligendamm (Prof.-Dr.-Vogel-Strasse 6, Bad Doberan-Heiligendamm, tel 49 (0) 38203 740-0, grandhotel-heiligendamm.de); Heringsdorf (tourist information: tel 49 (0) 38378 4771-10, heringsdorf-info.de); Zingst (tourist information: tel 49 (0) 38232 810-0, zingst.de)

On the Prom at Warnemünde

In contrast to exclusive Heiligendamm, **Warnemünde,** a short drive along the coast, is a seaside town for all. Locals come here to enjoy freshly smoked fish at the pier, see it being smoked as soon as the fishermen unload their catch, and watch the cruise ships go by from the promenade's Teapott Café—a fantastic example of East German 1960s futuristic architecture.

DAY SKIING FROM MUNICH

One of the things Münchners love best about their city in winter is that they can be out on the ski slopes by the time most people are getting out of bed. On weekend mornings from November through May, ski-carrying locals pack the concourse at Munich's Hauptbahnhof, around the same time as dazed nightclubbers are making their way home.

JOINING IN: The first train to Garmisch-Partenkirchen, gateway to a ski area with 41 runs and 43 miles (69 km) of pistes, departs at 6:30 a.m. To make the most of a day on the slopes, skip breakfast—grab a giant pretzel from one of the station cafés instead—and hop aboard. Less than 90 minutes later, you are there.

WHERE TO GO: The train stops at the bottom of the Hausberg cable car, which whisks skiers into the Garmisch-Classic ski area. Find your ski legs on 25 miles (40 km) of groomed pistes before testing your nerves on the Kandahar World Championship downhill run, which sweeps through the trees for 2 miles (3 km). Later, catch the funicular from the bottom of the Kreuzeck lift in Garmisch-Partenkirchen to the Zugspitze ski area for Germany's highest (and only) glacier skiing and all the off-piste powder your heart desires.

WHERE TO EAT: The Gletscherbahn lift up the glacier brings you to Gipfelalm, Germany's highest restaurant (9,685 feet/2,952 m). Refuel with goulash soup, mushroom chicken on butter *Spätzle* (noodles), or spinach and cheese *Knödel* (dumplings)—save room for the apple strudel—while admiring the views.

LOCAL KNOWLEDGE: Buy a combo ticket for the train. This includes a one-day lift pass, allowing you to avoid the lines at the ski lifts on arrival.

■ *Essentials:* Garmisch-Classic (mid-Dec.–mid-May); Zugspitze (Nov. through May, zugspitze.de/en/winter/berg); transport: bahn.com

Skiers prepare for an afternoon in the Zugspitze ski area.

Münchners pack the benches inside one of the festival's massive tents.

MUNICH, GERMANY
FOR BEER LOVERS

The Bavarians may not have invented beer, but they have perfected its enjoyment—and beer drinking reaches its peak during the Munich Oktoberfest, or Wies'n as they call it. A chance for men to squeeze into *Lederhosen* (leather trousers) and women to dust down their *Dirndls* (peasant dresses), the festival has been going strong since 1810.

WHAT TO EXPECT: The festival runs from late September to the first weekend in October. Book a table in one of the 14 Wies'n tents to avoid lining up with the tourists. Each tent has its own atmosphere: Local band Slow Comets head for the Augustinerzelt. They join friends, linking arms and swaying to the most traditional of the Wies'n brass bands.

HOW TO ORDER: Draught beer is served in 2-pint (1 L) glass mugs (called *Masskrug*)—ask for *"ein Mass, bitte."* Locals breakfast on *Weisswurst* (veal sausage); lunch on *Brathendl* (rotisserie chicken) or *Schweinhaxe* (pork knuckle); and enjoy *Kaiserschmarr'n* (shredded pancakes) for dessert.

MORE: Munich Beer Gardens

Augustiner Grossgaststätten: This historic building houses a beer hall (open year-round) and a courtyard beer garden. Neuhauserstrasse 27

Augustinerkeller: One of Munich's oldest beer gardens, this year-round establishment has 100 chestnut trees. Arnulfstrasse 52

FITTING IN: Learn some traditional German drinking songs and remember before you drink to say *"Prost!"*, clinking glasses with everyone at the table and making eye contact: To look away is rude.

■ *Essentials:* Oktoberfest (Theresienwiese, Bavariaring, oktoberfest.de/en, Tues. is family day)

MAY DAY MERRIMENT

The tradition of erecting a *Maibaum* (May Pole) is alive and well in the small towns of Bavaria. Some places erect a Maibaum each year; in others, groups of four or five nearby villages take turns hoisting a pole and hosting the May Day celebrations—each village wants to have the tallest pole and the best celebration. The whole event is the responsibility of the unmarried 18-year-old boys and 16-year-old girls of the village, but what was once a marriage mart is now just good fun.

POLE POSITION: Over the winter, the boys find and cut down a pine tree, remove the bark, and paint it in the traditional Bavarian blue and white stripes. Early on May Day (May 1) morning, the boys pick up the pole and hitch it to a tractor, which tows the pole (and the 20 or 30 excited and already slightly tipsy local boys sitting astride it) to the site where it will stand. A large crowd gathers to watch the pole go up. The beer is already flowing and most spectators clutch a tankard. Until recently, the poles, often 90 feet (30 m) high, were put up using a combination of rope, sticks, and brute force, but most villages now use cranes. "By the end everyone is pretty drunk and it's only 11 a.m. It's crazy!" according to Jonas Blitz from Ebenhausen, a small town outside Munich.

PARTY TIME: Once the pole is up, the festivities really get going. After a hearty Bavarian breakfast, the boys and girls line up to find out who their dancing partner will be for the day. They have been planning for this day and practicing Bavarian folk dances all winter, and bonds have formed.

Guarding the May Pole

Beginning in February, the tree is kept under 24-hour guard by local lads, for it's at risk of being kidnapped by boys from neighboring villages. Pairs of boys take turns at guard duty, staying overnight in a barn or hut nearby. Local girls cook them dinner; friends and neighbors stop by to keep them company and share a beer (for a modest fee). If the tree is stolen, a ransom, *Freibieren*, must be paid in, yes, more beer.

Says Jonas, "Everyone's really nervous because you don't know who you'll get. If it's someone you like, it's traditional to let out a loud yell and throw your hat in the air."

JOINING IN: The dancing continues all day and far into the night. Everyone in the village, from toddlers to grannies, struts their stuff on the dance floor, and any willing outsiders will be swept along in the mayhem. Brass bands alternate with tunes from an accordion player, and even those who aren't dancing clap along to the music.

WHAT TO WEAR: For local boys, lederhosen, often inherited from granddad; for girls, dirndls with aprons are de rigueur. Boys sport Bavarian hats, girls wear their hair up in a traditional style, topped with a fetching feathered hat. But the Maypole dancers are not the only ones who dress up. Even tiny tots go Bavarian in mini-dirndls or lederhosen.

WHAT TO EAT: For breakfast, it's *Weisswurst* (white sausage) and *Weissbeer* (white beer). As the day goes on, the pork products keep coming—more sausages (bratwurst) for lunch, then *Schweinbraten* (roast pork) and *Knödel* (hearty dumplings) for supper, washed down with dark *Maibock* (May beer) that is specially brewed for the occasion.

■ *Essentials:* May Day celebrations are advertised in the local press, or find one through the Bavarian tourist board (bavaria .by/popular-customs-bavaria-germany)

"If no one tries to steal a village's tree, that place is uninteresting. It's good when one gets stolen." —LUKAS SALZEDER, RESIDENT OF STIERBERG

Dancing is a key feature of the May Day festivities. Opposite: A young couple in traditional Bavarian dress

KOLPING
2007

HEIDELBERG, GERMANY
THE SPIRIT OF CHRISTMAS

The air is crisp with frost and heavy with the aroma of cinnamon and spices as people warm their hands around mugs of *Gluehwein* (mulled wine). Children tug excitedly at parents' hands, and groups of high-spirited university students walk arm in arm singing Christmas carols. On a hill overlooking the city, rose-colored Heidelberg Castle is bathed in spotlights while down below groups of shoppers explore the city's Christkindl Christmas markets.

WHERE TO GO: Heidelberg's Christmas market of 140 stalls spreads over six historic market squares. At Karlsplatz, directly below the castle, you can take a spin with the locals around one of Europe's most scenic ice rinks, surrounded by trees decorated with fairy lights, to the rousing sound of traditional Christmas music.

At Universitätsplatz (the largest of the markets), children can ride an antique Christmas carousel and you can stock up on Christmas gifts. The unusual German crafts and Christmas decorations—glittering stars, colorful trees, trumpeting angels, and nativity figures—make unique souvenirs. Marktplatz houses the three-story revolving *Weihnachtspyramide* (Christmas pyramid) depicting famous figures from Heidelberg's history. The lower level houses a stall selling Gluehwein and other Christmas treats.

WHAT TO BUY: The traditional Weihnachtspyramide decorations are popular gifts, and take the form of miniature carousels with several levels of Christmas motifs such as angels, shepherds, or manger scenes. The rising heat from candles set in the carousel causes a propeller atop the pyramid to spin madly. Or buy a few handmade miniature ceramic houses and other buildings lit from within by tealights and build your own town.

WHAT TO EAT: Each square offers plenty of opportunities to refuel. Gluehwein and *Feuerzangenbowle* (rum and mulled wine) wash down hearty meals of bratwurst and sauerkraut. Adults and children alike are drawn to stalls selling roasted almonds, *Schweinsteak* (pork fillet sandwich), crepes, cinnamon stars, *Christstollen* (fruit cake), and giant gingerbread hearts. Local Sharon Holton-Schmitt thinks it's a "delicious way to start the holidays."

■ *Essentials:* Bismarckplatz, Karlsplatz, Universitätsplatz, Marktplatz, Kornmarkt, Anatomiegarten (last week in Nov. until the weekend before Christmas, heidelberg-event.com)

The giant, brightly lit *Weihnachtspyramide* spins at the center of Marktplatz.

VIENNA, AUSTRIA
SING SILENT NIGHT

On Christmas Eve the air is crisp, clear, and icy as you huddle together with the local crowd on Stephansplatz, your hands wrapped around a *Wiener melange* (a brew similar to cappuccino) for warmth. Towering above you are the soaring Gothic spires of St. Stephen's Cathedral in the heart of Vienna. At 11 p.m. the great bells start to ring, the doors swing open, and the faithful stream into the majestic interior, which is lit with multicolored spotlights that turn every arch and statue into a Christmas decoration. The strains of the pipe organ reverberate through the cathedral along with Christmas music sung by the choir. Shortly before midnight, Austria's biggest bell, the Pummerin, starts to toll, signaling the start of the Midnight Mass.

JOINING IN: The service—a highlight of the cathedral's annual program—proceeds at a stately pace. On the stroke of midnight, the priests enter in procession to the sound of the organ and choir. The chandeliers along the aisle light up as the priests progress through the cathedral. Only when the Archbishop has arrived at the pulpit can the Mass begin, interspersed with many well-loved Christmas carols. The priests say Mass in German, repeating some portions in English, French, and Italian. The service always finishes with a spellbinding a cappella performance of *Stille Nacht* (Silent Night), Austria's most famous Christmas carol.

WHEN TO GO: Midnight Mass takes place annually on December 24. The event is hugely popular with the Viennese, so although the service doesn't start until midnight, arrive by about 10 p.m. to make sure you get a seat. Otherwise, it's standing room only.

■ *Essentials:* Stephansdom (1 Stephansplatz, tel 43 (0) 1 515 523 767, stephanskirche.at)

The spire of St. Stephen's Cathedral dominates the Vienna skyline.

Mountaintops dwarf tiny Chapel Bichl in Virgental.

EAST TYROL, AUSTRIA
PEAKS OF PERFECTION

Stressed with everyday life? Then follow the Austrian locals to the Virgental valley for some healthy, exhilarating, and relaxing hiking. While cross-country skiers head for Virgental in winter, summer brings walkers of all ages, who trek between alpine *hütten* (huts)—the mountain lodges that ring the valley. This dramatic unspoiled gem nestling between the Lasörling and Venediger mountains certainly filled hiker Hans Schneider with amazement. "The valley was bathed in bright sunshine, yet a menacingly dark cloud with flashes of lightning hung over a nearby peak. It was quite surreal."

WHERE TO GO: Use the village of Virgen as a starting point and try the complete the Lasörling Höhenweg trail, a four-day, well-marked hike, with spectacular views of patchwork fields, tree-clad mountain slopes, and snow-capped peaks. The trail may be described as "strenuous" but it's not difficult, with a dozen huts along the way.

LOCAL KNOWLEDGE: Rather than trek for three hours up the first 6,500 feet (1,980 m), many locals drive up to the Wetterkreuzhütte lodge, where they join the trail. You can arrange for a mountain taxi at the Virgen tourist office.

WHEN TO GO: Between June and September, although don't miss early summer, when you can feast your eyes on the carpets of red alpenroses, white oxeye daisies, and other wildflowers on the high alpine meadows.

■ *Essentials:* Lasörlinghütte (89/6 Virgentalstrasse, Virgen, tel 43 (0) 664 975 8899, lasoerlinghuette.com)

DIGGING DEEPER

"Hut" doesn't do justice to the hiking shelters. The octagonal Lasörlinghütte in the shadow of Lasörling mountain can house 65 hikers, who will enjoy a rustic dinner, such as dumpling soup with rye bread followed by *apfelstrudel* (apple strudel), all washed down with cool Austrian beer.

BRUSSELS, BELGIUM
MAROLLES ANTIQUING

The center of Brussels has always been mainly a working-class neighborhood. And no quarter has a longer, grittier tradition of working-class life than the Marolles, a 15-minute walk to the south of the Grand Place. The area has a bohemian edge, stemming from its fame among Brussels residents as the go-to place for unusual antiquities, bric-a-brac, and vintage clothing. The draw is the flea market (held daily, but bigger at the weekends) in the place du Jeu de Balle. In its wake, shops, cafés, and restaurants have followed, all relishing the enclave's new bohemian cool.

WHAT TO BUY: Junk-shop furniture, light fittings, retro clothing, jewelry, china, paintings, gramophone records, old cameras and radios, jukeboxes, arts and crafts—it's all here, laid out beneath open skies on the place du Jeu de Balle, or ready for serious browsing in the numerous shops that pack the Marolles' two main thoroughfares, rue Haute and rue Blaes.

LOCAL FAVORITES: Two huge bric-a-bric and antique operations stand out. The more upmarket and antiquey Passage 125 Blaes spreads across four floors—"Just like Ali Baba's cave," says local schoolboy Basile Debroux, excitedly, "but without the 40 thieves." Stefantiek has two labyrinthine outlets, the larger one on the place de la Chapelle with a bizarre facade festooned with junk. Fans of vintage clothing and textiles go to Modes, where you'll find dresses, suits, shoes, hats, gloves, lace, fans, buttons, tablecloths, curtains, and more.

TAKING A BREAK: Café La Brocante (*brocante* means "bric-a-brac") by the flea market is a great place to pick up the Marolles atmosphere with a local *gueuze* beer and light lunch. There's live music on Sunday afternoons.

■ *Essentials:* Passage 125 Blaes (121–125 rue Blaes, tel 32 (0) 2 503 1027); Stefantiek (6 place de la Chapelle and 63 rue Blaes, tel 32 (0) 2 494 100 589, stefantiek.com); Modes (70 place du Jeu de Balle, tel 32 (0) 2 512 4907, modes-antique-textiles.com, closed Mon.); Café La Brocante (170 rue Blaes, tel 32 (0) 2 512 1343)

Flea market in the place du Jeu de Balle

The Belgians' favorite comfort food

BRUSSELS, BELGIUM

DON'T HOLD THE MAYO

Mussels with fries—*moules-frites*—are just about Belgium's national dish. The shellfish are eaten in vast quantities in Brussels, served in steaming casseroles—one casserole per person—with a big bowl of crispy, golden-brown fries and mayo on the side. It's simple, hearty fare, best served in restaurants with no pretensions. The fact that the mussels actually come from Zeeland in the Netherlands or from Normandy in France doesn't diminish the Belgians' enthusiasm. The season generally runs September to February.

HOW TO ORDER: Moules-frites is served as a main course, with about 2 pounds (1 kg) of mussels per person. The classic recipe is *moules marinière*: Fresh mussels steamed with chopped celery, onion, and parsley. There are more complicated versions, but most Belgians believe the simpler the better. The superlative quality of fries comes from using freshly cut potatoes of a selected variety (normally Bintje), and frying them twice in clean beef fat. For a real hands-on approach to eating mussels, do as the locals do: Use an empty pair of shells as a pincer.

LOCAL FAVORITES: Le Pré-Salé, in the city center, is the classic setting for moules-frites: tiled walls, wooden tables and benches, and a busy open kitchen at the rear. Just up the street, La Marée is an understated but highly regarded fish restaurant; moules-frites is a specialty. Larger, but equally down-to-earth, is Bij den Boer, overlooking the site of the former fish market in place Sainte-Catherine.

■ *Essentials:* Le Pré-Salé (20 rue de Flandre, tel 32 (0) 2 513 65 45, closed Mon.–Tue.); La Marée (99 rue de Flandre, tel 32 (0) 2 511 00 40, closed Sun.–Mon., lamaree-sa.com); Bij den Boer (60 Quai aux Briques, tel 32 (0) 2 512 61 22, bijdenboer.com, closed Sun.)

"Moules-frites is all in the quality of the ingredients, simply cooked. The dish is the essence of Belgium."
—MARTINE VANDERVENNET, SUSTAINABILITY ADVISOR

AMSTERDAM, THE NETHERLANDS
KING'S DAY

It's party time in Holland—a mad night and day of nonstop fun, when all ages fill the streets, dancing, busking, and carousing, everyone drenched in the color orange. Koningsdag is the great national holiday, held on April 27 (or April 26 if the 27th falls on a Sunday) to celebrate the King's birthday. But this really is the people's day, and it's very Dutch: low-key, sociable, good-natured, tolerant, tongue-in-cheek. "People party all over the country, with food, drinks, and free concerts in the streets," says Francien van Bohemen, a public affairs officer. For the biggest Koningsdag party of them all, head for Amsterdam and join a million others thronging the canals and parks, partying on the canal boats, listening to live bands, and dancing to pop-up DJs.

LOCAL FAVORITES: Look around for a traditional *vrijmarkt*, or free market, where locals empty their homes of junk and sell it in the street or nearby parks. "You'll find the best bargains ever among old stuff turned out from attics and basements," says van Bohemen. On top of this, food stalls spring up, DJs play on public squares, and decorated boats cram the canals, lending a carnival-like atmosphere everywhere you go.

WHEN TO GO: Everything really kicks off the night before, as people set up shop and the partying begins. The excitement is infectious. Then it rolls on into the day itself, in—with luck—glorious, bright spring weather. The partying ends between 8 and 9 p.m.—time to get everyone home and rest those tired feet.

WHAT TO WEAR: Anything orange, the color that's associated with the Dutch and their royal family. T-shirt, jacket, cloak, tutu, hat, wig, glasses—make it as silly as you like. This is when the Dutch really let their hair down.

WHERE TO GO: For the best vrijmarkten, go to the Jordaan district, west of the city center and within walking distance of Centraal Station. Or try the area around Apollolaan Avenue in south Amsterdam. The Vondelpark is famous for its children's market and showplace, while the Museumplein hosts outdoor concerts.

LOCAL KNOWLEDGE: Transport is a nightmare in Amsterdam on Koningsdag. There's no public transport in the middle of town, and all trains from out of town are packed. It's better to arrive the day before and stay somewhere central for a couple of nights, so that you can walk everywhere, following the pedestrian routes marked in color.

■ *Essentials:* koninginnedagamsterdam.nl

Amsterdam's canals are a sea of partygoers.

I ♥ My City

Pancras Dijk
Editor, NG Traveler, Netherlands

It always starts the night before. Back in my younger days, my friends and I gathered in the old city center. On King's Day Eve (Queen's Day back then), the narrow streets are lined with impromptu bars serving Oranjebitter liqueur. At midnight, the street sale of unwanted household stuff starts, creating a lively market vibe. It might be the best night out in Amsterdam. A King's Day hangover is as much a tradition as King's Day itself. I'm now a father of two, but King's Day still starts one night before—by baking 40 little cakes and arranging them on a decorated plate. The next day, we take the plate to a nearby park. "Who wants a cupcake? Fifty cents!" yells my four-year-old. Within an hour, she manages to sell the full stock.

Poffertjes sizzle on giant cast-iron griddles.

THE NETHERLANDS
SWEET AND PIPING HOT

Go to any Dutch market on a cold winter's day, and you'll be drawn by the delicious smell of sweet, fried batter wafting through the air. The source will be a stall making *poffertjes*, little fluffy pancakes, each about the size of a golfball. A line of customers in padded coats and hats will be patiently waiting their turn.

Making poffertjes is performance art. Bakers pour liquid batter made from buckwheat flour, ordinary flour, warm milk, eggs, salt, and yeast, sweetened by sugar syrup into a griddle's indentations. The poffertjes quickly rise, turning golden brown on the hot, oiled surface, the bakers deftly flipping them with a fork to cook the other side. The bakers fork them onto a plate or into a carton, a dozen at a time, dab them with slabs of butter while still hot, and sprinkle them lavishly with *poedersuiker* (powdered sugar). Poffertjes are designed for swift consumption.

JOINING IN: Some stalls offer additional accompaniments, such as sugar syrup, or a whole-cherry sauce, topped by generous squirts of whipped cream. But many of the Dutch are purists when it comes to poffertjes: Butter and poedersuiker, and no more.

■ *Essentials:* Look for poffertjes at markets and fairs. Or try Pim's Poffertjes en Pannekoekenhuis (19/21 Nieuwstraat, Dordrecht, tel 31 (0) 78 631 27 09, pimspofenpan.nl, closed Mon.–Tues.), or In de Salon (1 Karnemelksloot, Gouda, tel 31 (0) 182 51 21 15, closed Mon.)

"The best thing about poffertjes is that you can share a whole plate of them with your friends." —PIP FARQUHARSON, AMSTERDAM RESIDENT

THE NETHERLANDS
ICE-SKATING ON THE CANALS

When winter temperatures drop below freezing and bitter winds scud in from the Baltic, northern Europe shudders. But the Dutch feel a frisson of excitement. Could it be cold enough to freeze the canals? As soon as the ice is thick, strong, and safe enough, out come the brooms to sweep away any surface snow; out of the attics and boot cupboards come skates. The canals soon teem with schoolkids carrying ice-hockey sticks, skating moms pushing baby-buggies, tiny tots in balls of padding, gliding grannies, sleds, skittering dogs, and steaming pop-up stalls, called *koek en zopie* (cake and drink), selling hot drinks, soup, snacks, and even shots of Dutch gin. Irene Wolters, a librarian from The Hague, says, "I love it when the canals freeze over—I can go to work on my skates!"

Longer routes lead out through the countryside, linking the cities and creating a new travel network. No smooth-surfaced artificial rinks, these: Natural ice is bobbly, cracked, lined with reeds, and watched over by disconsolate ducks and herons. But it offers a chance to see the world from a different angle—the backs of farms, windmills, and church spires across the fields, picked out against the slate-gray skies. Don't be surprised if stooped, lycra-clad speedsters whoosh past, rhythmically swinging their leading arms and dusting the ice with their knuckles.

JOINING IN: Local papers publish a *Schaats Kalender* (skate calendar) listing the best places to skate, with daily updates. In long cold spells, well-signposted tours are laid out, linking towns and famous sights. Don't skate alone: Stay where there are other people in case of accident. Also, be careful under bridges, where the ice can be thinner. You can test out your skating legs first at one of the outdoor ice rinks that pop up in city centers in winter.

WHAT TO WEAR: Woolly hats, scarves, gloves, thick winter jackets, and old trousers (the ice is rough). Most people use long-bladed speed skates (not figure skates), and sometimes old-style skates that you strap onto boots. Skates are hard to rent—especially when the canals are frozen. Blade protectors are useful for walking from one canal to another or going around a bridge.

FARTHER AFIELD: The question on everyone's lips is: Will it be cold enough for The Elfstedentocht? This members-only race, around a 125-mile (200 km) canal circuit in the northern region of Friesland, happens only rarely, when the cold is very intense—but when it does, the sight of 16,000 hardy competitors braving the ice is unforgettable.

■ *Essentials:* General information: holland.com. For information on ice rinks in Amsterdam, visit amsterdamsights.com; for the Hague, visit denhaag.nl

Youngsters in Amsterdam practice their skating skills.

Always book ahead for a meal at Le Garet, a Lyon bouchon.

LYON, FRANCE
LOCAL BISTROS

In a country famed for its cuisine, the city of Lyon is home to some of France's most sophisticated restaurants. But the most authentic places for local cuisine are its *bouchons*. These jovial bistros, where lawyers sit at one table and plumbers at the next, developed during the era of carriage travel as places where coachmen could grab a glass and a bite while their horses were brushed with bundles of straw called *bouchons*. Mostly family run, they are modest inside, but the food of a good bouchon will warm the coldest heart.

LOCAL FAVORITES: Lyon has 20 or so bouchons bearing the Authentique Bouchon Lyonnais label. With its original 1937 interior, Chez Hugon near Hôtel de Ville packs in the regulars. At La Meunière, start off your meal at the buffet table laden with salads: Olives, lentils, herring, potatoes and oil, and other regional specialties. Don't leave before sampling the Brie de Meaux cheese followed by apple tart.

HOW TO ORDER: Limited menus specialize in such hearty regional fare as sausages, tripe, roast pork, *oeufs en meurette* in a rich wine sauce, and black pudding with apples, usually washed down with a pot of Beaujolais wine.

■ *Essentials:* Chez Hugon (12 rue Pizay, tel 33 (0) 4 78 28 10 94, closed Sat.–Sun., Aug.); La Meunière (11 rue Neuve, tel 33 (0) 4 78 28 62 91, la.meuniere.free.fr, closed Sun.–Mon., mid-July–mid-Aug.); Le Garet (7 rue du Garet, tel 33 (0) 4 78 28 16 94, closed Sat.–Sun., Aug.)

DIGGING DEEPER

While in France's gastronomic capital, get valuable tips on how to shop, taste, and cook like a seasoned French chef from the Plum Lyon Teaching Kitchen (plumlyon.com). Its day classes include market shopping, cooking with herbs, and creating classic Lyonnais dishes.

TOULOUSE, FRANCE

Unlike much of the terrain on the Tour de France, the city of Toulouse, through which the great race sometimes passes, is mercifully flat—perfect for leisurely cycling. So why not take advantage, like thousands of Toulousains, of VéloToulouse, a citywide network of more than 250 automated docking stations where you can pick up and return a bicycle as many times as you like during the course of a day? As seasoned local cyclist Hughues Le Bras says, "Toulouse and its weather are cycling-friendly. I like to bike along the River Garonne and the Canal du Midi, my two favorite spots in the city."

WHERE TO GO: Just follow the throng of cyclists on the paths beside the Garonne, or along the canals that thread through the city. Tour the many layers of Toulouse, with its Roman remains, medieval churches, Renaissance merchants' mansions, 19th-century hydroelectric turbines, and museums that celebrate the city's place today at the heart of France's aeronautical industry. Or simply stop off and people-watch in the majestic place du Capitole, before enjoying a plate of cassoulet, a hearty stew of beans, duck, and Toulouse sausage, in a restaurant in the peaceful place Saint-Pierre or the bustling place Wilson.

WHEN TO GO: Late spring and early autumn are the most comfortable seasons for cycling, and there are few more magical sights than that of the Pyrenees mountains, some 50 miles (80 km) away, their peaks capped with snow, as you take a well-earned rest, sipping an aperitif with the locals in a riverside café. Since the docking stations operate 24/7, you can use the bike-sharing service to make the most of the city's lively nightlife too. Unlike many regional French capitals, Toulouse is a real party place, with university students swelling the city's population by almost a quarter during term-time.

Essentials: VéloToulouse (velo.toulouse.fr). A small fee per day buys an unlimited number of journeys.

The local red brick from which much of the city is built has earned Toulouse the title La Ville Rose (the pink city).

BORDEAUX, FRANCE
MARATHON IN THE VINES

Fine wines and foods are not something you would usually associate with physical exertion—unless you're French, that is. Each September, the Médoc Marathon follows a 26.2-mile (42 km) circular course from just south of the small town of Pauillac on the Gironde estuary through the vineyards of some of Bordeaux's top wine chateaus. Register as one of the lucky 8,500 runners, and hordes of excited schoolchildren and other locals will cheer you along the route, while regional producers ply you with samples of wines, cheese, oysters, beefsteak, and other specialties, served from more than 40 refreshment stands. Remarkably, no one crosses the finish line after the 6.5-hour limit set by the organizers. As one runner quipped, the Médoc Marathon is "a fun run, not for militants—a run for taking time, instead of making time."

JOINING IN: Painted faces and costumes, following a different theme each year, are de rigueur. Chateau workers run in teams, joined by hundreds of other locals. You can run as an individual or in a group, perhaps raising money for a charity. More than 30 wine estates offer refreshments, including the world-famous Château Lafite Rothschild, which provides a rest stop and medical station at the midway point. Back in Pauillac in the evening, a grand finale of food and music, with fireworks exploding over the estuary, caps off a memorable, if wacky, day.

LOCAL KNOWLEDGE: There are water stations along the route, but strap on a water bottle as some stands run out in hot weather. Hang around for Sunday to join a more leisurely vineyard walk, followed by a gastronomic lunch.

■ *Essentials:* Pauillac provides the race headquarters. Reserve a place in advance, and sign up for tickets to the Friday pre-run "Mille Pâtes" pasta party at marathondumedoc.com

MORE: Wine-country Races

Marathon des Vins de Blaye, France: This pre-Médoc vineyard run takes place on the right bank of the Gironde. marathondesvinsdeblaye.com

Napa to Sonoma Wine Country Half Marathon, California: Run from the Carneros regions of Napa Valley to Sonoma Plaza, sampling the fruit of the vine along the way. destinationraces.com

Médoc runners pass the Château Pichon Longueville.

C'EST FROMAGE

If you like cheese, you'll love Annecy, a place celebrated not just for its beautiful Alpine setting beside a deep blue lake, but also for its food. In particular, you'll appreciate, along with the lucky locals, the knowledge and skills of the town's award-winning *fromagers affineurs*—experts in the fine art of maturing cheeses. To ensure that the cheese is sold in tip-top condition, these gastronomic heroes tend to their carefully selected cheeses in temperature-controlled cellars, known as *caves*, before presenting them in mouthwatering displays in their shops.

The affineurs embrace varieties from all over France, but they will be more than delighted to introduce you to the revered local cheeses, such as Beaufort and Reblochon. Many of these are handmade on nearby mountain farms, where the richness of the Alpine pasture, infused with hundreds of different wild plants, helps to create milk with a subtly different flavor that finds its way into the cheese. And then there's a further twist. Summer milk—delicate and floral—comes from cows when they're grazing, bells tinkling, high in the mountains. Richer winter milk is produced when they're sheltering in barns in the valley, feeding on hay. Try cheese made with each kind of milk and you'll discover marked differences, season to season.

LOCAL FAVORITES: Alain Michel, a fourth-generation fromager affineur, runs the Crèmerie du Lac, with three shops selling his own-brand local cheeses. The fromager

affineur Pierre Gay, whose family business was founded in 1935, likewise offers a wide range, but specializes in the cheeses of the Haute-Savoie region, of which Annecy is the capital. You can spy on them through transparent panels on his shop floor as they mature in the cave below. Jacques Dubouloz is a fromager affineur who zooms from market to market in his van, packed with cheese, and also has a shop in Poissy on the outskirts of Annecy.

WHAT TO BUY: Look for local cheeses that are made with *lait cru* (unpasteurized milk). Reblochon is a semi-soft cow's-milk cheese, with an orange-pink, dry, and dusty washed rind, and distinctive, buttery flavor of hay and walnuts. Beaufort is a robust, hard-pressed cheese, with a firm texture and sweet aftertaste: The summer one is called Beaufort de Montagne, and the winter one Beaufort Laitier. There are various local semi-hard, pressed, gray-rind *tommes* (made from skimmed milk), such as Tomme de Savoie, or Tomme des Bauges. Goat's-milk cheeses from the area include the soft, almost sweet-flavored Chevrotin des Aravis, and the distinctive blue-veined Persillé des Aravis.

■ *Essentials:* Crèmerie du Lac (3 rue du Lac, tel 33 (0) 4 50 45 19 31, cremeriedulac.com, closed 12:15–3 p.m. and Sun.–Mon.; Pierre Gay (47 rue Carnot, tel 33 (0) 4 50 45 07 29, fromage-cheese.com, closed 12:30–3 p.m. and Sun.–Mon.); Jacques Dubouloz (30 route des Creusettes, Poissy, tel 33 (0) 4 50 22 89 84, cremerie desmarches.fr, closed 12:30–3:30 p.m. and Sun.–Mon.)

A Perfect Plateau de Fromage, Annecy-style

The key to a good cheese plate is quality not quantity. Ask the fromager affineur what cheeses are recommended today—those that have reached the perfect state of maturity. Just one fabulous cheese may be all you need: Savor it, and wonder at the ancient skills it embodies. Otherwise go for varieties of taste and texture in a selection of local cheeses: Perhaps a slice of semi-soft Reblochon, contrasting with the firmer, sweeter Beaufort, plus maybe a chunk of blue cheese like the thick-crusted Persillé des Aravis.

"In this region, where cheese is an essential food, you'll find a crémerie [dairy shop] on every corner." —MARIE-ANDRÉE MANCHELLE, ANNECY LOCAL

Duck livers—one of the market's specialties

PÉRIGUEUX, FRANCE
A GOURMAND'S MARKET

Through the winter months across southwest France, the specialty markets known as *marchés au gras* (literally, fat markets) draw chefs, cooks, and gourmets in search of fresh, fattened geese and duck—and, in mid-January, the finest examples of the rare and highly prized black truffles. Those in the know head for Périgueux's Marché au Gras in the place Saint-Louis, where producers display goose, duck, and truffle products under one of the longest tents you'll ever see.

WHAT TO BUY: Fresh eggs, pots of foie gras (duck or goose liver), cassoulet (duck baked with haricot beans), *confit du canard* (preserved duck), and terrines are good buys, as is a fat, juicy duck or goose for roasting—and of course those famous truffles. Stallholders are eager to share their tips on selecting and preparing a large goose or tender duckling, and offer samples of their terrines, pâtés, and preserved products to tempt your taste buds.

WHEN TO GO: The market takes place every Wednesday and Saturday morning, mid-November to the end of March. Do what local Marolyn Charpentier does and go in January when the holiday crowds have thinned, "to get closer to the vendors for advice on preparing foie gras."

EXPLORING FARTHER: From place Saint-Louis, make your way on old cobbled streets along rue Limogeanne to place du Marché for a delectable chocolate pause at La Maison du Chocolat et des Délices. Then continue to rue Denfert-Rochereau to join the winter shoppers browsing the stalls of fruit and flowers at this extension of Périgueux's weekly market.

■ *Essentials:* Marché au Gras (place Saint-Louis, tourisme-perigueux.fr, open mid-Nov.–end March); La Maison du Chocolat et des Délices (30 bis rue Limogeanne, tel 33 (0) 5 53 08 92 69, closed Sun.–Mon., delices-chocolats-perigord.com)

L'ÎSLE–SUR–LA–SORGUE, FRANCE
SUNDAY TREATS

Need a copper bathtub or a French rocking horse, or maybe vintage textiles, doorknobs, or cut glass? Between Avignon on the Rhône River and the hazy blue Luberon hills lies an antique aficionado's treasure trove. The town of L'Îsle-sur-la-Sorgue, crisscrossed by the River Sorgue and canals that once served a crayfish industry and powered silk and paper mills, now draws antiques specialists and collectibles vendors to its lively Sunday flea market. One savvy regular, Nathalie Gros, says, "I always arrive early, at about 9 a.m., for the Sunday market. I can look around and shop in peace, and by 10 a.m. I'm sitting down in a café, drinking a cup of coffee and watching the world go by."

WHERE TO GO: On Sunday mornings hundreds of bric-a-brac stalls spread along avenue des Quatre Otages, close to one of the canals. Around the corner, a dozen clusters of shops and galleries, like the Village des Antiquaires de la Gare in a converted textile factory, are crammed with all kinds of curios and objets d'art, jewelry, and vintage clothes, as well as larger pieces, such as carpets, statues, and wooden and wrought-iron furniture.

Buoyant Trading

On the first Sunday in August, join the food-lovers flocking to the **Quai Jean Jaurès** to taste and buy local produce such as wine, olives, and fruit. But this is shopping with a difference—you buy from little flat-bottomed, flower-covered fishing boats, called *nego chin* (meaning drowned dog).

LOCAL KNOWLEDGE: Bibliophiles go on the last Sunday of each month for the old Book Market in the gardens of the Caisse d'Épargne bank in place Gambetta.

WHERE TO EAT: Seek out Couleurs Café on rue de la République for fresh coffee, fine tea, and local pastries.

■ *Essentials:* Village des Antiquaires de la Gare (2 av. de l'Égalité, tel 33 (0) 4 90 38 04 57, levillagedesantiquairesdelagare.com, closed Tues.–Sun.); Couleurs Café (35 rue de la République, tel 33 (0) 4 90 21 41 61)

Clocks, bikes, and other curiosities fill the streets.

Browse among the statues at Madrid's Galerías Piquer.

ANTIQUES MARKETS

From vintage clothing to old bird cages, these antiques markets will supply every whim.

◼ Galerías Piquer Madrid, Spain

Near bustling El Rastro flea market, this calm courtyard is full of garden statuary: Think cute cupids and bronze walruses. Madrileños head here to buy fine antiques from the experts. *Calle Ribera de Curtidores 29, Rastro, esmadrid.com*

◼ Downtown, Delray Beach, FL

Locals stop by antiques emporium Alexander: A Delray Design (777 E. Atlantic Ave. Plaza), then head to Kismet Recycled, Vintage & Designer Clothing (157 N.E. 2nd Ave.) for new-to-you duds. *downtowndelraybeach.com*

◼ Bazar de Antigüedades, Mexico City

Set in a series of covered arcades, this bustling market is at its busiest on Saturday, and is a great place to look for mirrors, furniture, and glass. *Opposite Mercado Insurgentes, Zona Rosa, antiguedadas plazadelangel.com*

◼ Montpellier Quarter, Harrogate, England

Scope out the paintings at Sutcliffe Galleries or the oak furniture (1600–1850) at Elaine Phillips Antiques in the pretty center of town. Savvy locals check out Montpellier Mews Antique Centre for antique silver, crystal, and more. *montpellierharrogate.com*

◼ Ecseri Piac Flea Market, Budapest, Hungary

Get up early, then follow the crowds to this giant flea market. Do not be intimidated by its size—or the Communist-era surroundings; it's an experience you will never forget. There's plenty to buy, including souvenirs of the country's past. Be prepared to haggle hard. *District XIX, Nagykörösi út 156, Kispest, budapest-tourist-guide.com*

◼ Klip–Klap Antique and Art Market, Pretoria, South Africa

On the third Sunday of each month, vendors spread out their wares under umbrellas, and friends and neighbors stop to chat as they look at the bric-a-brac. Some buy, others sample the *potjiekos* (a savory stew cooked over an open fire). *78a Leander Rd., Olympus, klipklap.co.za*

◼ Dongtai Road Antique Market, Shanghai, China

In Shanghai, haggling is virtually an art form and you can test your skills on this little street where bargains include old bird cages, vintage buttons, and calligraphy. Offer 80 percent of the asking price and get ready to negotiate. Since there is no way to guarantee authenticity here (most things are not true antiques), buy for fun. *Dongtai Lu, meet-in-shanghai.net*

◼ Amcorp Mall, Petaling Jaya, Malaysia

Vendors display their wares on maroon-colored tablecloths at this packed weekend flea market which fills the mall's lower ground floor. Join the locals rooting through stamps, old pewter and porcelain, and vintage vinyl. Buyers and sellers mix and mingle creating a lively atmosphere. *18, Persiaran Barat, off Jalan Timur, amcorpmall.com*

Casa Placido in the Santa Cruz district serves fine sherries and traditional tapas.

SEVILLE, SPAIN
TAPAS BARS

Tapas bars are the life and soul of Seville. Here Sevillanos meet after work to socialize over a drink and graze on a few tapas. Hot, cold, salty, sweet—tapas bites can be the equivalent of a meal, but whether you choose small, medium, or large *raciones* (portions), "The best way to enjoy tapas is to spend the evening with friends sharing dishes," as the musician Ángela García López says.

HOW TO ORDER: Choose a couple of tapas, then do as the locals do and move on to another place—here the best anchovies, there the finest Huelva ham or the tastiest aioli potato. Local specialties include gazpacho andaluz, stewed bull's tail, baby squid, and spicy pork loin.

LOCAL FAVORITES: You can find some of the most popular bars along the lanes near the cathedral and in the Santa Cruz district. El Rinconcillo, the oldest in town, serves delicious ewe's cheese and spinach with chickpeas. On balmy evenings, its patrons pack the tables on the sidewalk, so be ready to move in as soon as someone asks for their check. Visit Las Teresas for cured meats; in Bodega Santa Cruz, the eggplant with honey melts in your mouth. Wherever you go, a tapas tour will make you feel like a local with, in the words of a Spanish proverb, "a full belly and a happy heart."

■ *Essentials:* El Rinconcillo (Calle Gerona 40, tel 34 (0) 954 223 183, en.elrinconcillo.es); Las Teresas (Calle Santa Teresa 2, tel 34 (0) 954 213 069); Bodega Santa Cruz (Calle de Rodrigo Caro 1A, tel 34 (0) 954 211 694); Casa Placido (Calle Mesón del Moro 5, tel 34 (0) 954 563 971)

DIGGING DEEPER

After you've eaten your fill, head for a gypsy bar, such as Casa Anselma (Calle Pages del Corro 49) across the River Guadalquivir in the Triana district, where the proprietress belts out soul music Sevillana-style from midnight until the early hours.

Sevillians turn out in traditional dress for the city's week-long party.

SEVILLE, SPAIN

FLAMENCO FOR ALL

Flamenco, food, and finery are on tap at the Feria de Abril de Sevilla. As one local, Gema Jurado Fernández, describes it, "The scent of orange blossom. The colors of costumes. The taste of wine—that's Feria to me." This whirl of flamenco dresses and equestrian chic takes place at the the Real de la Feria fairground on the western bank of the Río Guadalquivir opposite the old town.

LOCAL FAVORITES: During the week-long festival—which normally takes place a fortnight after Easter—the fairground transforms into a city of vividly decorated *casetas* (marquees) hosted by companies, labor unions, groups of friends, or families. A recent addition is La Calle del Infierno (Hell Road), a modern amusement zone with rides,

games, and raffles. During Feria, you can also watch bullfights at the La Real Maestranza, Spain's oldest bullring.

JOINING IN: Each day kicks off with a parade of horses and carriages through the fairground, followed by flamenco dancing, dining, and drinking in the casetas until late. Although most casetas are strictly private, about 15 are open to the public—try Er 77 and Los Duendes de Sevilla (the Goblins of Seville). Even if not in costume, locals dress to the nines—shorts and a T-shirt won't cut it. Once inside a caseta, sip a glass of manzanilla and take to the floor for the sevillanas (the local style of flamenco).

■ *Essentials:* General information: andalucia.com, spain.info

DIGGING DEEPER

Find your way to the Plaza de España (in the Parque de María Luisa), where many fairgoers decked out in *trajes de flamenco* (flamenco-style dresses) and the *traje corto andaluz* (short riding jacket) go to get their photos snapped against a backdrop of Andalusian architecture.

THE WORLD'S BEST HAM

Around dawn in the town of Monesterio, in southwest Spain's Extremadura province, the Puerta del Sol bar gears up for the day. Pilgrims getting an early start on the Vía de la Plata (Silver Way) from Seville to Santiago de Compostela rest their backpacks against the tiled walls while local workers hunch over coffee and *licor de bellota* (acorn liquor). The waiters set down breakfast—a baguette torn in two and a plate of paper-thin slices of cured ham colored deep purple and marbled with yellow-white fat. The flavors are rich, savory, and luxurious. Haunches of the region's prized Jamón Ibérico de Bellota hang behind the bar and from the ceiling of every restaurant in this small town. The ham comes from the local black Iberian pigs that live in the hills around Monesterio. The pigs snuffle out the acorns from the holm oak trees, a diet that gives the meat its extraordinary nuttiness. The ham, along with lard, bread, and liquor, is the traditional way in which the farm workers in this agricultural region start their day. Marisa Pemau Hernández remembers "breakfast underneath a grapevine with *la abuela* (grandmother) singing to us while cutting Jamón Ibérico."

JOINING IN: Almost all the bars and restaurants in Monesterio sell Jamón Ibérico by the slice. Locals may buy a whole ham but it's uberexpensive for the best—labeled *reserva* or *gran reserva*—which are aged up to four years. Before buying some it's usual to try a sliver or two.

■ *Essentials:* Puerta del Sol (Paseo de Extremadura 63, tel 34 (0) 924 516 274); for lunch and evening meals Restaurante el Rinconcillo (Paseo de Extremadura 67, tel 34 (0) 924 517 001)

A waiter cuts paper-thin slices of Jamón Ibérico de Bellota.

SONGS FROM THE HEART

Fado, Portugal's soulful native music, has been performed for hundreds of years in the streets and taverns of Lisbon. Sr. Fado, an intimate restaurant in the Alfama quarter, has become a fixture of the Lisbon fado scene since opening in 2008. Early in the evening, owners Ana Marina and Duarte Santos can be found working in the kitchen, preparing traditional dishes such as *cataplã*, a homey seafood stew. When the fado begins, with the sound of the viola de fado (played by Duarte) and the 12-string Portuguese guitar, Ana Marina emerges to sing and is transformed suddenly but subtly from cook to heartbreaker. As Duarte explains, "These songs—about love and loss, hope and regret—express the Portuguese *saudade*: the simultaneous sadness and happiness that our memories may conjure."

JOINING IN: On Wednesday nights, it's time for the *tertúlia*. "The door is left open for our friends to come and play the fado with us," Duarte says. Among these friends are the amateur singers and musicians who give the fado its cultural ballast, along with some real luminaries. Indeed, part of the surprise is wondering who will come through the door (or stand up in the restaurant) to sing or play next.

MORE LOCAL FAVORITES: Firmly established, Esquina d'Alfama has a tightly integrated collective of performers and a few surprise ones. Tasca do Jaime has an ever-rotating group of singers and lots of regulars. And for something more upscale, try Clube de Fado. Run by the veteran guitarist Mário Pacheco, it is a focal point for a generation of younger singers, musicians, and poets.

WHEN TO GO: Hours and dates change frequently, particularly during winter, so always call ahead.

■ *Essentials:* General information: visitportugal.com; Sr. Fado (Rua dos Remédios 176 in Alfama, tel 351 91 443 19 71, sr-fado.com, closed Mon. and Tues., reservations required); Esquina d'Alfama (Rua de São Pedro 4, tel 351 21 887 05 90, closed Tues.); Tasca do Jaime (Rua Graça 91, tel 351 21 888 15 60, closed Mon.–Fri.); Clube de Fado (Rua São João da Praça 86–94, tel 351 21 885 27 04)

Performers at Clube de Fado

Tiles on display at
Solar Antiques

LISBON, PORTUGAL
HUNTING FOR TILES

Walking through Lisbon's ancient Moorish Alfama district (the meandering web of cobbled alleyways surrounding the castle), you will by struck by two things: The laundry billowing out across alleys and squares from every apartment window, like oversize bunting; and the dazzling variety of panels of *azujelos*, the traditional, colorful, hand-painted ceramic tiles for which the city is famous. Every street provides glimpses of building facades on which zigzags, flowers, swirls, stars, and chevrons create a dazzling kaleidoscope of colors—iridescent green, blue and white, marigold yellow, deep purple.

WHERE TO GO: Many antique stores stock old tiles, or you can look for them in the Feira da Ladra flea market. Antiques expert Judith Miller says, "There is a lot of junk but there are bargains to be had here." When Judith is in Lisbon she joins the locals at Solar Antiques, in the Principe Real neighborhood, which specializes in antique tiles salvaged from Portugal's historic homes and buildings. Descend to the cool cellar to find endless rows, shelves, and stacks of them, grouped by century—15th to 19th—and by style—Moorish, art nouveau, and art deco.

LOCAL KNOWLEDGE: Prices for antique tiles vary widely according to age and condition—from around €1 ($1.30) per tile to more than €100 ($130) for a fine, rare antique tile—so do some research before shopping. From the 1730s until the devastating earthquake of 1755, Portugal produced tiles on an industrial scale and examples from that time may be less valuable; pre-1730 and post-1755, which saw a resurgence in artisanal tiles, are more valuable.

■ *Essentials:* Feira de Ladra (Campo de Santa Clara, Alfama, closed Sun.–Mon. and Wed.–Fri.); Solar Antiques (68-70 Rua de Pedro 35, tel 351 121 346 55 22)

VENICE, ITALY

VENETIAN THANKSGIVING

ondolas, luxury yachts, motor launches—boats of every size and description, festooned with garlands and colored paper lanterns—begin gathering around sunset in St. Mark's Basin. It's the third Saturday in July and the locals are out in force to celebrate the Festa del Redentore (Festival of the Redeemer), established in 1576 to celebrate the end of an outbreak of the plague. As the boats' occupants await the fireworks that kick off the festival, they feast on *sarde in saor* (sweet-and-sour sardine antipasto), *bigoi in salsa* (pasta with anchovy sauce), *salsicce* (sausage), *pincia* (bread pudding), and wine. The following day, the crowds return to cheer on competitors in the gondola regatta.

WHEN TO GO: The Festa del Redentore takes place on the third weekend of July, starting with fireworks on Saturday night at a half hour before midnight and concluding with the regatta on Sunday afternoon on the Giudecca Canal.

WHERE TO GO: Although you can get a good view of the fireworks from the waterfront around St. Mark's, the best place to enjoy them is alongside the locals on the water. Gather a group of friends and pre-book a gondola for the evening. After the fireworks, head to the Lido, where the local crowd stays up all night to wait for sunrise.

■ *Essentials:* Most of the activity centers around St. Mark's Basin and the Giudecca Canal. redentorevenezia.it, venicelido.it

Crowds enjoy the view from St. Mark's Square as boats gather for the festival in the Giudecca Canal.

GONDOLA SERVICE

MILAN, ITALY
SEARCHING FOR SHOES

Purchasing more than five pairs of new shoes every year, the Italians stand head and shoulders above the European average. Ardent shoppers, the Milanesi hunt for the perfect pair. Moira Ruiu, an Italian fashion designer, explains: "For garments, the Milanesi feel no embarrassment to shop in fast fashion and bargain stores, but when it comes to shoes no expense and energy are spared. Shoes require investment."

WHERE TO GO: When the citizens of Lombardy's capital look for the classical, refined, and contemporary, they turn to Vergelio, a high-end, multibrand boutique. Vergelio carries the Italian shoe superstars Casadei, Gucci, Giuseppe Zanotti, Sergio Rossi, and Cesare Paciotti, but also stocks glamorous international labels such as Stuart Weitzman. Vergelio's mid-market sister is Marilena, which features a carefully selected assortment of more casual lines.

Giuseppe Bruno, Italian fashion stylist, insists the holy grail for shoe shoppers towers over Piazza Duomo: "Years come and go, but Milano's La Rinascente remains THE destination, the mother ship to which shoe lovers flock." In January and July, particularly when new seasons launch and discount sales begin, hordes of locals descend on the department store's newly refurbished third floor, which is dedicated entirely to shoes.

■ *Essentials:* Vergelio (Corso Vittorio Emanuele II 10, tel 39 (0) 2 7600 3087, vergelio.it); Marilena (Corso Vittorio Emanuele II 15, tel 39 (0) 2 7600 0665, vergelio.it); La Rinascente (Piazza Duomo/Via Santa Radegonda 3, tel 39 (0) 2 88521, rinascente.it)

Après-shopping

After purchases have been completed and credit cards depleted, Milanesi enjoy the *aperitivo*, a late-afternoon drink-plus-snack devoted to chatting and people-watching, and savvy locals gravitate toward the bars of the old-world Brera neighborhood. If more substantial nourishment is called for, **Papermoon** (*Via Bagutta 1, tel +39 (0) 2 796083*) serves hearty fare, while **Maio** (on the top floor of La Rinascente) offers a great view of the Duomo.

Milan's shoe stores are worshipped by shoe-holics.

I ♥ My City

Federico Rocca
Fashion Editor
Vanityfair.it

I hate to admit it, but my shoes are battered and scuffed. I guess that makes me a real rarity in a world of shoe addicts. But what is it with this mania for shoes? Freud could have had a field day analyzing why people love shoes so much, but the way I see it, there are three types of people: people who just like shoes, those who collect them, and an elite who positively idolize them. For these women, and they are mainly female, shoes are almost a religion. But if women love to collect shoes, it's men who really take care of their shoes, and the temple of shoe-care is Turi Lacci e Lucidi, at Via Cerva 19. Inside is every type of wax, brush, and polish you could possibly need to keep your shoes in top condition. I sigh when I go by because, let's face it, I'm ashamed of my shoes.

Jesolo's plentiful shops have something for everyone.

TRAFFIC-FREE SHOPPING

Subtract cars and you'll find retail therapy much more relaxing.

■ **Piazza Primo Maggio, Jesolo, Italy**
Start your 8-mile (12 km) shopping marathon in the piazza in the heart of the seaside town of Jesolo, north of Venice. Then explore the network of pedestrianized streets and squares. More than 1,200 outlets—from chain stores to cutting-edge boutiques—draw discerning shoppers.
jesolo.it

■ **Lincoln Road, Miami, FL**
Lincoln Road is chic street, Miami, the place locals settle down in sidewalk cafés to watch the world go by. Running eight blocks east from Alton Road across to the Ritz-Carlton on Miami Beach, this stretch of the art deco district has nearly 50 bars and restaurants as well as boutique stores and

galleries to explore. The Sunday farmer's market answers the everyday needs of Miami folk, while, in December, at Art Basel–Miami Beach, the prestigious international art fair, it's time to splurge on a once-in-a-lifetime acquisition.
lincolnroad.org

■ **Strøget, Copenhagen, Denmark**
At more than a mile (2 km) long, Strøget is Europe's longest shopping street. Stretching through the center of Copenhagen between the two main squares, Rådhuspladsen and Kongens Nytorv, it has everything—from high-end boutiques to discount stores. When it's raining, locals hunker down at Illum, a large department store, until the skies clear.
visitcopenhagen.com

■ **Rua Augusta, Lisbon, Portugal**
The central thoroughfare in a grid of pretty 18th-century streets by the Rua Augusta Arch draws upmarket shoppers. Flower and chestnut sellers join the kiosks and café tables that line the mosaic-paved street, while buskers and mime artists keep the crowds entertained.
visitlisboa.com

■ **Váci Street, Budapest, Hungary**
This elegant shopping street runs parallel to the Danube River in the heart of ancient Pest. The souvenir shops may be hokey, so do like the locals and focus on the designer stores and the three-story Central Market Hall near Liberty Bridge for the real deal.
budapest-tourist-guide.com/vaci-street.html

■ **Temple Street Night Market, Hong Kong, China**
As dusk falls, crowds converge on Temple Street in Hong Kong's Kowloon district; traffic is banned so carts piled with goods appear. This is one of Hong Kong's largest flea markets. Its emphasis on menswear has given it the nickname Men's Street. Locals come here for the vibe and the great street food.
discoverhongkong.com

■ **Arcades and Lanes, Melbourne, Australia**
Once back entrances for tradesmen to properties on the larger main streets, today these old-fashioned arcades and narrow lanes are ground zero for Melbourne's trendy boutique shoppers and caffeine fiends.
thatsmelbourne.com.au

MODENA, ITALY
OPERA FOR ALL

The small Italian city of Modena is proud of many things—the Ferrari and Maserati works, balsamic vinegar, lambrusco wine, and a bucket stolen from Bologna in a raid 700 years ago—but most of all they are proud of native-son Luciano Pavarotti, whose name was added post mortem to the Teatro Comunale di Modena. The theater dates from the 19th century and outwardly blends with the surrounding buildings in an unremarkable city street. But inside, the perfect arc of ornate, tiered boxes designed for the well-to-do surround the auditorium above the stalls, and have all the baroque flourishes one would expect from a traditional Italian opera house. As local Daniel Palmizio says, "It's an unmissable experience to go to the opera in Modena. Verdi composed many of his operas not far from here. It's a special feeling to listen to the music around his people."

JOINING IN: If you buy tickets on the day of the show, you may be gratified to get a box ticket, only to find that it is in the rear of an upper-tier box. But peering over the other occupants has its benefits—expect to have exchanged names and numbers with them by the time you leave.

WHERE TO EAT: Most restaurants stop serving dinner long before the curtain falls so eat beforehand or the only thing you'll find will be a pizza off the Largo Garibaldi.

WHAT TO WEAR: Opera night must be date night in Modena, for the crowd is dressed to impress. Have a drink at the bar in the intermission and enjoy the fashion parade.

■ *Essentials:* Teatro Comunale di Modena (Via del Teatro n.8, tel 39 59 203 3020, teatrocomunalemodena.it, closed Mon., reservations recommended)

Local Lunch

Follow shoppers, businessmen, and workers in bright orange overalls up the stairs into **Trattoria Aldina** restaurant. A typical lunch is: Tortellini, a platter of sliced pork loin with potatoes and a side of spinach, followed by a fruit tart, handmade earlier in the day. This simple lunchtime restaurant is housed in two rooms in a building across from the Modena market, and will provide fuel for the evening's operatic endeavors. Via Albinelli 40, tel 39 59 23 61 06, closed Sun.

The Teatro Comunale di Modena provides a lavish setting for opera.

CASOLE D'ELSA, ITALY
VILLAGE HORSE RACE

Siena's Palio may be better known, but the annual horse race in the Tuscan hilltop village of Casole d'Elsa is just as hotly contested. Local passions run high as six horses and riders, representing Casole's six *contrade* (districts), compete for the honor that comes with winning the *drapellone* (painted banner). As the horses negotiate the sharp turns and uneven ground of a course marked out across gently rolling fields below the village walls, Casole's residents and neighbors roar them on with cries of *"Vai, vai. Avanti*—Go, go. Come on."

WHEN TO GO: The race takes place on the second Sunday in July and is the culmination of a weekend of feasts, concerts, and qualifying races.

WHERE TO GO: On Sunday afternoon, crowds pack the Piazza della Liberta in the village center to watch displays of flag-throwing and drumming by local performers dressed in medieval costumes. At 6 p.m., the horses, each accompanied by supporters dressed in the colors of their contrade, are led up to the Church of Santa Maria Assunta on the piazza to be blessed by the priest. Then the village empties of people: Just follow everyone else as

MORE: Tuscan Village Races

Bravio delle Botti, Montepulciano: In this barrel race, held at the end of August, pairs of runners representing the town's eight *contrade* push 175-pound (80 kg) wine barrels along an uphill course. montepulciano.com
Palio Marinaro dell'Argentario, Porto Santo Stefano: A rowboat race is held in mid-August between four teams representing the four districts of the Argentario peninsula in southern Tuscany. italian-islands.com

they make their way to the slopes below the little church of San Niccolò, beside the road winding up into the village. This will give you the best view of the course. Afterward, the winning contrada celebrates back in the piazza, and the evening ends with a grand firework display.

■ *Essentials:* turismo.intoscana.it, discovertuscany.com

Casole's Palio is a hard-fought bareback race.

Florence is at your feet from the hilltop town of Fiesole.

FLORENCE, ITALY
VIEWS TO DIE FOR

In summertime, locals looking to escape the heat of Florence head for the picturesque town of Fiesole—a former Etruscan hilltop settlement perched high on the hills above the city, with sweeping views across the Tuscan countryside. Most locals go up there in the late afternoon after work, or on clear weekend days when they can make the most of the impressive panorama. Local

Exploring Fiesole

Don't miss the chance to browse the small antique market that is held on the first Sunday of each month (excluding July and August) in the main square, **Piazza Mino da Fiesole.** Jewelry and old books vie for space with chairs, tables, and knick-knacks. Retro is big here and old telephones, record players, and radios tempt the local crowd to part with their euros.

writer Georgette Jupe says, "Let the cooler air and soft breezes of Fiesole relax you. You'll truly feel part of a different era; time moves as slowly as you'd hope in Italy."

HOW TO GET THERE: Fiesole is located about 3 miles (5 km) north of Florence. From Piazza San Marco, take the number 7 bus which will take you up to the town along a winding road in 20 minutes. Locals often stop at a supermarket first to pick up a bottle of wine and a picnic.

WHEN YOU ARRIVE: A charming, pedestrian-only street, Via di San Francesco, climbs steeply uphill from Piazza Mino da Fiesole. At the top by the monastery, you will be rewarded with stunning views of Florence. Find a shady spot to savor the vista along with your picnic.

A SWEET BREAK: Returning to the center of town, stop by Bar Pasticceria Alcedo. Sweet-toothed Florentines will go out of their way to come here in order to indulge in the freshly baked pastries.

■ *Essentials:* Bar Pasticceria Alcedo (Via Gramsci 39, tel 39 55 59349), fiesole.com

CORTONA, ITALY
TUSCANY'S BIGGEST BBQ

Villagers all over Tuscany come together for *sagras* (food festivals) at which seasonal ingredients take center stage from early summer (asparagus and cherries) through fall (chestnuts and truffles).

LOCAL KNOWLEDGE: The sagra is an Italian tradition that celebrates regional cooking and often also honors a saint. Villagers show off their cooking skills and their hospitality, while raising money for a local cause. In addition to dinner, there is usually dancing and a chance to buy local produce.

WHAT TO EXPECT: At the Sagra di Bistecca in the southern Tuscan village of Cortona, held in the Parterre Gardens annually on August 14–15, steak from the regal-looking white Chianina cattle is the star. Once used for pulling plows and carts on Tuscany's hilly farmland, this breed is now raised for its meat. Chefs stand in a haze of heat and smoke grilling hundreds of T-bones on an inferno of glowing coals. Teens and seniors ferry trays of steaks to customers sipping Chianti at communal tables. Later, everyone from babies to great-grandparents hits the dance floor.

WHAT TO EAT: The T-bone *bistecca* is cooked simply, served very rare, and seasoned only with salt and pepper. Local resident and web editor Luca Tiezzi explains, "In

---

MORE: Cortona Food Festivals

Calici Sotto le Stelle: Goblets under the Stars is a local wine-tasting event held in Cortona on the night of San Lorenzo (August 10), the best time to see shooting stars.
Sagra del Cinghiale: During the last weekend in July or first in August, try wild boar stew at this annual wild boar festival in Pergo, a hamlet on the edge of Cortona.
Sagra della Castagna: The village of Teverina, 1 mile (2 km) south of Cortona, holds an annual Chestnut Festival on the first or second weekend in October.

Tuscany, we like our steaks extremely rare, and served with a side dish of green salad, tomatoes, or *fagioli all'uccelleto* (beans with tomato sauce and sage)." This is truly food just like Mama used to make—and still does in Tuscany, where you, too, can be a local for a night.

■ *Essentials:* Cortona sagras: cortonaweb.net

The Piazza della Repubblica in Cortona. Opposite: Chefs tackle the T-bones at the town's Sagra di Bistecca.

Neapolitans love pizzas straight from the oven.

NAPLES, ITALY
NEAPOLITAN PIZZA

Let's not argue about whether Naples invented the pizza. Let's just say it's true, and that sometime after the arrival of the tomato from the New World, Neapolitan street stalls were selling baked and leavened dough covered with garlic, oil, tomato, and cheese and that the cult of the pizza was born. The first pizzeria is said to have been the Antica Pizzeria Port'Alba, which opened in 1830. It still pulls only two kinds of pie out of its oak-burning oven: the Marinara (tomatoes, garlic, oregano, olive oil) and the Margherita (tomato, mozzarella, basil), its colors said to mimic those of the Italian flag, in honor of Italian queen Margherita's visit in 1889.

LOCAL FAVORITES: At Trianon da Ciro, open since 1935, try the mushroom pizza. Di Matteo lures a regular clientele with its *pizza fritta*. Stuffed with ricotta, *provola* (a smoked cheese), and a smear of pork fat, it is a deep-fried masterwork. "I love Di Matteo because it's right in the heart of old Naples. Be prepared to stand in line around holiday time—the pizza is worth it!" says Neopolitan native Melania Capasso.

■ *Essentials:* Antica Pizzeria Port'Alba (Via Port'Alba 18, tel 39 81 442 1061, damichele.net, closed Sun. Oct.–Aug.); Trianon da Ciro (Via Pietro Colletta 46, tel 39 81 553 9426); Di Matteo (Via dei Tribunali 94, tel 39 81 455 262, closed Sun.)

MORE: Neapolitan Favorites

Féfé: Neapolitans come for the fresh seafood and sea views. Via della Shoah 15, Case Vecchie, Bacoli

Pasticceria Pintauro: This serves the best *sfogliatelle*—crispy pastries filled with vanilla-flavored ricotta and candied fruit—in Naples. Via Roma 275

Poseidone: Makes a delicious *spaghetti alle vongole:* Clams, chilli, garlic, and white wine. Via Partenope 1

Venetians take an evening stroll along the Zattere.

PASEOS AND PASSEGGIATAS

In Italy and Spain, join in the evening stroll between 5 and 8 p.m. to walk, talk, and drink.

■ **Venice, Italy**

"Andiamo a fare qualche vasca—Let's make some laps" is a frequent suggestion among Venetians, who step out for a stroll in the late afternoon. Locals dust off their best outfits and join friends on the sidewalk to catch up on the gossip. A favorite place is Zattere, the waterside quay that looks across to the island of Giudecca.
comune.venezia.it

■ **Catania, Italy**

Paved with lava from nearby Mount Etna, Via Etnea is a long, straight, part-pedestrianized street leading from Piazza del Duomo to the Tondo Gioieni in the heart of Catania. On balmy evenings, locals stroll the dark cobblestones, perhaps stopping for a drink in one of the many bars and restaurants that

cluster in the side streets.
turismo.provincia.ct.it

■ **Frascati, Italy**

Famous for its white wine, Frascati is also known for its *cantinas*—bars where locals gather to sip the cool, pale liquid. On summer evenings, waiters put tables out on the sidewalks for alfresco drinking. Most folks buy a *porchetta per la cantina* (a roast pork sandwich) from one of the many street vendors to accompany their Frascati.
laziofortourist.com

■ **Milan, Italy**

Milan is the home of Italian style, and the daily passeggiata is as good as a catwalk for spotting the latest fashions. The young and trendy head for the Brera district, where designer stores add to the browsing

possibilities. The Navigli canals are also a favorite with the locals, who come to drink in the cafés and bars, some lingering until the nightlife begins.
tourism.milan.it

■ **Alghero, Sardinia, Italy**

The entire population of Alghero seems to turn out for an evening walk along the narrow lanes of this walled medieval city. Locals often pause in the rustic bars and soak up the atmosphere.
alghero-turismo.it

■ **Siena, Italy**

La passeggiata is a daily performance in Siena, and locals flock to the beautiful, expansive main square and the Via di Città. Much of the center of this medieval Tuscan city is pedestrianized, making it the perfect place to people-watch and

linger over a slice of *panforte* (spiced fruit cake). From April to September there is a fiesta every Sunday, adding to the throng.
terresiena.it

■ **Madrid, Spain**

Nobody eats before 9 p.m. in Madrid and entertainment rarely starts before midnight, so the evening paseo is a chance to stop for tapas. Locals take to the Plaza Mayor and Puerta del Sol while Parque del Buen Retiro is ideal for a summer amble.
esmadrid.com

■ **Seville, Spain**

To escape the heat of summer, Sevillanos stroll over to Barrio Santa Cruz, where the narrow lanes of this former Jewish quarter are said to be a little cooler than the rest of the city.
visitasevilla.es

BUCHAREST, ROMANIA
STROLLING IN CIȘMIGIU

An oasis of calm in the heart of the city, Cișmigiu Gardens is where locals stroll among the statues in the Rotunda Scriitorilor (Writers' Rotunda) or play a leisurely game of chess or backgammon. It's hard to believe this leafy park was once swampland. Designed by Wilhelm Meyer, a former director of the Imperial Gardens of Vienna, Cișmigiu was inaugurated in 1854, along with a full set of rules—one of which famously prevented pedestrians from bringing hogs into the park. Those days are gone, but the old plane trees remain, as does an original 19th-century newspaper kiosk. Local writer Raluca Gavris says, "You can smell the past; the gardens mirror the history of Bucharest. They define Bucharest."

JOINING IN: The centerpiece is the beautiful lake, and on summer days rowboats and pedalos crisscross its surface. The locals can often be found drifting among the swans on the calm waters, or paddling under the little stone bridges. In the winter, the green water turns to white and ice skaters take to the lake in place of the boats. For local publishing executive Livia Stoia, the park holds happy memories: "When my children were little we played here on the way home from kindergarden."

WHEN TO GO: Year-round the gardens play host to public events such as concerts or performing arts, so there is no bad time to visit. During summertime, little huts sell local handicrafts and sweet snacks, and in winter you can stave off the cold with a glass of *vin fiert* (boiled wine) before putting on your ice skates. Even at night, Cișmigiu is alive with lovers taking romantic, nocturnal walks; skaters and cyclists gliding along the walkways; and the young getting together for drinks.

■ *Essentials:* Cișmigiu Gardens (Schitu Măgureanu Str./ Regina Elisabeta Blvd./Știrbei Vodă Str., mydestination .com/romania)

MORE: Outdoor Spaces

Grădina Icoanei Park Old Bucharest lives on in this quiet spot known as Icon's Garden. Dacia Blvd./Icoanei Str.
Herăstrău Park This big park has an open-air theater, an aquarium, and a yacht club. Aviatorilor Blvd./Kiseleff Str.

Boating is just one of the many activities on offer at Cişmigiu.

I ♥ My City

Adina Brânciulescu
Editor, NG Traveler, Romania

We live in Militari, an ugly neighborhood of Bucharest without any green spaces, but I escape every day to Cişmigiu with my three-year-old son, Vladimir. We take the subway to Izvor, near the Palace of Parliament (formerly the House of the People), cross the bridge over the Dâmboviţa River, and we're almost there. I prefer the quiet entrance on Schitu Măgureanu Street, next to the chess players' area, but I follow Vladimir to the main entrance on Regina Elisabeta Boulevard. We take the linden-lined Parterre Alley past the peacocks' shelter to Swan Lake. The guard here won't let anyone throw pieces of bread to the ducks and swans, but we trick him every time. Then we take our little shovels, rake, and bucket and go to the playground by the lake.

In the shadow
of New York's
Flatiron Building

Great Cities

Local favorites in 15 hot spots across the globe

Paris's Marché des Enfants Rouges, the city's oldest covered market

New York

Arts and Eats in the City that Never Sleeps

■ **Fresh Food for Miles**
On Monday, Wednesday, Friday, and Saturday, downtown's Union Square is a sea of white tents where local farmers, fishermen, and bakers come to sell top-notch goods and produce to a regular throng of New Yorkers in the know. Grab food for a picnic in the square or simply look out for stands offering free samples, such as sliced apples, pieces of cheese, or homemade jams and chutneys on cubes of thick bread. If Union Square is out of your way, there are 53 other green markets dotted through the city.
grownyc.org

■ **Time Travel** More than 100 blocks north of the Metropolitan Museum of Art is its lesser-known gem of an offshoot, the Cloisters. The museum houses medieval European art, including the famed Unicorn Tapestries, but even more of a draw than the collection is the building itself: a castle surrounded by gardens, with a view of the Hudson River. After your museum visit, stroll through Fort Tryon Park surrounding the museum.
metmuseum.org

■ **Parade by the Beach**
Dream up a parade and New York probably has it, but locals know that few are as spirited as the Mermaid Parade. It is "a blissful, gyrating, sweaty, hedonistic explosion of glitter and pasties, DIY floats, and fake fins," says Oriana Leckert, who runs the website Brooklyn Spaces. "It reminds you how unself-conscious and nonjudgmental New Yorkers can be." Plus, it's on Coney Island. What better reason to head down to the beach?
coneyisland.com/programs/ mermaid-parade

■ **Not Your Mama's Apple Pie** Imagine the offspring of sugar and fireworks and you'll have some idea of the tastes at Momofuku Milk Bar, New Yorkers' favorite offbeat dessert spot. The flagship store is in Williamsburg, Brooklyn, but at all five locations you can eat Compost Cookies, made with pretzels, potato chips, coffee, oats, chocolate, and more; Cereal Milk ice cream, which tastes exactly like the sugary milk left at the bottom of the bowl; and Crack Pie, which we'll keep a surprise.
milkbarstore.com

■ **Greenery in the City**
The New York Botanical Garden is worth the trip

Rebel lobster at the Mermaid Parade

Nature? New York City? Yup, if you know where to look. One of my favorite things is to ride the West Side bike path. It runs the entire length of Manhattan, more than 10 miles (16 km), alongside the Hudson River. The northern half is mostly trees, birds, and river views. At the end of the trail, Inwood Hill Park, a "Forever Wild" park, includes woods with hiking trails, shorebirds, caves, and a tidal marsh. All this is a few blocks from Italian, Japanese, Dominican, and other cuisine. I love the urban world and I love nature. I can have both in New York.

Bicycles are best.

New York Botanical
Garden, a cool find

to the Bronx, where locals go to see a dizzying array of plant life. Elena Willis, a resident at nearby Montefiore Hospital, drove by for years, "always wondering what was beyond those walls," she says. When she finally visited, she was stunned by the botanical array and bought a membership. The glass-enclosed Enid A. Haupt Conservatory houses the Orchid Show in the spring and the Holiday Train Show—with models of NYC landmarks, made of natural materials—in the winter, plus a year-round tour of some of the world's biospheres. *nybg.org*

■ **Beyond the Blockbuster** New Yorkers love indie art and Film Forum in West Houston Street is the only autonomous nonprofit cinema in the city. Its carefully curated slate of independent and foreign films hits the spot. Originally a space with a projector and 50 folding chairs, the Forum—which turns 50 in 2020—now has three screens and is open every day of the year. In 1992, the *New York Times* called Film Forum "New York's most prestigious, active and venturesome art-film theater." It still is. *filmforum.org*

■ **Books, Books, Books** New York's literati know that at Strand, "18 miles of books" isn't just a tagline. The East Village-based independent bookstore's collection is as expansive as it is extensive, and prices range from $1 for the used books lining the sidewalks outside to tens of thousands for some of the rare books on the third floor. A $10 or $15 gift card buys entry to one of the bookstore's regular evening readings. *strandbooks.com*

■ **A Flea for Every Season** For high-quality furniture, clothes, and crafts—and an encapsulation of what "hipster Brooklyn" means—head to the Brooklyn Flea, held outdoors in April through Thanksgiving and in a cathedral-esque old bank at other times. "Even when I know I'm not going to buy anything, I love wandering around," says Jillian Steinhauer,

a writer and editor who lives in Crown Heights. "To me, the Flea epitomizes Brooklyn." *brooklynflea.com*

■ **Listen, Picnic, Sunbathe** New York City is legendary for its music venues, from jazz clubs and concert halls to trendy nightclubs. But in the summer, locals flock to outdoor shows. At Celebrate Brooklyn, musicians perform for free at the Prospect Park Bandshell; the few concerts that cost are audible from the surrounding lawns. Bring a picnic, sit on a blanket, and soak in the sounds. *bricartsmedia.org*

Join in Brooklyn's free summer music fest.

Kids go wild at the Sculpture Garden.

Washington, D.C.

Where Politics, Poetry, and Pizza Collide

■ **Neapolitan Pizza at 2 Amys** You know you are eating the real deal when your pizza is made by a member of the Verace Pizza Napoletana Association. The nightly line out the door is also a good indicator of 2 Amys' popularity among D.C. residents. The restaurant is a 15-minute walk from the closest metro station, Cleveland Park. *2amyspizza.com*

■ **Founding Farmers** Promoting sustainable agriculture and the American family farmer, Founding Farmers restaurant serves food fresh from local fields and waters. It's just a block from the Foggy Bottom metro and a 10-minute walk from the White House. Kyle Cheney, a political reporter, says that while the large menu can be daunting, the "mussels are a must-have start to any meal." Make a reservation, as tables sell out weeks in advance. *wearefoundingfarmers.com*

■ **Dumbarton Oaks Garden** Perfect for an afternoon with friends, these 10 acres (4 ha) of gardens, trails, and fountains off Wisconsin Avenue surround a 19th-century mansion and museum containing Byzantine and Pre-Columbian collections. *Washingtonian Magazine* staff writer Melissa Romero escapes here on the weekends. "When I need a quiet getaway for a few hours," she says, the "lush landscape, with plenty of paths for trail running, is a hidden gem." *doaks.org*

■ **Sculpture Garden** Tucked away from the crowds on the National Mall, the National Gallery of Art Sculpture Garden is a haven for locals looking to picnic with friends or collect their thoughts by the fountain. With ice-skating in winter and free jazz in summer, it provides a wonderful reprieve from hectic Constitution Avenue. *nga.gov*

Washington is a longtime center for bluegrass music and lately its young, global, and hipsterish population has spawned a new bluegrass with an indie sensibility. I like to hear this (and lots of other music) in the up-and-coming Atlas District on H Street, N.E. Instead of bourbon and barbecue, start the evening with *moules frites* at Granville Moores, or grab falafel sandwiches or Vietnamese pho before walking down to Argonaut, where bluegrass plays on Thursday night and the bartenders pour mugs of DC Brau, Flying Dog, and other local ales.

One of the staples of the D.C. music scene

■ **Late-night Falafel**
With its perfectly made tabouleh and moist falafel, Amsterdam Falafel always hits the spot. It features 21 sauces and toppings to fuse its Dutch and Middle Eastern influences. And, open till 4 a.m. on weekends, it's a hit among the late-night crowd. It's located in Adams Morgan half a mile (1 km) from the Woodley Park metro stop (Red line). *falafelshop.com*

■ **Eastern Market** For Washingtonians who live on "the Hill," the residential neighborhood behind the Capitol, as well as plenty of others, Eastern Market is a regular haunt. Selling jewelry, clothes, home goods, books, and fresh

For home-baked goods, head to Eastern Market.

fruit and vegetables, it's conveniently located at its namesake metro stop. The indoor food market is open Tuesdays through Sundays, and the outdoor art and farmers' market on weekends, when live music wafts among the rows of tents. *easternmarket-dc.org*

■ **Politics and Prose**
Awarded the 2013 Readers' Choice as D.C.'s Best Bookstore, this independent bookstore and coffee shop has a book (or five) for any and every interest. Located on Connecticut Avenue, it's a

bit off the beaten track—a few miles northwest of downtown. Now that it serves beer and wine, it's possible to toast your favorite writers, as they host author talks and book signings, some of which are aired by C-SPAN Book TV. *politics-prose.com*

■ **Cruise on the Potomac**
Departing from the Georgetown waterfront, this guided cruise mixes locals sipping Chardonnay on a breezy escape from D.C. with tourists snapping shots of the monuments. The boat sails 45 minutes down the Potomac River to the shops, bars, and restaurants of Virginia's Old Town Alexandria, with views of the Capitol, the Washington Monument, Roosevelt Island, and more, en route.

You may find yourself among a bachelorette party—it's a fun way for brides-to-be and their friends to celebrate the upcoming nuptials. *potomacriverboatco.com*

■ **Spiritual Sustenance**
Busboys and Poets feeds your mind and body with locally sourced eats and eclectic culture. Named with the poet and social activist Langston Hughes in mind (Hughes bussed tables in the 1920s), the restaurant's four area locations host poetry readings and slams, open-mike nights, and live music. *National Geographic* staff contributor Hannah Lauterback recommends the "delectable lamb Mediterranean burger with a side of perfectly crisp sweet potato fries." *busboysandpoets.com*

Politics and Prose

The beat goes on in Pedro do Sal.

Rio de Janeiro

Feijoada *by Day and Samba by Night*

■ More Beans, Please
Cariocas love Saturdays—not just because they can spend a whole day at the beach, but because it's *feijoada* day. Although everybody and their *mamãe* claim to prepare a version of the national stew of beans, pork, and sausages, one of the most succulent is served at the Armazém Cardosão, an unpretentious general store/bar in the residential neighborhood of Laranjeiras. "This is one of the city's best-kept feijoada secrets," says TV producer Consuelo Cruz, who arrives at the bar early, before the impromptu samba jams begin and the cauldron runs dry.

■ Favela Dining The installation of U.P.P. (Police Pacification Units) in many Rio favelas has brought some security to these hilltop communities, with drug-related shoot-outs giving way to "favela dining." One of the brightest stars of this gastro trend is Bar do David in Chapéu Mangueira (where the classic 1959 film *Black Orpheus* was shot). A former fisherman, David serves dishes rustled up by his sister and mother, including shrimp croquettes and R$10 daily lunch specials. Saturday's seafood feijoada (with white beans) comes with live pagode music.
rioguiaoficial.com.br

■ Monday Night Samba Special With Lapa's sizzling nocturnal scene having reached the boiling-over state, hardcore sambistas have decamped to the up-and-coming port zone, particularly Rio's historic Saúde neighborhood, the birthplace of Carioca samba. On Mondays in the picturesque square known as Pedra do Sal, locals who cut out early from work get down to business at the traditional *rodas de*

Shrimp croquettes, from a favela recipe

I ♥ My City

Fabrício Boliveira
Film and television actor

My favorite neighborhood in Rio is Santa Teresa, the *bairro* where I live. A mixture of colonial town and artists' community, it is paved with *pedras portuguesas* (cobblestones) and has a very Brazilian feel. The best thing about Rio is the way it combines an urban setting with so much nature. One of my favorite things is to go to Paineiras, on Corcovado mountain. You start off amidst all the traffic and then suddenly you're in the middle of a tropical forest filled with waterfalls. By car, it's only 10 minutes from Santa Teresa. I often stop to take a dip in a waterfall before I go to work. It's so refreshing.

samba (samba circles) that quickly morph from impromptu jams into open-air festas. The namesake *pedra* (boulder) is an ideal perch for swaying and shimmying while sipping the killer caipirinhas that are sold at numerous makeshift stands.

■ **Blue Lagoon** The alter-ego to Rio's famous beaches is the equally scenic Lagoa de Freitas. Residents of Rio's swanky Zona Sul (South Zone) keep enviously svelte by walking, running, and biking around its landscaped shores. Its waters beckon wakeboarders and water-skiers, not to mention languorous types whose ideal form of exercise involves tooling around in swan-shaped *pedalinhos* (pedal boats). Post-exertion, chill at one of the Lagoa's many kiosk bars; the hippest *ponto* is Oke Ka Baiana Tem, which serves spicy delicacies from Bahia.

■ **Finds From the Madding Crowd** Saara is Portuguese for Sahara—an appropriate name for the souk-like district of narrow streets in old downtown Rio that are cluttered with shops and stalls specializing in Carnaval costumes and paraphernalia. Apart from enough feathers and glitter to keep a samba school (or chorus line of drag queens) in business for decades, there are scads of cheap finds ranging from discounted Havaianas to fridge magnets in the shapes of tropical fruits. "Despite the noise and the knock-offs, it's a fun place to go because you have every kind of person from all over Rio buying something," says dancer/choreographer Luiz de Abreu, who shops for interesting props and costumes amid the mayhem.

■ **Bossa Copa** While some gringos associate bossa nova with Frank Sinatra, Ella Fitzgerald, and 1970s elevator music, the real deal is alive and well in this wood-paneled bar in the bairro where it all began—Copacabana in the Zona Sul. "Every Tuesday and Saturday, there's always someone singing live bossa nova," says Sandra Almeida, an actress who also works in a health food restaurant in nearby Botafogo. "It's frequented by a local Copa crowd, and you'll never see a tourist here. Prices are cheap, service is good, and the beer is always *estupidamente*— stupidly—icy."

■ **Sunday in the Park with the Redeemer** Only a ten-minute stroll from Rio's star eco-attraction of Jardim Botânico in the Zona Sul lies the oft-overlooked Parque Lage. Stroll through the park's tropical foliage, then take a look around

Fast Facts

■ Brazil's second largest city (after Sao Paolo) is post-card perfect, with Sugarloaf Mountain a dramatic back-drop. Many of Rio's affluent residents live just west of Sugarloaf in tony waterfront neighborhoods like Leblon and Ipanema.

■ Laranjeiras is a local gem—an old world, tree-lined residential neighborhood that's also home to the city government.

the palace. Built by 19th-century industrial magnate Henrique Lage, today it is occupied by Rio's School of Visual Arts. Dominating the school's inner patio is a swimming pool in whose blue waters the reflection of Christ the Redeemer, high on the hill behind, floats prominently. Contemplate the vision while savoring gourmet sandwiches, homemade ice cream, and brunch served at the courtyard's D.R.I. Café, a favorite haunt of local residents as well as the resident art students.
eavparquela ge.rj.gov.br

Everything you need for Carnival in Saara

D.R.I. Café, a shady
sanctuary in the
School of Visual Arts

Tokyo
Sushi, Sake, and Skyscrapers

■ Eat and Drink like Locals *Izakayas* are great places to try everyday Japanese comfort food accompanied by sake, beer, shochu, or even Japanese whiskey. Shin Hinomoto is an authentic old-school izakaya in the Yurakucho area serving high-quality seafood at reasonable prices. It's been around for nearly 70 years. The only thing that's not typical about it is that the current proprietor is British! *andysfish.com/Shin-Hinomoto*

■ Spoiled for Choice 109, or Ichimarukyu, is a department store dedicated to young fashionistas. The choices can be overwhelming, but for new trends this is the place to go. *shibuya109.jp/en/top shibuya109.jp*

■ Party Under the Cherry Blossoms During the few days when the *sakura* (cherry) trees bloom, everyone parties under the blossom with food and sake. The festivities go on well past midnight. "My favorite spot is Sumida Kouen," says chef Takasaki of Masaru. "I've been going there since I was a kid." Other notable *ohanami* spots are Yasukuni Shrine, Hibiya Park, Ueno Park, and Yoyogi Park.

■ Eat with True Edokko *Unagi* (fresh-water eel) has been popular among *edokko*—old-school Tokyo natives—since the 18th century. Masanori Irokawa is the seventh-generation chef/owner of Irokawa *(tel 81 (0) 3 3844 0590)*, a restaurant specializing in unagi in Asakusa, the Shitamachi area of Tokyo. One of the last true edokko—brusque and impatient on the outside but warm-hearted inside—he is loved for his character as much as his food.

■ Humble Food that Strives for Perfection *Tendon* (tempura served over rice with a sweet and savory sauce) is another

The 109 department store at Shibuya intersection

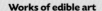

Works of edible art

Cherry blossom—so pretty you want to reach out and touch it

classic Tokyo dish. One would think the owner of Masaru (tel 81 3-3841-8356), another culinary gem in the Asakusa area, has deliberately hidden his restaurant so no one can find it. Despite its location, a long line forms every day for their meticulously made works of edible art. Note: Masaru is only open for lunch, and when chef/owner Yoshinori Takasaki cannot find ingredients that meet his high standards, he will not open the shop that day. It's best to reserve ahead.

■ **Sing Your Heart Out**
Karaoke is a Japanese word meaning empty orchestra or orchestra without a singer. Karaoke studios are everywhere—since the 1970s, it's been

a very popular Japanese pastime. These days most studios are owned by large companies with multiple locations—Big Echo has more than 100 Tokyo studios, while Pasera has 16. (Their websites are in Japanese only, so check with locals for the best options.) Most have rooms in a variety of sizes, from single-sized booths for those who want to practice on their own, to large spaces where groups can party.

■ **Traditional Bathhouse**
Public bathhouses (sentou) have been an integral part of Tokyo life since the Edo period (1603–1868). The number of sentou is dwindling, but you can still find classic bathhouses

tucked away in the city streets. Ooedo Onsen Monogatari is a sentou on steroids. If someone made a theme park based on sentou culture, this would be it.
ooedoonsen.jp/higaeri/english

■ **Textiles and Tableware** When they need inspiration, fashion designers frequent Nuno, a textile shop in Roppongi. They design and manufacture their own fabrics using ancient techniques and materials, as well as modern cutting-edge technology. Many of Nuno's products have made it into the permanent collection of New York's Museum of Modern Art. You can find bargains on tableware and small

Fast Facts

■ Officially, 13.2 million Japanese reside across 386 square miles (1,000 sq km) in 23 municipalities, or "special wards," northwest of Tokyo Bay.

■ Kichijoji, a favorite residential neighborhood anchored by Seikei University, is home to cafés, bars, shops, and the large Inokashira Koen park.

kitchenware, from sashimi knives to a sharkskin wasabi grater, at Kappabashi ("Kitchen Town") near Asakusa. This is where restaurant industry people go to buy their kitchen utensils.
nuno.com

■ **Depachika** Short for "basement of a department store" in Japanese, these department-store food meccas are packed with edibles from around the world. Everything from $1 rice balls to $150 melons are sold in dazzling displays. Takashimaya and Isetan are great Tokyo options.
takashimaya.co.jp, www.isetan.com

Teapots for sale in "Kitchen Town"

Sydney

More Than Just an Opera House

■ **Jaw-dropping Beach**
Every Sydneysider has a favorite beach or three, with miles of white-sand Pacific coast or harbor coves to choose from. Those in the know avoid tourist-trampled Bondi for more secluded spots such as Shark Beach in genteel Vaucluse. Perhaps the name deters the crowds—though nets keep out the rarely sighted beasties and local realtors prefer to call it Nielsen Park beach, after the surrounding parklands. These include an 1852 sandstone mansion and a café for refreshments. Midweek is best for beach lounging, sheltered swimming, and fine harbor views without the crowds. Another beach favored by locals is Maroubra, 30 minutes south of the city. "I surf there at least two or three times a week," says Cameron Kerr, director of the Taronga and Taronga Western Plains zoos. "The family dog and I arrive just as the dawn light comes up over the ocean. It's magic."
nationalparks.nsw.gov.au

■ **Melting-pot Cuisine**
As Australia embraces the "Asian Century," its economy, buoyed by exports to booming Asia, Sydney can increasingly lay claim to being an Asian melting pot. For buzzing Asian street life and great Vietnamese food, head out west to the suburb of Cabramatta, Sydney's Little Saigon. In central Sydney, Chinatown has branched out beyond old Cantonese favorites to embrace other Asian cuisines. One recommendation is Mamak, where Malaysian chefs twirl and stretch dough into giant paper-thin sails before folding and slapping them onto the griddle. The ensuing crisp, flaky roti bread is perfect for dipping in rich coconut curries.
mamak.com.au

■ **Dirty Dancing** It's hard to move in the city parks for all the walkers, cyclists, and personal trainers, but for something different, fitness fans are heading to the old wharves at Walsh Bay. The waterside once sweated with commerce but now houses the city's arts hub—including the Sydney Dance Company, which runs drop-in ballet, jazz, hip-hop, and other dance classes. Ramon Doringo, an instructor at the school, notes that the classes "bring together people of all ages, from diverse backgrounds, giving them an opportunity to feel included in our

Shark Beach— don't be deterred by the name

I ♥ My City

Christine Forster
Councillor, City of Sydney

Unlike London or Dublin, Sydney is a young city, not known for having great pubs. But you could throw a blanket over my neighborhood in the inner-city suburb of Surry Hills and cover a dozen terrific watering holes, each with its own special character and clientele. Wandering the square bounded by Oxford, Bourke, Crown, and Cleveland Streets will take you past The Clock, with its first-floor balcony full of beautiful people wanting to see and be seen; The Carrington, with its dark ambiance and great tapas; and The Beresford, with the buzziest backyard in town. Step down Fitzroy Street and you'll find the quirky Cricketers with its mix of young hipsters and old locals. Each one is uniquely "Sydney."

community." Beginners are welcome, or the rumba-shy can enjoy waterfront views at the café-bar, popular with leotard-clad students. *sydneydancecompany.com*

■ Million Dollar Views

Like ants to honey, visitors flock to the arches of the Sydney Opera House, but few know that beneath the building, in the lower concourse, lies the fanciest food court in town—the Opera Kitchen showcasing some of Sydney's best known gastronomic outlets. The wagyu burgers may be a tad expensive, but the harbor views are priceless. Alissa Breit, who works at the Opera House, points out that "sometimes we Sydneysiders forget to appreciate where we live and work. Until, that is,

we take a seat at Opera Kitchen to soak up the view, have a drink and a bite to eat." Highlights: the sushi bar at Kenji, plank-roasted king salmon at Cloudy Bay Fish Co., and tiger prawn and green mango rice paper rolls at Misschu. *operakitchen.com.au*

■ Island Life

Why take a harbor cruise when a ferry provides the same views for a fraction of the price? Cockatoo Island has become Sydney's favorite daytrip on the harbor since the former convict prison and dockyards opened to the public. Tour the heritage buildings, take in a concert or art exhibition, or join the hubbub at the Island Bar at sunset. Accommodations, from exclusive cottages to camping, are also offered. *cockatooisland.gov.au*

■ Illuminating Event

Sydney loves a party, from its Gay & Lesbian Mardi Gras in February to the New Year's Eve fireworks show, but one event highlights the city like no other. In June, buildings such as the Opera House, Harbour Bridge, and Customs House become canvases for stunning lighting effects during the Vivid Festival, showcasing art, music, and ideas at venues around the city. Vivid has a strong music program thanks to curators such as Lou Reed and Brian Eno, but the light installations steal the show. *vividsydney.com*

■ Market Economy

The inner suburbs of Paddington, Newton, Woollahra, and Surry Hills offer Victorian-era streetscapes lined with

indie shops, but markets are fun for hunting out vintage gems, handicraft, and fashion. Passengers from visiting cruise ships browse the weekend market in The Rocks, and Saturday's Paddington Markets also packs them in, but Bondi Beach Markets on Sunday gets the nod from locals. Come here for unique gifts and fashion from up-and-coming designers looking to graduate from market racks to celebrity wardrobes. If you tire of shopping and the cool young things, the famous (though most likely crowded) beach is nearby. *therocks.com, paddingtonmarkets.com.au, bondimarkets.com.au*

The Island Bar on Cockatoo Island

Crowds swell
Sydney's Opera
House during the
Vivid Festival.

Drinking in the city views at Char

Shanghai

Bigger, Better, Faster, and Newer

■ **Dramatic Degustation at a Secret Restaurant**
When Shanghai gourmands want to be wowed, they turn to Paul Pairet. The French chemist-turned-chef has made Shanghai his culinary playground for almost a decade and recently realized his wildest fantasies at the secret-location restaurant Ultraviolet. In-the-know gastronomes book ahead for one of the ten nightly seats at the 20-course feast, where each dish is paired with multi-sensory experiences, such as 360-degree wall projections, scent diffusions, and DJ soundtracks. "One evening we had a table of chefs with ten Michelin stars between them—and got a standing ovation," grins Pairet. *uvbypp.cc*

■ **TCM Time-out**
What's the secret to balancing body and mind in a frenetic city of 23 million? Locals favor TCM (Traditional Chinese Medicine), including centuries-old treatments like *tuina* massage, acupuncture, and fire cupping. "Some treatments may seem archaic but they are very holistic and really do work," says Shanghai resident Ivy Ling, waiting at Body Talk for her moxibustion (burning mugwort) therapy. Body Talk, in a former French Concession villa, offers diagnosis and traditional therapies in a spa environment (limited English is spoken). For no-frills, well-priced *tuina* massages and reflexology, head to Green Massage, which has English-speaking service and four branches around the city. *greenmassage.com.cn*

■ **Night Skies** For twinkling views of Shanghai's soaring skyline and waterfront, city brokers head for the terrace of Char on the 30th floor of Hotel Indigo Shanghai on the South Bund. It's the place to take in the vista over a cocktail or two then tuck into steak or seafood. *char-thebund.com*

■ Fashion Fancy

While tourists swarm the Fabric Market for counterfeit Chanel jackets, fashionistas find inspiration in the chic, tree-lined alleys of the former French Concession, where independent boutiques tucked away in heritage residences are a fine hunting ground for interesting fashion. Leading the pack is Dong Liang (180 Fumin Lu, tel 86 (0) 21 3469 6926), which fills an 80-year-old converted lane house with tailored capsule collections, plus funky clutches, jewels and specs, by hard-to-find independent designers.

"Dong Liang set a precedent for showcasing China-born designers, which is a relatively new evolution here," says Shanghai fashion editor Patsy Yang.

■ Go for a Twirl at the Paramount Ballroom

In the swinging 1930s, Shanghai's art deco Paramount Ballroom (218 Yuyuan Lu, tel 86 (0) 21 6249 8866) opposite Jing'an Temple was the hottest dance hall in the Far East. Today, coiffed dance aficionados take the mirrored elevators to the fourth floor, where the belle epoque dance hall remains. Buy a ticket to join the couples spinning on the sprung-wood dance floor, or simply poke your head inside to travel back in time to Shanghai's golden era.

■ Mixology with Chinese Characteristics

Flashy cocktail lounges abound in Shanghai, but Yuan (17-2 Xiangyang Bei Lu, tel 86 (0) 21 6433 0538), just off the main drag of Huaihai Road, is shaking up the scene. Created by Shanghai native Stephy Zhu, Yuan is a funky homage to the 1980s. The stylish mix of retro ruby and emerald furnishings, Shanghai textbooks, and old Chinese cartoons are fun, but it's the cocktails infused with indigenous Chinese liquors and herbs such as ginseng, ginger, and hawthorn that are the real draw.

■ Rally to Propaganda Art

In the basement of a nondescript apartment block in west Shanghai (ask the concierge for directions), the Propaganda Poster Museum displays hundreds of government posters, produced from 1949 to the late 1970s. "It brings back memories of my youth," says Shanghai resident Guo Lan. *shanghaipropaganda art.com*

■ High Tea in a French Concession Garden

Among the many beautiful garden villas in the former French Concession, Yongfoo Elite, in the one-time British Consulate on Yongfu Lu, recaptures the heady decadence of 1930s Shanghai with its exquisite Chinese or Western high teas. Regulars know to reserve ahead for the best seat in the house—an ancient opium bed beneath a magnolia tree. Alternatively, head to the Tea Garden in the backyard of Urban Tribe boutique on Fuxing Lu for a restorative infusion. *yongfooelite.com urbantribe.cn*

Traditional Chinese medicine in action

Taking a dip in Lifta's springs

Jerusalem
Cool Springs, Hot Clubs, Sweet Halva

■ **Spring Dip** Once a lively Palestinian village in western Jerusalem, Lifta today is a place where families take a stroll on clear Shabbat afternoons, the Jewish day off. Come here to get a sense of the complex history of this unique yet abandoned Arab village, while enjoying its traditional 19th-century Ottoman-style architecture, shady paths, fig trees, and centrally located spring pool. Springs are common in the mountains surrounding Jerusalem; architect Tal Nahmani likes the Even Sapir Spring path in the southwest part of the city. "One of the more magical crystal-clear springs is inside a cave, just off the path. Even Sapir Spring is a great place to end a walk in the mountains of Jerusalem," he says.
liftasociety.org/about

■ **Holy Drinking** As the sun sets, Jerusalemites cover themselves and go out for a drink. For a true local experience, head downtown to the area around Nahlat Shiv'a Street. Start with an Israeli Goldstar beer at the dark Sira dance bar, where anything can (and will) happen. "It's the only place in Jerusalem where one encounters the whole diversity of this city at once," says Maximilian Peters, a German graduate student living in Jerusalem. "Secular students who just want to enjoy the music, orthodox Jews who want to see the 'other side,' and Arabs from East Jerusalem going for a drink," he explains. From there, continue to Al-Bir, a small bar on Aristobulus Street where you can still smoke next to the counter while drinking your Taybeh, the only Palestinian beer around. Jerusalem has an interesting and kicking underground scene. Follow the techno parties organized by Berlin-inspired Pacotek in different venues around town. For a more

Jerusalem is a chaotic and intense city—and that's what I love about it. I walk in Mea Shearim neighborhood to see ultra-Orthodox Jewish men shopping for the Shabbat dinner, covering their eyes when a not-so-modest female passes. I cross the street to East Jerusalem with its many markets, giving space to a herd of goats. Later I'll head to Mahane Yehuda market for a Goldstar beer with colleagues or a German friend who migrated here. Before heading for bed I'll get the perfect kebab at Damascus Gate.

Brewed in Israel

varied experience, try the events of Taltalistim, a group of entrepreneurs who take over abandoned locations—from a synagogue to a rundown hotel—to host parties, often combined with art installations. *pacotek.com*

■ Going to the Shuk
The colorful and lively Mahane Yehuda market, between Jaffa Road and Agrippas Street, dates from the end of the 19th century and is still evolving. Stroll around its narrow alleys packed with hundreds of fruit, vegetable, spice, and prepared-food stalls, serving families from all over the city. Sample the sweet halva (confections

made from sesame paste) offered to the shoppers to spark their appetites, before stepping into the famous Rachmo Restaurant for a warm plate of freshly made hummus. Or nibble on a selection of tapas, with a digestif of arak, an anis-based alcoholic spirit, at the market's hip Casino de Paris Café. *machne.co.il*

■ Damascus Gate
For the most intense feeling of the Arab presence in the city, head to the Damascus Gate area. Practically a huge parking lot and one of the main entrances to the Old City, it's packed, loud, and intense—but you will not want to leave. Ogle the many butcher

Freshly baked and ready for the rush

shops, distinguished by the huge chunks of bloody meat hanging in their storefront windows, and shop for herbs freshly harvested from the gardens of the old women sitting on the street corners. Don't think twice before buying the best (and cheapest) kebab pita sandwich

in town from one of the carts, and drink a three-shekel-strong Arab coffee from the stall in the middle of it all.

■ Mount Scopus Sounds and Views
On Sunday evenings during the summer, head to Mount Scopus in north Jerusalem, home to Hebrew University, a satellite of Brigham Young University, to experience one of the most impressive views of the city. Book a free ticket in advance to the Sunday night classical music concert (*concert@ jcbyu.ac.il*). After the encore, find the parking lot of the 7 Arch Hotel. Check if the bagel cart (very different from the NYC style) is still around. Then walk to the observation deck facing the Dome of the Rock and join the hand-holding couples admiring the most romantic view in town. *7arches.com*

Damascus Gate

Strolling the Nevsky

St. Petersburg

Bikes, Bridges, and Three Million Pieces of Art

■ **Biking the City**

Fifteen years ago, only hardcore adventurers or masochists bicycled in St. Petersburg. Now, automobile drivers have become more accustomed to cyclists and are more willing to share the road with them. Biking alongside the Neva River during the "White Nights," an annual festival celebrating the season of the midnight sun, is an experience not to be missed, but some of the most peaceful biking roads are north of the city, in the region where city dwellers for generations have maintained their *dachas*, or summer homes.

Christian Courbois, an American businessman who has lived in St. Petersburg since 1993, says one of his favorite summer outings is to take his bike on a local train, get off at a stop, and then bike to a different station. *peterswalk.com, skatprokat.ru*

■ **On the Nevsky**

From the inception of St. Petersburg, the commercial focus has been on Nevsky Prospekt. It's down this broad avenue that Gogol's beleaguered clerk wandered, seeking his lost overcoat, in the short story "The Overcoat." It's the street strolled by all classes of St. Petersburg residents, browsing historic stores such as Dom Knigi and the Gostiny Dvor shopping complex.

■ **City Views**

St. Petersburg native and photographer Sergei Grachev says one of his favorite ways to relax in the city is to linger on some of its 342 bridges. "The views from many of these bridges is just fantastic. You can really appreciate the design of the city."

■ **Great Galleries**

St. Petersburg is famous for the Hermitage, of course. The former Winter Palace of the tsars

They say St. Petersburg is all about museums, and culture, and beauty. But it takes a bad case of myopia to say this. No, it's a city of drama, comedy, and tragedy. Examples of this? The city's planners put Italian architecture (best viewed in sunshine) in a gray and foggy swamp, so that it can only be properly enjoyed a few days a year. And they built a beautiful city on numerous islands connected by cast-iron bridges that are raised during the White Nights so that people can't get home and are forced to endure the city's beauty until morning. When someone said "Beauty knows no pain," he was thinking of St. Petersburg, a place where emotions clash, causing one to suffer and yet love more through this suffering.

contains a collection of more than three million pieces of art. In recent years, however, the city has become known for its contemporary art. Maria Kasyanenko, a St. Petersburg painter and sculptor, recommends The Loft Project (*Ligovsky Prospekt 74*). It contains gallery space on several floors, as well as a café and hostel. Another favorite of Kasyanenko's is Erarta (*29th Line, Vasilievsky Island 2*), the largest independent modern art gallery in Russia. "It's very encouraging that there is a place especially created for contemporary Russian art," she says.
loftprojectetagi.ru, erarta.com

■ **Live music** The Hat jazz bar (*Ulitsa Belinskogo 9*) books high-profile musicians during the weekend, but some of the most interesting performances can be heard on evenings in the middle of the week, when the club hosts running jam sessions. Local jazz musicians, many of them world-class, often amble up to the stage to join in. The lucky bar patrons, meanwhile, pay no special admission charge to listen.
facebook.com/The HatBar

■ **Club HQ** If you prefer a younger scene, head over to Ligovsky Prospekt 50. After passing into the

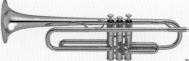

For jazz, head for The Hat.

courtyard, the visitor is confronted by an array of club and bar choices. "It is like a whole country," says Irina Kruzhilina, a writer for *Forbes Russia*. "Walking into the yard is like opening the door to Narnia, a different world." Choices include a biker bar called The Hooligans; a venue for underground artists called Dushche; and Jesus, a dance club.

■ **Food Favorites**
For years, poor value, poor food, poor service, and drunken patrons characterized Russian restaurants. However,

the dining scene has improved in recent years, and there are now lots of places worth recommending. A favorite for freelance photographer Grachev is Caffe Italia (*Bakunina 5*). "They have a real Italian chef, and serve real Italian food," he says. English speakers be forewarned: The menus are available in Italian and Russian only. If a visitor is craving borscht, however, Grachev recommends Teplo (*Bolshaya Morskaya 45*). The name means "warm," and the restaurant is known for its cozy ambiance. Its menu includes Russian specialties, but also other European and Southeast Asian dishes.

The art scene includes pop-up exhibitions. This one celebrates literary protest in the Soviet era.

Istanbul

Baklava, Backwaters, and Other Turkish Delights

■ **The Bosphorus** This wide blue waterway parting Asia from Europe gives the city its unique character. "Inhaling the Bosphorus air is good for anyone" is the common assurance of the locals. Eating fresh fish on the waterfront is an essential part of most people's weekend. Catch your own with simple tackle or go to one of the many good fish restaurants that line both waterfronts. Ismet Baba in Kuzguncuk has a great terrace, while the Suna'nin Yeri *(tel 90 (0) 216 332 32 41)* next to a little quay in Kandilli is modest in appearance but big on atmosphere. If you're lucky enough to snag a table right on the water, the wake of a ship may swell to your feet. *ismetbaba.com*

■ **Karakoy Cool** Karakoy, an old settlement with new renovations near the Golden Horn in the heart of the city, is getting trendy with its hip restaurants. Try some of Istanbul's best baklava at Güllüoglu. *karakoygulluoglu.com*

■ **Bebek Breakfasts** Bebek Café, with its shabby seats and hip location *(Cevdet Pasa Caddesi No. 137)*, is a hot spot for young professionals as well as freelancers for a simple breakfast of *simit*, the Turkish bagel, and tea. "My day is somehow incomplete if I don't start it with a cup of tea and some friendly chat here early in the morning!" says journalist Murat Sabuncu.

■ **Live Music** Trendy clubs jammed with a diverse crowd of young professionals, students, artists, or stylish society types and pulsing with live music are located in Pera and in Ortaköy. At Babylon, rock is on the menu; Curcuna throws thematic parties, and Indigo is popular for its famous iDJs. *babylon.com.tr*

■ **Island Getaway** The Princes Islands in the Marmara Sea, where horse-drawn carriages substitute for banned cars, are a ferry ride away from Kabatas, the main pier on the European side, and Bostanci, on the Asian side. Büyükada is the largest island, offering urban comforts amid old wooden buildings and elegant villas, well-kept gardens and idyllic side streets, as well as some modest beaches and simple restaurants. *ido.com.tr*

■ **Coffee-shop People** The contemporary version of the 16th-century coffee shop thrives at the cool street cafés of Cihangir, one of the gentrified bohemian neighborhoods with a view of the old city, and at the chic cafés of lively downtown Nisantasi, filled with fashionistas

Pistachio-packed baklava

I ♥ My City

Gul Irepoglu
Art historian, architect, and author

This multifaceted city is like a diamond, and its many moods, views, and pleasures thrill me. Looking down from the Bosphorus Bridge, connecting Europe and Asia, I feel like a Byzantine empress. Walking under the old pine trees of Büyükada on the Princes Islands, accompanied by the sound of waves, makes me feel immortal. And always, the vibrant crowds amaze me. Istanbul inspires art and literature, but it is the small pleasures that I love, such as its fragrances—roses, spices, coffee—or taking the boats across the Bosphorus. Sailing from Europe to Asia in minutes excites me, like the energy of this East–West hybrid.

Drink coffee the Turkish way.

The Princes Islands
—a local idyll

and paparazzi. On the Asian side, cafés like The Divan, with its delicious cherry cake, are longtime meeting spots for locals. *turkeytravelresources.com, divanpastaneleri.com.tr*

■ **Tulips in Istanbul**
The tulip gardens in the parks of Emirgan, an old district on the Bosphorus, are stunning in spring. Kiosks that once belonged to the sultan serve as cafés and add to the romantic setting.

■ **Music Festivals** These attract so many people

Tile detail in Topkapi Palace, a fine setting for concerts

that it's a source of pride to get tickets to concerts such as Mozart's *Abduction from the Seraglio* in the 600-year-old Topkapi Palace, or a concert in 1,500-year-old St. Irene Church, in the courtyard of the same palace. *turkeytravelresource.com*

■ **Shopping Fever** In the Nisantasi district, the well-heeled spend a fortune on world brands, while in Pera—the Brooklyn of Istanbul—trendy young Istanbulites hunt for astonishing pieces at low prices in the Terkos Passage or at one of the vintage stores. True fashion mavens hit Gönül Paksoy's Ottoman-inspired clothing and jewelry store *(Atiye Sokak No. 1/3)* in Nisantasi.

theguideistanbul.com, elacindoruknazanpak.com, istanbul.com.tr

■ **Go Organic** For sweet oranges, apricots, pomegranates, and artichokes at low prices, residents choose open-air markets in residential neighborhoods. Erenköy Market on the Asian side and Ulus on the European side are among the best. "It's been my habit to get my vegetables here every Thursday for 30 years. The goods are so good!" says beauty parlor owner Nazan Tore.

Music festival in front of the Sultanahmet Mosque

EMİNÖNÜ BELEDİYESİ

Fast Facts

■ Divided by the Bosphorus Strait, Istanbul is Turkey's cultural hub and largest city, with 14 million inhabitants. The city touches two continents—its western half lies in Europe, its eastern half in Asia.

■ Locals flock to Bebek, a historic residential neighborhood along the Bosphorus on the European side, to dine on the waterfront, shop, and taste some of the city's best marzipan.

Enjoying the Good Stuff

Berlin

Playing to the Beat

■ **Underground Supper Clubs** Sophisticated pop-up restaurants are thriving in Berlin, a city that loves cachet and artsy intrigue. Diners pledge to cloak-and-dagger secrecy. "Please don't tell anyone where you're going," reads the Shy Chef's email confirmation, revealing an address in the bohemian Kreuzberg district. Popular supper clubs (often held in gorgeous living rooms and listed heritage buildings) include the Good Stuff Supper Club, with sensitive pairings of Latin and Middle Eastern flavors with fine wines, and Fisk & Gröönsaken, for wallet-friendly, meatless dining. *theshychef.wordpress.com,* *facebook.com/Good.Stuff .Supper.Club, groonsaken .wordpress.com*

■ **Life's a Beach** On balmy summer days, the 54 volleyball courts of BeachMitte, in north Berlin, echo with the slap of bronzed hands on leather, while onlookers sip caipirinhas and Weizenbier. Pretensions are thin on the ground. "We play awful and nobody cares," says Silvia Flores, a Berliner and sometime volleyballer who works at a nearby office complex in the district. *visitberlin.de*

■ **Listen to the Music** The tradition of classical music is alive and well in Berlin, which has eight large symphony orchestras including the Berliner Philharmoniker. But if you want to tap into the community spirit, join music fans at summer concerts in the Greek-style Waldbühne amphitheater, in the far west of the city, near the Olympic Stadium. "We drove an hour and stood in line for an hour even with tickets, but it was totally worth it," enthuses Heike Kornfeld, a resident of the northern Reinickendorf district. Unlike at the mainstream concert halls, locals bring picnic baskets and light candles for the finale, bathing the gallery in a soft, flickering glow. *waldbuehne-berlin.de*

I ♥ My City

Robert Rückel
Director of the DDR Museum

Every corner of Berlin has figured in a major historical event, and there's so much history to explore. Yet the city does not live in the past. In a state of constant change, it throbs with life. Some of my favorite transformed places are the East Side Gallery, an old stretch of Berlin Wall that became an art space; the Burgermeister, a popular snack bar housed in a former public lavatory; and the lively Turkish market on Maybachufer, near the former East–West border.

Slice of a former life—the Berlin Wall

■ **Boutiqueville** Glamorous Friedrichstrasse and Kurfürstendamm may empty more wallets, but it's the pint-size fashion boutiques that mint the real Berlin look. Prowl the lanes of northern Prenzlauer Berg, Friedrichshain, and Kreuzberg and you'll find dozens of hole-in-the-wall studios—not high-end designs, but fresh, street-flavored creations for Berlin's chain-phobic consumers. "You can actually afford to buy clothes here!" marvels Justin Evans, an American musician who lives in Friedrichshain's shop-filled Wühlischstrasse. *fashionhain.de*

■ **Dig for Buried Treasure** Berlin turns out its collective attic at the Mauerpark Flohmarkt, a massive flea market in Prenzlauer Berg that sprawls along a onetime stretch of the Berlin Wall. Every Sunday, while weekend tourists are sleeping off the previous night, thousands of sharp-eyed locals rummage through nearly 500 stands of GDR memorabilia, antique furniture, and vintage clothing. "People come from miles around," says flea-market manager Lars Herting. Stick around until 3 p.m. and join lively karaoke sessions in the "bearpit" amphitheater next door. *mauerparkmarkt.de*

■ **Dancing in the Streets** There's never a dull moment on the capital's storied streets, which double as stages for lively events. A popular highlight is Kreuzberg's Carnival of Cultures, a street festival featuring outlandish costumes, exotic eats, and Rio-style floats every May. Plenty of Berliners take off from work to join in. "With 1.4 million visitors, the whole neighborhood does nothing but party for four days," says organizer Philippa Ebéné. The show-stopper is the enormous Whitsunday street parade with dancers, acrobats, and musicians from around 80 countries. Want to get in the groove? Do like the locals do and come in homemade costume. *karneval-berlin.de*

■ **Java Jive** As locals will tell you, the capital's best gourmet coffees are available at ex-pat-run cafés, which source the world's finest beans. No blend is too exotic or wacky (think banana or Nutella latte) for the uberbaristas of Bonanza Coffee Heroes, Godshot Coffee Club, or The Barn Roastery, all performing their dark arts in the hipster quarter Prenzlauer Berg. *bonanzacoffee.de, godshot.de, thebarn.de*

■ **Soak in a Spa** Berlin has dozens of wellness spas for all budgets and body types. In the Liquidrom, office workers from Potsdamer Platz get rubbery in the Himalayan salt sauna, ice bath, and Finnish steam room. Then everyone floats mindlessly in the 43-foot (13 m) saltwater pool, framed by a ceiling oculus and arches bathed in psychedelic patterns, while soothing tunes are piped in underwater. *liquidrom-berlin.de*

Browsing the Mauerpark Flohmarkt

Londoners converge on September's Thames Festival.

London

Kippers and Sausages, Antiques and Parkland Strolls

■ First Stop for London Foodies

A decade ago, Borough Market, one of London's oldest, gained a new lease on life when a group of stallholders began selling specialist foods. Londoners flocked to the site and visitors followed. Then there were problems with rents and many stalls moved on, finding new homes in nearby Maltby Street and Spa Terminus, now London's hottest foodie destination. "It's a joy to be working with like-minded people," says Alison Elliot, who runs the Ham and Cheese Company. "Everyone is passionate about what they sell, whether it's bread, beer, or ice cream."
www.spa-terminus.co.uk

■ One-stop Shopping

Renowned for its quality, service and fair prices, John Lewis, a local department-store institution, lacks the glitz of some more famous competitors—but that is its great appeal. There are few London homes without some household items from this store.
johnlewis.com

■ River of Fire

The Mayor's Thames Festival takes place between Westminster Bridge and Tower Bridge over ten days in early September, its events all inspired by the Thames, London's river. The festival grows from year to year, expanding beyond its traditional limits, as Londoners increasingly take it to their hearts. Events and performances (which are usually free) vary annually—anything from films, art, barge-racing, and night carnival to circus, live music, and classic boats—but always conclude with a rousing firework display over the water.
thamesfestival.org

■ A Walk in the Park

On a sunny Sunday morning, Londoners love nothing better than a stroll in the park, but not so much the obvious ones such as Hyde Park, Green Park,

I ♥ My City

Alan Kingshott
Chief Yeoman Warder, Tower of London

Over the course of a long military career I have lived in many different parts of England, but as Chief Yeoman Warder of the Tower of London I currently live in the 13th-century Byward Tower within the walls of the Tower itself. As well as being rich in history, this unique address also allows me to indulge some of the things I love most about my city. One of my passions is going to the theater. The Tower is so centrally located that I can be in the West End—Theaterland—in no time. I go regularly with my wife to see anything from opera to musicals and everything in-between, never mind all the superb shops and restaurants you can fit in before or after a show.

Classic London bus

Gardens, or St James's, as the smaller and more peripheral green spaces. Locals love Holland Park, near Notting Hill, to the west of the center, or Primrose Hill in the north, with its fine views over the city. Farther north still stretch the lofty expanses of Hampstead Heath, where you can walk for an hour or more and then breakfast or lunch at Kenwood House in the adjacent Kenwood estate. *rbkc.gov.uk, royalparks.org.uk, cityoflondon.gov.uk, hampsteadheath.net*

■ A Little Night Music
The Green Note in Camden Town, one of London's many "villages," is the type of cozy, candlelit music club only locals know about. James Studholme, the singer with Police Dog Hogan, regular performers at Green Note, is a big

fan: "Although London is known for live music, there are few venues like this. Not only do they treat their musicians well, but the vibe and intimate atmosphere are spot on. Turn up on any night, and you know you are going to hear something interesting and often exceptional." *greennote.co.uk, policedoghogan.com*

■ Best for Breakfast
"If I want to give visiting friends a treat, a glimpse of Londoners at work and play—and a good breakfast into the bargain—I'll often book a table at The Wolseley on Piccadilly," says Simon Horsford, a journalist with the *Daily Telegraph*. "You'll see all sorts: business people, distracted lovers, the odd celebrity, party people who haven't gone to bed, and many more." The buzz is great, the

setting—a former luxury car showroom—striking, and the classic British food (haggis, kippers, kedgeree, porridge, Cumberland sausages, and more) is hard to beat. *thewolseley.com*

■ Meat the Locals
Londoners have been voting with their stomachs for years when it comes to traditional British food by visiting St. John, housed in a former smokehouse near Smithfield, London's historic meat market. Founded in 1994, the restaurant is a touchstone for longlost or reinvented dishes such as Welsh rarebit (grilled cheese on toast), potted beef and pickled beetroot, or roast chicken and braised turnips. *stjohngroup.uk.com*

■ North on Portobello
Most visitors know Portobello Road market, but

Fast Facts

■ The City of London is the financial hub, Westminster the home of government, and the West End the center of arts and entertainment. Most of the city's 8.2 million residents live in communities outside the center of town.

■ The Tube—London's Underground—carries 2.67 million passengers a day on 11 color-coded lines.

as Jane Lambert, a local resident for 25 years, points out, "Londoners avoid the street on a Saturday because it becomes so busy you can hardly move." Visit on a Friday instead, when the crowds are thinner and the range of stalls is more eclectic—the vintage clothes, in particular, are outstanding. Lambert also suggests heading to the emerging Golborne Road area for coffee and Portuguese pastries at Lisboa or lunch at Pizza East Portobello, a big new favorite of the Notting Hill crowd. *portobellomarket.org, pizzaeastportobello.com*

Hampstead Heath in the fall

Est 1887

ALICE'S

Fridays are best
for treasure-
hunting on
Portobello Road.

The Mosquée
de Paris's opulent
restaurant

Paris

A Movable Feast for the Culture Aficianado

■ **Garden Tea** Next to the Jardin des Plantes on the Left Bank, La Grande Mosquée de Paris (*place du Puits-de-l'Ermite, tel 33 (1) 45 33 97 33*) is the spiritual center of the city's Algerian community. It features a charming open-air tearoom, a fig-tree-shaded garden where students from the Sorbonne like to come to drink shot glasses of mint tea served by waiters in vests and ties. An indoor restaurant serves plates of couscous on ornately engraved metal tables, below elaborately decorated ceilings, and there's even a steam bath where patrons can get a massage (though men are only admitted Tuesdays and Sundays; the rest of the week is reserved for women).

■ **Buttes-Chaumont** This eccentric park in northeast Paris (*1 rue Botzaris, tel 33 (1) 44 52 29 19*) was a 19th-century dump before it was transformed into a wonderland of stalactite-studded grottoes, duck-filled ponds, and Disneyesque passages through artificial cliffs. It is a pleasing alternative to the better known—and more crowded—Tuileries and Luxembourg gardens in the center of Paris, and the colonnaded temple at the hilltop has one of the finest panoramas in the city. Best of all, you can picnic without being whistled off the grass by a frowning guard.

■ **Pari Roller** Every Friday at 10 p.m., up to 40,000 inline skaters gather outside the Gare de Montparnasse to follow a fast-paced, 16-mile (26 km) circuit through the boulevards of Paris (the route changes weekly), ignoring red lights and one-way streets along the way, and escorted by a dozen uniformed *gendarmes*, themselves on wheels. The (French-only) website posts the exact route each Thursday night. *pari-roller.com*

■ **La Ferme Saint-Aubin** "Berthillon, schmertillon!" exclaims Derek Thomson, editor at France24.com, who vastly prefers the dairy products from this artisanal cheese shop down the street (*76 rue Saint-Louis en l'Île*) to its more famous ice-cream-selling brethren. "La Ferme Saint-Aubin buys cheeses fresh from producers around France, then ages them in its cellar," he explains. "The flavor sharpens as the cheese dries and contracts. A three-week-old Pont d'Yeu from the Loire region is a nice balance. It's creamy

Inline skaters rule the rues on Friday evenings.

I ♥ My City

Diane Johnson
Novelist and essayist

After their obligatory time at the Louvre or the Eiffel Tower, I always recommend that visiting friends step off the tourist trail for some time far from the madding crowds. An out-of-the-way afternoon could begin at the Bibliothèque Nationale—its fabulous displays range from book binding to Victorian porn. Afterward, walk over the Seine on the Simone de Beauvoir footbridge to the park around the Cinémathèque, the French film museum. This was the American Center until the U.S. government lost interest in this Frank Gehry building and sold it to the French.

The real deal—eating croissants in Paris

and smooth, like a fresh *chèvre*, but with a sharp, arresting flavor." *fromager-ferme-saint-aubin.fr*

■ **Markets** Join the Parisians in shopping for fresh food at one of the city's many neighborhood markets. Some of the most popular include Marché d'Aligre (*daily except Mon., metro: Ledru-Rollin*), Marché Biologique (*Sunday a.m., metro: Sèvres-Babylone*), rue du Poteau market (*daily a.m., metro: Jules-Joffrin*), and the Marché des Enfants Rouges (*daily except Mon., metro: Temple*), the oldest covered market in Paris. *marchedaligre.free.fr, paris.fr*

■ **Roue Libre** Every Sunday, the notoriously aggressive streets of Paris become bicycle friendly. The banks of the Seine, the cobbles of the rue Mouffetard, and a long stretch of the Canal St.-Martin are closed to automobiles, giving bicyclists the run of much of the town. The RATP, the local metro and bus company, rents five-speed bicycles from several outlets, including its central location in the Forum des Halles. *rapt.fr*

■ **Vintage Craze** Don't pay top dollar for high fashion. Do as the Parisians do—purchase last year's designer fashions at the many *dépôts-ventes*, consignment shops. Or join a younger crowd at trendy vintage shops, many of them in the Marais quarter. Violette et Léonie (*7 rue de Poitou* and *1 rue de Saintonge*) offers a good selection of recent clothing, as does GoldyMama, though it's more far-out—stylistically and geographically (*14 rue du Surmelin*). *violetteetleonie.com, goldymama.com*

■ **Palais-Royal** Commissioned by Cardinal Richelieu in the early 17th century, this enclave is an idyllic retreat from the hectic Right Bank. Pull up a metal chair to the fountain and peruse the day's *International Herald Tribune*, examine the sculptures studded through the six acres (2.5 ha) of grounds, or scan the upper-story apartments to pick out where Colette and Jean Cocteau once lived. Then linger before shop

Vintage at GoldyMama

■ The River Seine separates the bohemian Left Bank from the glamorous Right Bank.

■ Twenty *arrondissements* (districts) spiral out from the city center, each with a distinct personality—the 5th and 6th are popular for their parks and lively cafés.

windows pricing Shiseido perfume, toy soldiers, and the *tête de veau* at Le Grand Velour, one of the fanciest restaurants in town. *palais-royal.monuments-nationaux.fr*

■ **Quartier d'Été** Quartier d'Été has been entertaining Parisians since 1990. Opening on Bastille Day (July 14), the month-long celebration features performance art in venues throughout Paris and neighboring Essonne, most with free admission. Past shows have been held in the streets, on steps, and even in pools and trucks. The festival showcases actors, musicians, circus performers, and dancers. *quartierdete.com*

Fast Facts

Exhilarating views over the Eternal City

Rome

Living La Dolce Vita

■ **Authentic Food and a Great View** How about a splendid lunch, dinner, or late afternoon *aperitivo* in the shadow of Trajan's Column, the magnificent monument glorifying that emperor? Enoteca Provincia Romana (*Foro Traiano 82*) is a restaurant and wine bar in Centro Storico showcasing local products. "The food is great but to eat looking out at one of Rome's major monuments makes it even better," says Roberto, a local geologist. Good for lunch after visiting the Forum (ask for a window table) or the Provincia's Roman Houses exhibit at nearby Palazzo Valentini.
enotecaprovinciaromana.it, palazzovalentini.it

■ **City Steam** *Hammam* is a Turkish word but how appropriate to have one in Rome, where the use of water for steam bathing, cleansing, and relaxing was probably perfected: "The ancient Romans were geniuses in the channeling and distribution of water, so where better to relax and get clean?" says Laura Farr, an archaeology and hammam lover. With its interconnected warm, hot, and cold rooms, Acquamadre (*Via di Sant'Ambrogio 17*), open every day but Monday, has brought this pleasure back to the Eternal City. Here, stressed-out Romans soak and sweat, then enjoy a vigorous body scrub and a herbal tea. Massages and other beauty treatments are also available.
acquamadre.com

■ **Via dei Coronari** On Sundays, many Romans like to shop, or just plain window-shop, for antiques—furniture, paintings, and objets d'art. The best place is the charming Via dei Coronari, a pedestrian street built in 1475 to help pilgrims get to St. Peter's more quickly. Later named after the *coronari*, the makers of rosary beads and other religious objects that pilgrims might buy, its interesting shops and galleries are on the ground floor of lovely medieval and Renaissance palaces.

■ **Local Festa** Every year, residents of Trastevere look forward to the summer Festa de' Noantri when this former working-class neighborhood is given over to parades, food and drink stands, bands, jugglers, theater, and, of course, prayers. The object of religious veneration is a richly dressed statue supposedly hauled out of the Tiber River in 1535 and dedicated to Our Lady of Mount Carmel. On July 16, the statue is taken from the Sant'Agata church in Trastevere, sailed on the river accompanied by a flotilla of small craft, paraded though the streets, and then put on view for eight days in the imposing church

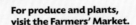

For produce and plants, visit the Farmers' Market.

of San Crisogono. *festadenoantri.it*

■ **Musical Magnet** Roman music lovers flock to the Parco della Musica, an arts complex in the Flaminia district. The Auditorium, as it is commonly known, has three concert halls and an outdoor amphitheater that seats 3,000, and studios for smaller events or rehearsals. It stages concerts—from classical and jazz to rock and gospel—as well as theater, dance, exhibits, and lectures. A large bookstore,

art galleries, and two cafés also draw the artsy crowd. *auditorium.com*

■ **Homegrown** On Saturdays and Sundays, Romans in the know flock to the Farmers' Market (*Mercato di Campagna Amica, Via San Teodoro 74*) in the glass-covered structure near the Circus Maximus. It was designed to promote agriculture from the Lazio region, and local farmers set up stands to sell their produce, which ranges from bread, cheese, honey, and fruit to plants and flowers. There are tables for those who want to eat their purchases on the spot. *mercatocircomassimo.it (Italian only)*

■ **Indulgent Desserts** Romans living near the old Jewish Ghetto buy their desserts at the Boccione bakery (*Via Portico d'Ottavia 1, tel 39 (0) 6 687 8637*), even if they have to stand in line. Homemade (and they look it) specialties include the ricotta cakes—chocolate or *visciole* (sour cherry). There are also cinnamon and almond cookies, and *pizza ebraica* (Jewish pizza) a flat, marsala-flavored cookie bar topped with pine nuts, raisins, almonds, and candied fruit. "It's all too fattening," moans Angela, a Boccione fan who lives nearby in the neighborhood, "but I keep coming back."

Eat like a Roman in Trastevere.

The old working-class neighborhood of Trastevere

In summer, free light shows illuminate the Palau Nacional.

Barcelona

Getting Down in Gaudí's Town

■ **A Village Within A City** Close to the center but a world away from the sightseeing crowds is the congenial district of Gràcia, incorporated into the city in 1897. "It's like a village in the morning and a city at night," says long-time Gràcia resident, Mercè Batalla. "Everybody knows everybody." The open, relaxed vibe attracts artists, international students, and families to this eclectic neighborhood, which is home to one of the oldest, thriving Catalan Roma communities. La Parada, outside the Abaceria market, has a speaker's corner on Saturday mornings for artists and poets. Daily routines include having morning and afternoon coffee in one of the many plazas, such as Plaça de la Revolució (Revolution Square), or the tree-lined Plaça de la Vila. In the evenings, bars draw in the crowds, serving beer and tapas until the small hours. For a meal, Famen (*Carrer de Ramis 2–4*) near the Plaça de John Lennon serves up good local fare. *bcn.cat*

■ **Main Street Bcn** Large department stores and malls exist, but the main street of each *barri* (district) is where most people choose to shop. "That's where you get more variety and the best buys," says salon owner Anthony Llobet. El Born, in the area of the Old Town behind the beach, is the place to hunt for trendy clothing and local crafts. Mid-town shoppers hit Passeig de Gràcia and Rambla de Catalunya. Crisscross the streets between these two main boulevards for boutique shops, art galleries, plus cafés where you can sit in the shade. *sitamurt.com, pasteleriasmauri.com*

■ **Comfort Food** Packaged baked goods are shunned in Barcelona, as most people buy their daily loaf at the local *forn*, or

I ♥ My City

Lynn Baiori
Barcelona Metropolitan *magazine* editor

Barcelona is a place of dreams. The downtown area, particularly El Born and the ethereal basilica of Santa Maria del Mar in La Ribera, have a mystical attraction. Every stone seems to hold the memory of the hope and struggles of this beautiful city. I also love the narrow back streets of El Call, the old Jewish quarter and its tiny synagogue. Even the festivals have a dreamlike quality. A favorite of mine is the Festa Major de Gràcia in August, when the community turns the streets into a colorful fantasy world. I love the spirit of this town. People really do love their city, and Barcelona bountifully responds.

Detail, Santa Maria del Mar

oven. Hot spots include Turris in Eixample; Forn Europa and Fortino, both in Gràcia; Baltà (*Carrer de Saints, 115*) in Sants–Montjuïc; and Mistral (*Ronda de Sant Antoni, 96*), in El Raval —all selling a tempting assortment of bakery items. "When I was a girl, the scent of croissants baking from the Forn Mistral would wake me in the morning," Paquita Satorra recalls as she buys a croissant for her grandson. "And they're still good."
turris.es, forneurope.es, fornfortino.com

■ Kid Friendly
Traveling with children? Join local families for some kid-friendly fun: Up on Tibidabo, the city's hilltop amusement park, ten-year-old Barcelonan Elisenda says the rollercoaster is *the best* as she runs off for a second go; when the heat starts to rise, a favorite getaway for grown-ups and children is the Olympic-size pool on Montjuïc (*Avinguda de l"Estadia, 30–38*); in the Jardins de la Torre de Les Aigües, in an Eixample courtyard, you'll find moms sunning themselves while little ones splash in the pool; and, for a fantasy-inspired adventure, head to the Parc del Laberint (*Pg. dels Castanyers, 1*) and discover its walking trails, waterfall, labyrinth, and small palace with

wandering peacocks.
tibidabo.cat

■ Our Gal
Barcelona is a city that knows how to put on a show, from summer light shows at the Font Màgica in front of the Palau Nacional to the many festivals. The city's patron, La Mercè, is lavishly honored each September with a cultural festival that attracts nearly two million people. With more than 600 activities and some 2,000 local and international artists taking part, La Mercè is a nonstop carnival of both traditional and modern theater.

The Gothic quarter becomes the stage for the celebration, with dancers, musicians, technological displays, exhibitions, and performances day and night for a week. Most spectacular is the Correfoc, or fire run, when costumed "devils" dance through the old town carrying poles of whirling fireworks.
merce.bcn.cat/en

■ Pedal Power
You may think of Amsterdam as a biker's paradise, but Barcelona locals love to ride, too. You'll see parents taking kids to school, workers en route to the office, young and

old on wheels. The town council is continually adding new bike lanes to improve mobility. "The Carretera de les Aigües is a beautiful route," says cyclist Joan Castellví. "From there you have Barcelona at your feet." The lane runs along the Collserola hills, offering a bird's-eye view of the city. Inner-city routes include The Diagonal, Carrer Enric Granados, and the Passeig Marítim—the waterfront, with its new architecture, Frank Gehry's spectacular fish sculpture, beach bars, and fish restaurants.
budgetbikes.eu, rentabikebarcelona.com

La Concepcio is Eixample's neighborhood market.

Capetonians let their hair down at the annual Carnival.

Cape Town
Confetti-filled Jols and Picnics by the Sea

■ **In the Swim** Right in the heart of Cape Town, hidden behind an unprepossessing façade on the corner of Long Street and Orange Street, lies one of the city's best-kept secrets: the shabby-chic Long Street Baths. Stressed out by tramping the sights? At the baths, surrounded by faded Edwardian elegance, you can swim a few laps, enjoy a massage, or sweat away your cares in the steam room. "I love this place!" enthuses aid worker Jennie Martin. "When things get too much, I hire myself a cubicle and lie around for hours, reading, and dozing."
capetown.gov.za

■ **Bree: the New Long Street** "Since Long Street has become totally touristy," says magazine editor Daniela Massenz, "Bree Street in De Waterkant, south of the Waterfront, is where I like to grab a meal." Park your Vespa, then breakfast on an almond croissant and a flat white at Café Frank. Or lunch on sushi, sandwiches, or slow-roasted lamb with the hipsters at Jason Bakery, right across the road. Be warned: Bree Street can get hectic around midday when the lawyers, office workers, and students in the area take their lunchtime break.
cafefrank.com, jasonbakery.com

■ **Biggest Party in Town** Capetonians can be a reserved bunch, but once a year they run wild at the Cape Town Carnival. "I was there this year, and it was a total blast," laughs writer Kai Tuomi. Celebrating the city's cultural diversity, dancers sashay, musicians blow their horns, and revellers caper all along Somerset Road and the Fan Walk. Watch the performers and papier-mâché creatures go by or, better still, get involved yourself. Put on a mask, fling a handful of confetti, and have a *jol* (party), as they say in this part of the world.
capetowncarnival.com

I ♥ My City

Margie Orford *Crime novelist, journalist, and film director*

To know Cape Town you must walk it. If you walk it you will fall in love. The call of the muezzin at prayer time floats above the streets of Bo-Kaap, an area of the city built before cars. The cafés, the wine bars, the vendors selling single cigarettes and vegetables in the center. The artists' studios and galleries in gritty District Six. Most magical is the fact that this busy port city is contained by the natural world. Look one way down the end of the canyoned city streets, and you'll see the Atlantic; turn around, and you will see the quiet majesty of Table Mountain.

Zulu bead art in Bo-Kapp

■ **Feast Your Eyes**
At the laid-back Haas Collective on Rose Street in the old Bo-Kaap Malay quarter, you can run your eyes over local design while eating a breakfast or a light lunch and sipping coffee made from Brazilian, Colombian, Guatemalan or Ethiopian beans. Haas showcases the best in local design, including ceramics, jewelry, sculpture, graphics, and soft furnishings. If you're a fan of all things kitsch, snap up one of their Tretchikoff-print cushion covers or bags. *haascollective.com*

■ **Whale of a Time**
In spring and early summer, smart locals ask for a table with a sea view at Octopus' Garden restaurant in the coastal suburb of Muizenberg. From this venue, wrapped around St. James railway station, they know they have every chance of spotting a whale breaching or dolphins and seals surfing the waves. The décor may be New Age glittery, with mirrors and brightly colored walls, but the food is simple and delicious. "Best pizzas in town," raves Odidi Mfenyana, a cabaret artist. "Try the Marilyn Monroe; it's *to die for!*" In the daytime, kids can play in the garden. Friday evenings, jazz or light rock entertains the crowd. *facebook.com/octopus gardenrestaurantstjames*

■ **Going for the Record**
Drop in to Mabu Vinyl, in the Gardens quarter, near the city center but off the main tourist drag, to shop for vintage records and CDs. Chat with proprietor Stephen "Sugar" Segerman, a lifelong fan of singer Sixto Rodriguez. Segerman hit the headlines as the unlikely hero of the Oscar-winning documentary *Searching for Sugar Man* (2012), which focused on his hunt for Rodriguez. "Ever since the Oscar," Segerman smiles, "things have been crazy around here—but crazy in a nice way!" In his small shop, he is happy to track down that long-sought vinyl album for you. *mabuvinyl.co.za*

■ **Park Off** For the urban outdoors, forget about Kirstenbosch in the foothills of Table Mountain and head for Cape Town's newest green space, Green Point Urban Park, west of the Waterfront. Laid out in 2010 as a complex of jogging tracks, cycle paths, lawns, and playgrounds, the park has become a huge hit with the locals (so much so, that it's best visited on weekdays). Parents with young kids will love the climbing ropes, swings, and trapezes. Nature enthusiasts will enjoy a ramble through wetlands. Feeling lazy? Then bring a picnic and blanket and doze in the sun. *capetownpartnership.co.za*

In spring, whale-spotting is on the menu at Octopus' Garden restaurant.

The ultimate
flotation tank—the
Dead Sea in Israel

CHAPTER 4
AFRICA & THE MIDDLE EAST

ST. LOUIS, SENEGAL
ALL THAT JAZZ

During its annual Jazz Festival in late May, the sleepy town of St. Louis on the Senegal River is all about the music. Jazz fills the air and spills out of every bar and restaurant. On the main stage on the place Faidherbe some of the biggest names in jazz and African music perform over five evenings. Senegalese greats such as Cheikh Lô or Baba Maal might share the bill with American saxophonist Pharoah Sanders or South African jazz great Hugh Masekela. Other regulars include the African Roots Quintet, which unites expressly for the festival, and Ablaye Cissoko, probably Senegal's most famous exponent of the *kora* (an African stringed instrument). The festival's sponsors ensure that poor youths in the town can attend for free.

JOINING IN: At 2 a.m., as you leave the venue, the streets are a festive hodgepodge of people gabbing, food vendors and merchants hawking their wares, and vehicles belching diesel fumes, all against the colorful background of everyone's Saturday best. The night is young by local

MORE: Sounds

L'Embuscade: Down a Gazelle beer or three while listening to local musicians jam at this popular haunt on rue Abdoulaye Seck. Tel 221 (0) 33 961 8864
Quai des Arts: This nightclub on avenue Jean Mermoz is the place to catch top Senegalese musicians, and not just during the festival. Tel 221 (0) 33 961 5656

standards, and there's more music to hear. Follow the flow to one of the post-concert improv sessions in the town's bars, restaurants, and other nooks and crannies where the party goes on till dawn.

■ *Essentials:* Place Faidherbe (tickets: tel 221 (0) 33 961 2455, saintlouisjazz.org)

Festival performer Ablaye Cissoko (left) plays the kora with guitarist Claude Guillabert.

Ashanti musicians trumpet the arrival of the king.

KUMASI, GHANA
ROYAL AUDIENCE

It is 1 o'clock in the afternoon and hundreds of people mill around in the courtyard of the Manhyia Palace in Kumasi, capital of Ghana's Ashanti region. Suddenly the murmuring ceases and the momentary silence is broken by a chorus of horns and flutes and a throbbing of drums. It might seem chaotic but this is *Akwasidae*, one of the most grandiose *durbars* (receptions) in Africa, a festival for the Ashanti to honor their ancestors and an chance for the Ashanti sub-chiefs discuss regional matters.

WHAT TO EXPECT: The King of the Ashanti enters on a palanquin. Otumfuo Osei Tutu II greets his honored guests before sitting down to receive his subjects. Pride of place is reserved for his golden stool, which sits by his side on a throne of its own, for it is said to contain the spirit of all Ashanti both living and dead. Accompanied by music and a fusillade of rifle fire to show power, the sub-chiefs, dressed in their ceremonial dress of Kente cloth, pay their respects to the king. Says Kumasi native Tina Asiamah, "When I walk towards the festival I hear the musicians playing drums and blowing Ashanti horns. The aroma of the spices from the food prepared for the Gods lingers in the air as the chiefs chant prayers to their ancestors in the stool room."

WHEN TO GO: Akwasidae takes place every 40 to 42 days, starting on a Friday with private rituals and culminating in the public ceremony on the Sunday to which visitors are openly invited; in fact, you might be one of the chosen few to be presented to the king.

WHAT TO BUY: Boldly patterned Kente cloth is sold at the Ashanti village of Bonwire, 12 miles (20 km) northeast of Kumasi, where the cloth is woven, and at Bonwire Kente Cloth Shop in Bank Road, Kumasi.

■ *Essentials:* General information: manhyiaonline.org

Workers in a cooperative process argan nuts by hand.

ESSAOUIRA, MOROCCO
BERBER BEAUTY SECRETS

Looking for a miracle? If you head away from Marrakech toward the Atlantic coast you may just find one—a skin-care miracle, that is. The pretty resort of Essaouira is home to one of the world's rarest oils: argan nut extract. Used by local women for generations to nourish the skin and erase blemishes, the "liquid gold" now goes into anti-aging creams, soaps, moisturizers, lip balms, facials, and massage oil. When skin-care expert Liz Earle first experienced the regenerative feel of Morocco's argan oil on her skin, she pronounced it the "best facial I ever received." Berber brides rub the oil into their hair before washing it and use the oil on their nails.

LOCAL FAVORITES: Argan oil is sold in small—2 to 4 fluid-ounce (60-120 ml)—quantities. You can buy it from roadside cooperatives such as Tamounte on the Marrakech-Essaouira road. In Essaouira's little medina, Arga d'Or sells soap and moisturizing cream. Prices are fixed at the cooperatives, but you might be able to bargain in the medina. Savvy locals know to beware low prices as they indicate that the oil is not the real deal.

Rose Water

Another local beauty product, rose water (a by-product in the extraction of rose oil), also provides flavor for local dishes. Not only do Moroccan women dab it on their skin—cooks sprinkle it over platters of fresh strawberries, use it to pep up salads, and stir it into the sticky nut-and-honey mixture that fills favorite pastries.

LOCAL KNOWLEDGE: The oil is also good enough to eat. Praised for its "delicate taste" by top chefs, it is sometimes used in the local cuisine to add flavor. Most often, it's dripped into tagines and couscous dishes or used as a dip for fresh, warm Moroccan bread, either for breakfast or with a glass of mint tea in the late afternoon.

■ *Essentials:* Tamounte Cooperative (Imin'Tlit, Essaouira province); Arga d'Or (5 rue Ibn Rochd, Essaouira)

IMILCHIL, MOROCCO
SEPTEMBER ROMANCE

A Berber love story sparked the founding of this famous *moussem*, a festival-cum-market-cum-marriage fair held in September high in Morocco's Atlas Mountains. "September romance" is the informal title of this unique event at which Berber tribes exchange love and livestock in and around the village of Imilchil. Visiting the three-day gathering today, you can witness engagement rituals followed by marriages that take place around the tomb of the local saint, Sidi Mohammed Maghani.

JOINING IN: Part homecoming celebration for shepherds who have spent the summer with their sheep and cattle in the moist upper meadows and part marriage fair, the moussem, which used to be closed to visitors, now welcomes guests. Men wear white turbans and young women dazzle prospective partners in colorful dresses and elaborate silver jewelry as they dance long into the night. As you mingle with other fairgoers, take care: A nod and a wink between marriage candidates is all it takes to initiate a formal family sit-down around a pot of mint tea in one of the thousands of *khaimas* (tents) sheltering as many as 30,000 Berbers on the lake plateau of the Middle Atlas range.

■ *Essentials:* **General information:** guideinmorocco.com, travel-exploration.com

Brides of the Aït Haddidou tribe at Imilchil

MARRAKECH, MOROCCO
FEASTING THE NIGHT AWAY

As they say in Marrakech, "The best Moroccan food is home-cooked," and it's rare for Moroccans to visit restaurants. But they do eat at the food stalls on the Jemaa el-Fna, the Square of the Dead, in the center of old Marrakech. When the sun sets over the nearby Koutoubia Mosque, dozens of stalls appear out of nowhere, tables and benches pop up, lights flicker all around, and clouds of smoke rise under the stars. "I've been coming here since I was a boy," says computer manager Said M'samri, sliding onto one of the shared benches and ordering a bowl of snails in a cumin-flavored broth. "It was special. You never knew who or what you would find on the Jemaa. I'm now over 50, and bring my own family."

JOINING IN: Business is brisk, and the busy crowds can be confusing: Which way to go? Which stalls serve the best food? Just watch the locals as they move from stall to stall, here for meatballs, there for spicy sausages, lamb kebabs, or freshly fried squid and shrimps.

WHAT TO CHOOSE: Pick from sweet peppers and eggplants, thin potato cakes, olives and sesame bread, tomato dip, couscous, and rows of tagines, described by English chef Jamie Oliver as "stew with attitude." Diners pack the benches, smells of garlic and smoke fill the air, and on a raised stand the snail man ladles out generous helpings. Hearty *harira* soup, made with lamb, lentils, chickpeas, and generous quantities of herbs and spices, is popular during Ramadan. Later on, munch on nougat or almond pastries and watch snake charmers, storytellers, acrobats, and musicians performing on the square.

LOCAL KNOWLEDGE: On a chilly night, eat indoors at Chez Chegrouni on the edge of the square. It sells simple, local food such as harira soup, couscous with chicken, and tagine of lamb and prunes at low prices.

■ *Essentials:* Jemaa el-Fna (Old City); Chez Chegrouni (46 Jemaa el-Fna, tel 212 (0) 24 654 7615)

Dozens of food stalls pack the square each evening.

SALT, MUD, AND RELAXATION

Yes, the clichés are true: You can easily read a book—or fiddle with your iPad—while floating on your back in the waters of the Dead Sea. "An afternoon floating in the sea makes a wonderful respite from the streets of Tel Aviv, and kids love playing in the mud," says Miran Epstein, who has been coming to the Dead Sea beaches for many years. The science is simple: a salt content that averages between 30 percent and 35 percent creates enough buoyancy to support a human body.

What's more, the Dead Sea isn't actually a sea, but a huge desert lake between Israel and Jordan. And the water is anything but dead—recent scientific diving expeditions have revealed what researchers call a "fantastic hot spot for life" deep below the surface.

WHAT TO EXPECT: While you can just turn up on the shore of the Dead Sea and take a dip, there is no natural shade and locals prefer to pay an entrance fee to one of the hotels or kibbutzim to access changing facilities, showers, first aid, lifeguards (it's hard to sink but you can choke on the salt), and restaurants, as well as health and beauty treatments and gift shops.

WHERE TO GO: Mineral Beach, halfway down the Israeli shore, balances nature and development. As well as floating in the lake, and smothering yourself in mineral-laden mud, you can swim laps in an indoor freshwater pool, splurge on spa treatments, and eat lunch at the cafeteria-style restaurant. There is also a lakeside amphitheater that stages live entertainment on Israeli holidays.

Perched on the other cliffs above the beach is Metzoke Dragot, a small desert resort with accommodations and incredible views to Jordan on the east bank.

■ *Essentials:* Mineral Beach (Mitzpe Shalem, West Bank, tel 972 (0) 2 994 4887, dead-sea.co.il); Metzoke Dragot (West Bank, tel 972 (0) 8 622 3012, metzoke.co.il)

MORE: Hotels and Kibbutzim

Kalia Kibbutz Near the lake's north end, this kibbutz offers food, lodging, and a Dead Sea beach, plus the option of volunteering to help around the kibbutz. You can also visit nearby Qumran, where the Dead Sea Scrolls were discovered. kaliahotel.co.il

Leonardo Club Hotel Dead Sea, Neve Zohar Among a cluster of hotels at the southern end of the lake, this high-rise hotel is popular with Israelis. fattal-hotels.com

HOLON, ISRAEL
A CHILDREN'S PARADE

Where else can you see 10-foot-long (3 m) beasts made from flowers, Benjamin Netanyahu reigning as king of a giant chessboard, and Angry Birds dancing atop a flatbed truck? For a family take on the springtime holiday of Purim there is no better place than the large city of Holon, where Israelis of all ages go wild. Noisy crowds gather to see costumed musicians, acrobats, magicians, and dancers accompanied by larger-than-life floats and puppets depicting animals, politicians, and celebrities. Fireworks, extravagant makeup, streamers, and fancy dress add to the mayhem.

WHERE TO GO: While the exact route and schedule differ each year, the Adloyada parade generally winds through Sokolov Street and Weizman Street around midday. Doron Shalom, Culture Department Director of Holon Municipality, recommends taking up a viewing position along the route: "The parade is most impressive when you can see all the floats in the procession marching

MORE: Purim Partying

Bezalel Purim Circus, Jerusalem: Students at Bezalel Academy of Art and Design hold an open party each year, often with a circus theme. gojerusalem.com
Zombie Walk, Tel Aviv: Fake blood-covered revelers—zombie Michael Jacksons, zombie chefs, and dreadlocked zombies—parade up and down the city's central boulevards while downing anise-based *arak*. touristisrael.com

in a long row." Afterwards, street performances and activities at the Municipality complex continue until evening.

■ *Essentials:* General information: holon.muni.il

Holon's kids take center stage in the Adloyada parade.

Vibrantly colored spices in Akko's shuk

AKKO, ISRAEL
SHOPPING FOR SPICES

In the sleepy port town of Akko, where the ships of ancient Greece once docked and Knights Templars fought, a pan-Middle Eastern *shuk* (souk) spreads out along Market Street—a warren of booths and stalls operated by the same families for generations.

LOCAL FAVORITES: The shuk is well stocked with shoes and clothing, housewares, toiletries, and handicrafts, as well as food—carrot and citrus juices squeezed to order, fish straight off the boats, dried figs and dates, olives, and roasted coffee beans—but one of the main reasons why locals come here is to buy spices.

WHERE TO GO: The Old City of Akko's main thoroughfare, Market Street, runs from the Hospitallers Gate in the north toward the old port at the other end. Toward the south, on a prominent corner, sits a modest shop called Kurdi and Berit. Here, wooden chests of drawers and racks of vials and jars store countless varieties of pungent, savory, spicy, and sweet seasonings, sourced from all over the world. Proprietor Kurdi Hamudi learned his trade from his mother and is in the process of apprenticing his son in the family's secret blending methods and recipes, including creating a dozen varieties of curry. Blending is done in the shop itself and always in small batches. Hamudi's signature product is a custom-roasted and blended Turkish ground coffee infused with ground cardamom imported from India. "It's the best quality," he asserts. "Spicy—full aroma."

WHAT TO EAT: Look out for Hummus Said, a landmark hummus joint in the center of the shuk. If you come at lunchtime, don't despair if the line is long—service is swift and it moves fast.

■ *Essentials:* shukbites.com; Kurdi and Berit (tel 972 (0) 4 991 6188); Hummus Said (tel 972 (0) 4 991 3945)

TEL AVIV, ISRAEL
DESIGNER DESTINATIONS

Locals often refer to Tel Aviv as the "Bubble," because its heady mix of youth-driven prosperity and urban hedonism is not representative of the rest of Israel. Tel Avivians march to a different beat, and this is reflected in its fashion industry. "We are a young country, and we don't rely on history for passion and culture," says fashion buyer Galit Reismann. "We're still defining ourselves. Most of the designers here are young."

WHERE TO GO: Favorite places include Common Raven in the old town of Jaffa for well-cut innovative design; Tamar Prinak, in the center, for minimalist chic; Shani Bar, on Dizengoff in the center, for shoes inspired by birds and racecars; and Yosef Peretz, also on Dizengoff, for dresses with post-urban prints. There are plenty of mall-style clothing chains, but for the high end, there are no big stores to buy complete outfits. "We mix and match, and explore juxtapositions, like vintage with modern," Reismann notes. The hottest designers, often graduates from Tel Aviv's Shenkar College, host sales in their apartments or their workshops. "Smart designers do the combined studio-boutique thing," adds Reismann. Bigger events take place at bars and clubs, often in the afternoon, while pop-up stores in old Bauhaus-style buildings in the Jaffa Flea Market offer collections from multiple designers.

JOINING IN: Word gets around via fliers, social media, or blogs. First-time Tel Aviv boutique shoppers are often surprised to find windows that are decorated either starkly or not at all. Boutiques are workspaces, where designers are busy breaking fashion's boundaries while at the same time schmoozing with their devoted clientele.

■ *Essentials:* Fashion news: dreedtea.com; tlvstyle.com; Common Raven (19 Beit Eshel St., tel 972 (0) 3 774 1058, cmrvn .com); Tamar Primak (25 Gordon St., tel 972 (0) 52 263 0564, tamarprimak.com) Shani Bar (151 Dizengoff St. tel 972 (0) 3 527 8451, shanibar.com); Yosef Peretz (213 Dizengoff St., tel 972 (0) 3 529 8991, yosefperetz.com)

> *"Hunting down the coolest designs is at the essence of the boutique scene."*
> —GALIT REISMANN, FASHION BUYER

Checking out the latest designs in the Neve Tzedek area

The red rocks of
Wadi Mujib

HAMMAMAT MA'IN, JORDAN
HOT SPRING HAVEN

Like a secret garden, the hot springs of Hammamat Ma'in lie in the deep cleft of Wadi Zarqa Ma'in off Wadi Mujib in western Jordan. Surrounded by a jagged fence of orange-red rocks, waterfalls tumble down into deep blue ponds half-hidden under rising sheets of steam. "We come here to relax and get away from the city streets," says weekend visitor Sayid Yusef as he lifts his two-year-old daughter Noor into the spring.

Hammamat Ma'in is a relaxing day-trip within easy reach of Amman, Jordan's capital. On Fridays and Saturdays (the Jordanian weekend) families flock here, bringing picnics of crispy *fattoush* salad, *fatayer* (pastry parcels of cheese and spinach), hummus, and stuffed vine leaves.

WHAT TO EXPECT: The admission charge permits access to a complex of pools. The main attraction is the steaming waterfall cascading out of the cliff above at a bath-like temperature of 113°F (45°C). This is open to everyone, including children, who whoop in delight as the water pummels their backs. Stick your toe in the water and inch by inch immerse yourself up to your neck, easing into the water's warm embrace. The mineral-rich sulphuric waters are said to have therapeutic properties. Male soakers up for the challenge of considerably hotter temperatures can take a dip in the men-only pool and waterfall nearby.

JOINING IN: Jordanian women enter the pools fully clothed. Although it is acceptable for foreign women to bathe in a swimsuit (there are on-site changing rooms), it's best to wear a T-shirt and shorts or sarong over the top.

■ *Essentials:* General information: visitjordan.com

"The kids can play in the pools and the waters are wonderfully soothing." —SAYID YUSEF, AMMAN RESIDENT

DUBAI, U.A.E.
ALL THAT GLITTERS

Emirati women (and quite a few men) love gold. It is traditionally the most important part of the bride price, and to this day any bridegroom worth his salt provides his bride with a heavy gold belt, headdress, earrings, and necklace. Historically, this was her security should the marriage founder.

Dubai's Gold Souk is one of the biggest in the world. The rumor goes that at any one time it holds more than 11 tons (10 tonnes) of gold. It is located in the Deira district: To get there, pay a *dirham* to the ferry man and take an *abra* (wooden boat) across the Dubai Creek from Bur Dubai. Surprisingly for such a treasure trove, it is a dusty place where old ceiling fans attempt to cut through the baking heat along its covered wooden walkways.

WHERE TO GO: Jewelry shops range from established chains to small outlets. During the wedding season—June and July—the whole souk will be mobbed. Smaller shops have workshops at the back where craftsmen are on hand to create customized pieces. Precious stones and pearls can also be bought unset. If you are looking for a special gift, try international jewelers Liali.

MORE: Jewelry Shops

Gold and Diamond Park: Escape the heat for this air-conditioned market in west Dubai, and the convenience of almost 100 jewelers under one roof. Interchange 4, Sheikh Zayed Rd., Al Barsha

Meena Bazaar: You'll find jewelers, including Meena Jewelers, in this local market among shops selling food and clothes. Al-Fahidi St., Bur Dubai

LOCAL KNOWLEDGE: Rigorous local laws control the quality of gold, so pieces are certain to be authentic. With more than 700 gold and jewelry stores in Dubai and more than 300 in the Gold Souk itself, haggling is expected.

■ *Essentials:* Gold Souk (Sikkat al Khail St., Deira, closed Fri. a.m.); Liali Jewelers (Ground Level, Gold Souk, Sapphire Rd., tel 971 (0) 4 434 0461)

Handcrafted gold bangles in Dubai's Gold Souk

UNITED ARAB EMIRATES
SANDBOARDING

Sandboarding may have been invented on California's coastal dunes, but the sport reaches new adrenalin-packed heights on the rolling dunes of the Sahara, where young Emiratis and thrill-seeking members of the U.A.E.'s vast expat population have embraced the sport.

WHAT TO EXPECT: The boarder glides down a sandy slope on a plank about the same size and shape as a snowboard. Although diehard sandboarders stand (like surfers) as they're running the dunes, novices lie on their back or stomach. The best sandboarders can achieve speeds of 40 miles an hour (64 km/h).

WHERE TO GO: On the edge of the Sahara's Rub' al Khali, or Empty Quarter—the world's largest sand desert—the Emirates is the perfect place to learn or master sandboarding. Several good areas are found on the outskirts of Dubai, but the holy grail of the sport is Liwa Oasis, a collection of Bedouin villages to the southwest of Abu Dhabi. The ocher-colored dunes surrounding the oasis include a sandy giant called the Tal Moreeb (Scary Hill) that towers 900 feet (300 m) above the desert floor.

JOINING IN: Adventure outfitters in Dubai and Abu Dhabi offer guided sandboarding trips. Or you can buy a board, rent a 4WD vehicle, and choose your own dune. You'll need wider and longer boards than standard for running big dunes. Sandboards must have an upturned tip to keep the board from plowing into the sand. You can wax the bottom of the board to make it run more smoothly.

WHEN TO GO: Given the triple-digit temperatures usual in the U.A.E. in summer, sandboarding is best in late fall, winter, or early spring. Even then, wear sunscreen, long-sleeves, long pants, and a hat. Anyone contemplating a glide down Tal Moreeb should invest in a helmet.

■ *Essentials:* Liwa Oasis; 95 miles (150 km) south of Abu Dhabi, off the E11 motorway; Tal Moreeb: 15 miles (25 km) from the village of Mezaira'a in the center of the oasis; abudhabisesertsafari.net

The U.A.E. offers ultra-smooth dunes for sandboarding.

Diplomatic Quarter Parks, Riyadh, Saudi Arabia

URBAN OASES

Where locals go to take the heat out of hectic city living.

■ Diplomatic Quarter Parks, Riyadh, Saudi Arabia

Between the burning desert and the pollution of Riyadh are some 30 parks where children can play freely and families catch their collective breath. There are lawns, groves, flowers, and streams, and a 12-mile (20 km) walking track circles the parks.
DQ main entrance on Makkah Road (Route 40 W.)

■ Lan Su Chinese Garden, Portland, OR

This walled garden fills an entire city block. Plants and trees native to China set off Asian pavilions, bridges, and walkways. Join Portlanders in the tea room for a snack before attending one of the garden's talks or workshops.
239 NW. Everett St., lansugarden.org

■ Georgian Garden, Bath, U.K.

In this tiny garden in Bath, garden historians have re-created an original town garden first laid out in the 1760s. Its plants, paths, and trellises look much as they might have done in Jane Austen's time. Peaceful and secluded, it's the perfect spot for an afternoon with a book.
4 The Circus, Bath, visit bath.co.uk

■ Botanical Garden, Antwerp, Belgium

This garden in the heart of Antwerp originally grew herbs for the local hospital. Nowadays workers picnic on the benches in summer or dip into into the tropical greenhouse on cold winter days. There's a changing exhibition of sculpture.
Leopoldstraat 24, visitantwerpen.be

■ National Gardens, Athens, Greece

Where else can you sit among Corinthian capitals in the heart of a city? At lunchtime, workers from the Greek Parliament building next door come to enjoy the garden's elegantly arranged palm trees, delicate pergolas, and fragments of ancient architecture. American writer Henry Miller said of these gardens in 1939: "It remains in my memory like no other park I have known."
Amalias 1, greece-athens.com

■ Chi Lin Nunnery, Hong Kong, China

Lotus ponds, Buddhist relics, and Tang era-style temples all jostle for attention in the midst of Hong Kong's high-rise Diamond Hill district. Each rock, tree, and shrub has been placed according to the ancient Chinese principles of feng shui, creating a sense of harmony. Soak up the peace and quiet then join the locals for lunch on the terrace of the park's highly popular vegetarian restaurant overlooking a lily pond.
Chi Lin Road, Diamond Hill, discoverhongkong.com

■ Legaspi Park, Manila, Philippines

Every lunchtime and evening this little park in the beating heart of Makati in Manila fills with exercising workers. On weekends, it takes on a more relaxed character. Children clamber over the jungle gym while their parents watch them from under the shady trees.
Rada Street, Makati, Metro Manila

A Bhutanese
dancer celebrates
in style.

ARTVIN, TURKEY
BATTLE OF THE BULLS

In Artvin province in Turkey's far northeast, amid forested mountains and high alpine pastures wedged between the Black Sea and Georgia, farmers look forward to a day that comes but once a year. The bullfight.

This raucous, thrilling event originates in the annual bullfights that took place every spring as farmers moved their livestock from winter quarters up to the high pastures. Here, the bulls would battle each other for supremacy before settling down to eating the rich grass in the proper pecking order. It was a dangerous affair, with much bloodshed and even death. So over time, the farmers introduced a series of controlled bullfights to pre-empt these high-altitude disputes. Today, these fights have become the centerpiece of a fun summer festival.

JOINING IN: The bullfights take place in the Kafkasör meadows, 5 miles (8 km) from the provincial capital, Artvin. Sit with the large crowds that pack the rough wooden stands of the arena and feel the tension as it builds through the day, culminating in the final battle.

The last two beasts, eyes red, nostrils flaring, lock horns. The crowd falls silent, watching, waiting. Suddenly the stronger animal forces its adversary into flight. Amid a cacophony of cheers, rasping bagpipes, accordions, and oboe-like zuma, the announcer comes over the loudspeakers bestowing the title of *basboga* (chief bull) on the winner.

WHAT TO EXPECT: Most years, some 200 bulls compete, divided into six categories based on chest width. Umpires and owners bring the bout to a close if an animal appears to be at risk of injury. In practice, it seldom gets to this stage—there is much snorting and pawing up dust as the bulls eyeball each other from across the makeshift arena, but less physical contact. And to protect them, the bulls' horns are filed down pre-combat.

WHEN TO GO: The Kafkasör Festival (sometimes called the Caucasus Culture and Arts Festival) extends over four days during the third week of June. The bullfights take place on one day only. The rest of the festival celebrates the traditional culture, still very much alive in this out-of-the-way corner of Turkey, with folksinging and dancing, wrestling and vast amounts of local food and drink.

■ *Essentials:* General information: kultur.gov.tr

Two of Artvin's bulls vie for top position.

The *hammam* in Bursa's Kervansaray Termal Hotel

BURSA, TURKEY
SCRUB, WASH, AND SOAK

Your deep-cleanse in a *hammam* (Turkish bath) begins with a half-hour steam to loosen all the dirt and old skin. After that the attendant gives you a head-to-toe scrub (during which you may be horrified to see dead skin sloughing away in black rolls that look like pencil shavings), followed by a thorough soaping, and a massage. Next, it's time to take a break from the heat. Do as the locals do: Cover up in brightly colored wrap, rest, chat, and enjoy the social side of the hammam. "No one remains a stranger for long," says Katherine Belliel, a regular visitor from her home in Istanbul. Then take a final soak in the hot pool before getting dressed.

WHERE TO GO: The therapeutic waters of the city of Bursa, 55 miles (90 km) south of Istanbul, have been attracting bathers since Roman times. Its baths are fed by hot springs from the Uludağ Mountain and vary in temperature according to the season, from steamy in summer to moderately hot in spring. Almost all of the best hammams are in Bursa's Çekirge district. For a classy atmosphere and plenty of local flair try the baths at the Kervansaray Termal Hotel.

WHAT TO WEAR: Locals wear bathing suits or underwear; baring all is not done by either sex. Hotel hammams provide towels; public baths do not, so bring your own.

JOINING IN: Order a full cleansing package—an exfoliating scrub (*kese*), a wash with olive oil soap, and a massage.

■ *Essentials:* Kervansaray Termal Hotel (16080 Çekirge Meydani, tel 90 (0) 224 233 93 00, kervansarayhotels.com)

"Wear sandals in the hammam or risk comment: Many believe that walking barefoot endangers the kidneys." —KATHERINE BELLIEL, ISTANBUL AUTHOR

AN EXPLOSION OF COLOR

Add a rainbow of colored powder to water, apply liberally, and watch the mayhem unfold. This is the north Indian springtime festival of Holi. In Hindu mythology, Holi marks the victory of good over evil and, in common with many spring festivals, it also announces the end of winter and the banishing of darkness and negativity. As Jaipur native Rohan Sinha says, "Everyone loves Holi—it's a great unifier. It means meeting friends and family, unadulterated fun, good food, and a riot of colors." Traditionally even royals could be pelted with paint.

WHEN TO GO: Holi takes place across the Jaipur region usually in March. This is a great time to visit for the stifling pre-monsoon heat has yet to arrive and the city is at its most exuberant. The two-day party is rowdy, messy, and joyous: A raucous celebration with a real carnival atmosphere.

SPECIAL ATTRACTIONS: The Elephant Festival happens on the day before Holi at the Rambagh Polo Ground, near the Taj Rambagh Hotel and opposite the Sawai Man Singh Stadium. The pachyderms, elaborately painted and festooned with an assortment of bells, bangles, ear danglers, and gold-embroidered fabrics, parade before the crowds before a winner is chosen in an elephant beauty contest. The party ends with a display of fireworks.

JOINING IN: On the night before Holi, generally after midnight, people light ceremonial fires to mark the beginning of the festival. The lighting of the fires is heralded by a deafening fusillade of firecrackers.

The following day, set off early, while it is still cool, to join the thronging crowds around the City Palace and the Palace of the Winds. The locals go to Holi with friends and you should, too. It's more fun and safer (some people consume a lot of alcohol at this festival). The frenzied paint-throwing activities generally start around 8 a.m. Choose a good vantage point to watch the action unfold, arm yourself with a supply of colored powder, and prepare for a vivid encounter. The wonderful chaos can last until mid-afternoon, after which things quieten down fairly rapidly.

LOCAL KNOWLEDGE: Holi also celebrates the downfall of a legendary ogress who preyed on children. In honor of this story, children are allowed to play pranks on this day.

WHAT TO WEAR: The brightly colored powder will stain, so old clothes are essential. Some of the paint is mildly toxic—protect your skin either by covering up, by applying layers of sun block, or by smearing oil on yourself before venturing into the mayhem, and wear sunglasses to keep paint from getting in your eyes. Also, although you may be tempted to take your camera with you, don't as the chances are it will get damaged. Instead, buy a disposable one for the occasion.

■ *Essentials:* General information: rajasthantourism.gov.in; Rambagh Polo Ground (Bhawani Singh Rd., Rambagh); City Palace (Kanwar Nager, Pink City); Palace of the Winds (Johari Bazar Rd., Badi Choupad, Badi Chaupar)

MORE: A Smaller Holi

To the north of Agra and east of Jaipur, the city of **Mathura** and neighboring **Vrindavan** hold a quieter, more traditional Holi. The festival, devoted to Lord Krishna, who was born in Mathura, takes place in either February or March and can go on for a week. It usually starts several days before the main festival across the rest of northern India. holifestival.org

"Holi is the simplest of all Indian festivals, and anyone can join in— rich or poor, no matter what religion." —ROHAN SINHA, JAIPUR NATIVE

Dressed and ready for the Elephant Festival. Opposite: Powder paint fills the shops at Holi.

Business proceeds at a leisurely pace at the Pushkar camel market.

PUSHKAR, INDIA
CAMEL FAIRS

Dressed in their traditional festival finery, villagers, merchants, and pilgrims from all over the Indian state of Rajasthan gather in the small town of Pushkar to barter, strike marriage deals, and meet up with relatives. It's the Kartik Purnima festival, held in the month of Kartika (late October to mid-November), when Hindu pilgrims come to bathe in the town's holy lake. Local salesman Vishwas Makhija says, "The turbans of the Rajasthani men are elegant: Elaborately wrapped and in a rainbow of brilliant colors." During the first five or six days of the ten-day celebration, up to 50,000 camels also arrive in town to be bought and sold, as well as raced.

WHEN TO GO: Arrive at the start of the festival, when the camel market is in full swing. Sellers make sure their animals look their best—shaving, grooming, and decking them out in colored halters. Buyers inspect them, checking their mouths and feet, then barter to get the best price.

WHERE TO STAY: The herders sleep on the ground alongside their charges, cooking bread and stew over open fires of dried camel dung. But there are rooms in town for those who prefer a bed.

■ *Essentials:* General information: rajasthantourism.gov.in; luxury tents: orchard.in

DIGGING DEEPER

To witness the frenzied buying and selling of more four-legged creatures, travel to the small town of Nagaur, around 35 miles (55 km) north-west of Pushkar, for the eight-day animal fair held each January or February, when some 70,000 cattle, horses, and camels are traded.

MADURAI, INDIA

TEMPLE OF TRANQUILLITY

Once a year a flower-garlanded barge floats across the vast temple tank in Madurai to the temple island in the middle. All around the tank's perimeter, huge crowds worship the goddess Meenakshi and her consort Lord Sundareswarar, whose icons sit within the barge. The festival reaches fever pitch after dark, when the barge, the temple, and even the walls surrounding the tank are lit up by every variety of light from tiny candles to LED lights, fluorescent tubes, and fireworks.

WHERE TO GO: The Vandiyur Mariamman Teppakulam in Madurai is some 1,000 feet long by 950 feet wide (300 m by 290 m). It is one of the largest tanks in India, and is supplied from the Vaigai River via underground channels.

LOCAL KNOWLEDGE: A temple tank is a large reservoir known as a *pushkarini* (literally, a tank). The rainwater collected in the tank provides the temple's—and in some arid areas, the local community's—water supply. The tank is also used for *abhishekam* (ritualistic bathing) by devout Hindus. To bathe, people descend the broad, stone steps and immerse themselves in the cool, dark water, emerging cleansed, purified, and spiritually uplifted.

JOINING IN: Before entering a temple tank, wash your legs and hands in the pool and sprinkle some water on your head. The water quality is very poor in Indian temple tanks, so don't get water in your mouth, or bathe if you have any cuts. It's unusual for women to enter the water.

WHAT TO WEAR: Men should always have some form of wrap around the waist, such as a towel that extends to the knees—swimming shorts or trunks on their own are not acceptable. Temple tanks are not used for swimming, and you shouldn't take wet clothes into the temple with you after bathing. As in all temples, you must remove your shoes and you should not wear or carry leather.

WHEN TO GO: The Float Festival takes place in January or February, when the moon is full. The tank fills up during the monsoons from September to November, but at some other times of year, even the Vaigai River dries up, and the tank is so dry that it is used to graze cattle or even by children playing cricket.

■ *Essentials:* General information: tamilnadutourism.org; Vandiyur Mariamman Teppakulam (Teppakulam W. St.)

The Float Festival at the Vandiyur Mariamman Teppakulam

MUMBAI, INDIA

AS THE SUN SETS ON JUHU BEACH

Everyone in Mumbai loves Juhu, so it isn't surprising that the beach makes a cameo appearance in the most famous novel set in the city. In Salman Rushdie's *Midnight's Children,* the protagonist boasts about the feats his childhood crush has pulled off on Juhu Beach: Winning camel races, drinking vast amounts of coconut milk, and being able to open her eyes underwater.

Though the camels have since disappeared (thanks to animal-rights' activists), and swimming isn't advisable (the water has become too polluted), the coconut vendors are still around—and thousands of Mumbai residents buy their wares every day, after they've taken a jog or been through a rigorous yoga workout on the sands early in the morning.

WHAT TO EXPECT: The coconut men draw even more customers in the evening, especially on weekends. As the sun goes down, Mumbai residents flock to the shore to fill their lungs with the salty breezes (a pleasure locals refer to as "eating the air"), chat with friends, play cricket and soccer, and devour snacks at the stalls by the parking lot. When it gets dark, vendors pull fluorescent toys out of their bags and the sky fills up with blurs of red and blue as phosphorescent helicopters are catapulted into the air. It's every bit as magical as a Rushdie novel.

WHAT TO EAT: Juhu is street food central: *Bhel puri* (a tangy mix of puffed rice, deep-fried chickpea noodles, sweet date sauce, and a hot cilantro chutney); *pav bhaji* (a spicy mash-up of vegetables accompanied by warm loaves of bread, slathered with butter); *kulfi* (thick ice cream); and *gola* (shaved ice dipped into a variety of syrups).

WHAT TO WEAR: Shorts are acceptable for both women and men, but women may be made to feel uncomfortable if they're just in swimsuits.

■ *Essentials:* General information: maharashtaratourism .gov.in; Juhu Beach (Juhu Tara Rd.)

"Juhu is Mumbai's Central Park and Coney Island rolled into one." —NARESH FERNANDES, MUMBAI-BASED WRITER

The sun sets over the Arabian Sea.

When I was a child, Juhu Beach was in a distant suburb and we visited it for weekend breaks. We played in the water, ate coal-roasted corn-on-the-cob, gulped down sugarcane juice. And then I did not go there for almost two decades until four years ago when I started taking my three-year-old daughter. Through the excited eyes of a child, I experienced the joy of Juhu all over again. Like her, I looked beyond the crowds, to the pretty shells, the horse rides, sand sculptures, and the man selling monkey-shaped balloons. With the water gently lapping the shore in the early morning, young boys enjoy games of football, the elderly take walks, and I hear my daughter's joyful squeals as the rising tide starts to fill the hole she has dug in the sand.

AMRITSAR, INDIA
SHARING THE LOVE

A Sikh prayer, "May the iron pots of the *langar* [community canteen] be forever warm," is granted every day at the Golden Temple (*Harmandir Sahib* in Punjabi, meaning Temple of God) in Amritsar, northwest India. The temple is Sikhism's holiest *gurdwara* (shrine) and a major pilgrimage destination for Sikhs from all over the world. It also feeds up to 40,000 people a day in the world's largest free kitchen, which is run by volunteers (*karsewaks*) and funded by donations. Service to the community is a key tenet of the Sikh faith so the kitchen buzzes with helpers chopping, frying, rolling dough, and stirring cauldrons with wooden spoons as tall as a man. Later on, the volunteers wash dirty plates in long troughs, stack up dishes for the next sitting, and scrub the floors.

WHAT TO EXPECT: In the dining hall, pilgrims sit on the floor in long quiet rows. In this most sacred place everyone is equal regardless of age, sex, caste, country, or creed, and you could be sitting next to royalty on one side and a beggar on the other. Even the 16th-century Mughal emperor Akbar the Great pushed aside the silk rugs awaiting him and sat on the floor like everyone else. Says Neha Pande, a Sikh and regular visitor, "Each person accepts *chapatis* [flat bread] with their own hands as a sign of respect towards the karsewaks, rather than having the chapatis served onto plates." The meals are freshly cooked and generous, filling the air with the smell of garlic and spice. Pande adds, "A langar promotes the idea of oneness, harmony, sharing, and shunning all barriers of inequality. And the meal—it's simply delicious."

FITTING IN: Take a plate, cup, and cutlery and find a place to sit. Dress decently, cover your head, and remove footwear. Food is free, volunteering and donations are optional.

■ *Essentials:* Golden Temple (Golden Temple Rd., Amritsar, tel 91 (0) 183 255 3951, sridarbarsahib.com)

The Holy Book

Each evening at around 10 p.m., in a ceremony known as **Palki Sahib,** a procession escorts the Guru Granth Sahib, Sikhism's most sacred text, from the Golden Temple to the building where it is kept overnight.

An army of
volunteers prepares
the daily meal.

Silencing the world with an Iyengar yoga session

PUNE, INDIA

IN THE HEART OF YOGA

Pune, in India's Maharashtra state, is home to the Ramamani Iyengar Memorial Yoga Institute (R.I.M.Y.I.), founded in 1975 by internationally renowned yoga teacher B.K.S. Iyengar. With its emphasis on accessibility, Iyengar yoga uses blocks, belts, and other props to enable practitioners to achieve perfect alignment without physical strain as they do the asanas (yoga poses).

WHAT TO EXPECT: Bobby Clennell, author of many books on yoga and a frequent visitor to Puna, describes the center as "an oasis of calm amid one of the world's fastest growing cities. The institute speaks about yoga as eloquently as the Iyengar family members who teach there." The three floors represent body, mind, and soul, while the eight supporting pillars symbolize the eight limbs of yoga. A small Hanuman temple sits atop the building. Although this is the mother ship of Iyengar yoga worldwide, R.I.M.Y.I. is very much part of the surrounding community. Locals work here as well as attending classes alongside an international crowd.

JOINING IN: Yoga master B.K.S. Iyengar, now well into his nineties, his daughter Geeta, son Prashant, and a committed team of local yoga instructors run classes throughout the day. You can attend the general sessions but must be an experienced practitioner and book well in advance.

■ *Essentials:* R.I.Y.M.I. (1107 B/1, Hare Krishna Mandir Rd., Model Colony, tel 91 (0) 20 2565 6134, bksiyengar.com)

"The body is my temple; asanas are my prayers." — B.K.S. IYENGAR

MALDIVES

HOT SAND, WARM WATERS: TOTAL RELAXATION

Almost every culture has its own wellness rituals, and in the Maldives archipelago, local masseurs practice one of the simplest and most effective therapies—traditional sand massage. Although it's sometimes performed indoors, the most suitable, and indulgent, place to try it is on a beach, lying with your body half in and half out of the water, warm surf breaking over your legs as a skilled masseur kneads your muscles with a blend of cool sand and seawater.

WHEN TO GO: The time of day is key. Almost on the equator, the double chain of coral atolls that make up the Indian Ocean nation of the Maldives are sweltering hot at midday. Thus, sand massage is best in the cool of the early morning or late afternoon, with the coconut palms casting long shadows over the beach and a gentle breeze blowing in from Africa or India. Later the evening the water can be rough, so sand massage is not done after 6 p.m. The experience begins with a gentle, relaxing coconut oil massage.

Some therapists blend the coconut oil with indigenous ingredients such as crushed gandhakolhi leaves, used by islanders to cure minor aches. Then comes the sand. Pannia Chalvam, a spa manager says, "There are many different kinds of sand—for this therapy, we use very fine, soft sand."

WHERE TO GO: The Maldives is a conservative Muslim country and body contact in public is frowned upon more often than not. Unless you know a Maldivian family or a local professional masseur, it's difficult for visitors to enjoy a sand massage outside the confines of a resort hotel. Sand massage is a spa specialty at several hotels, including Madoogali on North Ari Atoll and Paradise Island Resort & Spa on North Male' Atoll.

■ *Essentials:* Madoogali (North Ari Atoll, tel 960 (0) 666 0581, madoogalimaldives.com); Paradise Island Resort & Spa (Lankanfinolhu, North Male' Atoll, tel 960 (0) 664 0011, villahotels.com)

The beach on Kunfunadhoo Island is the perfect place for a sand massage.

ELEPHANTS ON PARADE

As the summer full moon draws near, families from the surrounding villages throng the streets for the nighttime parades in honor of the Buddha's Tooth. This sacred relic is kept in the Temple of the Sacred Tooth (Sri Dalida Maligawa), Kandy's main temple. Kandy, the ancient royal capital of Sri Lanka, sees crowds 20-deep lining the streets each night.

WHEN TO GO: The festival runs for ten days in late July–early August with ever-larger torchlight parades each evening. On the final night, whip crackers and fire jugglers clear the way for hundreds of drummers, singers, dancers, flag bearers, and dozens of richly caparisoned elephants festooned with twinkling fairy lights.

JOINING IN: It's total immersion: Drumming so loud you can feel it through the soles of your feet, lights and colors so bright they are seared on your eyeballs. Arrive early in the day to get a good view. At the end of the two-hour parade, the excitement rises. Toddlers climb on their fathers' shoulders, the old and the frail are ushered to the front, others peep through the smallest gaps, then all fall silent as the sacred Maligawa elephant comes into view, tiptoeing, it seems, on the pristine white cloth unrolled in front of him. All eyes are on the casket carried on his back, symbolizing the Sacred Tooth that protects the country.

■ *Essentials:* General information: srilankatourism.org

An elephant draped in fairy lights leads a spectacular torchlight procession.

Locals stock up on marigolds for Diwali decorations.

KATHMANDU, NEPAL
FESTIVAL OF LIGHTS

Oil lamps, flickering candles, marigold garlands, and mandalas (graphic representations of the universe) brighten Kathmandu's sidewalks and doorsteps during Diwali, the Hindu festival of light, which celebrates the triumph of good over evil. In every corner of the valley, people pray for new beginnings as they invite Lakshmi, the goddess of wealth, to visit and bring material and spiritual blessings. Candles light doors and windows, while trails of marigold leaves lead from the mandalas into buildings to show the goddess the way.

WHEN TO GO: The five-day festival begins at an auspicious time in mid-fall, according to the Hindu calendar, with feeding the crows. On day two, people drape their dogs in marigold garlands, and on day three they garland the sacred cows. On day four, everyone decorates the thresholds of their houses with candles and mandalas. The lights are at their best that night to welcome Lakshmi, and bells tinkle and drums echo in every temple and shrine. Firecrackers and parades fill the streets. Finally comes Brothers and Sisters Day, when siblings exchange gifts and families and neighbors share a traditional feast.

JOINING IN: Everyone is welcome to join in, and if a friend or guide invites you into their home, don't hesitate to accept. On the fourth day, children go from door to door singing. It is traditional to give them money in return, so have small change ready.

■ *Essentials:* General information: tourismkathmandu.com

"Family is all-important in Nepal and Diwali is the perfect time to get together with my brothers and my sister, and their children. There's dancing, gambling—and lots of drinking."
—MEGH THAPA, FORMER GURKHA ARMY OFFICER

KATHMANDU, NEPAL
WALKING MEDITATION

On the eastern outskirts of Kathmandu lies the suburb of Boudha, home to the largest stupa in Nepal. The Bodhnath Stupa is a sacred hemispherical structure 118 feet (36 m) tall which followers believe holds relics of the Buddha. Below the prayer-flag-festooned spire, the eyes of the Buddha, painted on the four sides of the golden tower, look in all directions.

Every evening as dusk falls, locals emerge from the surrounding alleyways to perform the daily *kora* ritual at the white-domed stupa, now lit by the setting sun. Both a spiritual and social occasion, the kora is a walking meditation that brings people together to meet and chat at the end of the day, while also earning merits for the afterlife.

WHAT TO EXPECT: Women with babies on their backs, old folk leaning on bamboo staffs, young men with mobile phones and prayer beads, monks with alms bowls, families, and friends—all walk around the stupa seven times in a clockwise direction. Devotees turn the prayer wheels set into the wall as they walk. Chanting, gongs, and bells can be heard, along with the occasional clapping of wooden blocks as the most devout prostrate themselves along the way. Most worshippers are Tibetan refugees and their descendants, but everyone is welcome.

JOINING IN: Simply fall in step with the people walking around the temple and complete the full cycle of seven circumambulations. Be sure to walk in a clockwise direction and to complete an odd number of circuits. All around you, shopkeepers watch from their doorsteps while boys sell grain to feed the pigeons—an act of kindness. If you get tired, take a seat on one of the nearby benches.

■ *Essentials:* General information: tourismkathmandu.com; Bodhnath Stupa (Boudha Rd., Boudha)

Monkey Temple

The temple of **Swayambunath,** just west of Kathmandu, perches on a hilltop with breathtaking views of the valley below. To get there, climb the 365 steps to the top where Buddhist and Hindu pilgrims pray around a towering stupa. Chiming bells, chanting monks, and sacred monkeys vie for your attention around myriad shrines. simriknepal.treks.com

Child monks circling
the Bodhnath Stupa
at dusk

TEXTILE HEAVEN

Peek into courtyards in this Bhutanese city and you'll see women weaving in quiet meditation, usually using backstrap looms. In these small workshops or even on doorsteps, women use cotton, silk, hemp or nettle fiber, and wool dyed in vibrant colors to make lengths of patterned fabric. These pieces of cloth are used to form the national dress: The *gho*—a knee-length robe tied at the waist—for men; the *kira*—a rectangle of fabric wrapped and folded around the body to form an ankle-length dress, belted at the waist—for women. Both sexes wear them with ceremonial scarves on important occasions.

WHERE TO SHOP: When it's time to buy special new clothes, everyone heads for Norzin Lam, Thimphu's broad, tree-lined main street, and the adjoining Clocktower Square. Popular outlets include Norbooz Buray and Thridung Nima. The Kelzang Handicrafts Center stocks ready-made ghos and kiras. Bhutan's Seal of Excellence and Seal of Quality schemes determine the quality and authenticity of handwoven textiles, and bargaining will prove difficult.

JOINING IN: "People pick simple plaid patterns for daily use and intricate (*kushuthara*) types for special occasions," notes Pema Chhoden Wangchuk, a curator at the Royal Textile Academy. Her colleague, Karma Deki Tshering adds, "The tighter the weave, the better the quality, although people sometimes prefer a looser weave as it is more flexible and therefore more comfortable." Whatever you choose, you'll be sporting a work of art and skills that have been handed down from one generation to the next.

■ *Essentials:* General information: royaltextileacademy.org, tourism.gov.bt; Norbooz Buray and Textiles (Karma Khangzang Building, 2nd Fl., Norzin Lam, tel 975 (0) 1723 5332); Thridung Nima Namza (Shop No. 6, Thimphu Main Bazar, Norzin Lam, tel 975 (0) 1763 4627, thridungnimanamza.com); Kelzang Handicrafts (Clocktower Sq., Norzin Lam, tel 975 (0) 2 321353)

DIGGING DEEPER

For festive occasions, women wear a *kushuthara*, a highly colored silk fabric worn as a kira. For healing ceremonies, women may be told to wear the color of their astrological element: Green for wood, red for fire, yellow for earth, white for metal, and blue for water.

This page: Young men
wearing ghos at festival time.
Opposite: Weavers at
work in Thimphu

Farmhouses clustered in the fertile Paro valley

PARO VALLEY, BHUTAN
AT HOME IN THE HILLS

You wake to the call of a cockerel, the sound of cattle stirring in the stables, and someone softly tiptoeing into the Buddha's room to pour fresh water into the ritual bowls: A day in a Bhutanese farmhouse begins gently.

WHAT TO EXPECT: In west Bhutan's Paro valley, home to some of the kingdom's oldest temples and monasteries, old farmhouses are scattered among paddies and apple trees, and host families welcome guests who stay with them to sample rural life. With arched windows, carved eaves and frames, and notched logs climbing to the upper floors, the farmhouses reflect a centuries-old design tradition. Inside, bright rugs, cushions, and blankets add warmth and color.

LOCAL TRADITION: In the Paro Valley, there's more to taking a bath than just turning a faucet. A wooden tub is filled with cold water while large smooth stones from the river are heated on an open fire. Then in come the stones,

dropped one by one into the water at the foot end. Sizzling steam rises all around as you sink into the bath, blissfully relaxed as the mineral goodness softens your skin. Enjoy, but don't soak for too long, as the family may be waiting their turn. Nothing, not even hot water, is wasted.

JOINING IN: After guests have spent a day exploring, the family welcomes them into the fold with a delicious farmhouse feast. To accompany the meal, the father of the household might play the Bhutanese lute, an instrument with seven strings and a dragon's head. Outside, Buddhist prayer flags flutter in the breeze, prayer wheels tinkle along the stream, and thousands of stars light up the evening sky.

■ *Essentials:* Paro Valley farmhouses: tel 975 (0) 8 271941, bhutantourpackage.com. No independent travel is allowed in Bhutan. Find a registered tour operator at tourism.gov.bt.

CHOKHOR VALLEY, BHUTAN
BLESSED BY FIRE

People in the Chokhor valley in central Bhutan come to the second day of the Thangbi Mani festival with high hopes of a lucky year ahead. They aim to cleanse their souls and ensure an auspicious year to come through the *Mewang*, or fire-blessing ceremony. This annual festival is held at the small, 15th-century Buddhist monastery in the hamlet of Thangbi.

WHAT TO EXPECT: At first light, villagers from Thangbi and the nearby hamlets of Goling and Kharsath, dressed in their best, head for the monastery. In the courtyard, incense fills the air and chanting accompanies costumed dancers shuffling and twirling on the uneven flagstones. Next, the crowd moves to the open ground beyond the monastery gate, where everyone gathers around two tall piles of buckwheat stalks.

The reverberating sounds of horns, cymbals, and drums are said to dispel evil spirits as red-robed *gomchen* (lay priests) conduct purification rituals and light the fires. Ash and smoke fill the air, flames shoot toward the sky, and the crowds rush forward—mothers, children, young men trying to protect their hair, friends grabbing each other's hands. If you run through the fire three times your sins are forgiven, and luck, in the form of a year of good harvests and healthy children, will come to the community.

When the flames die down, the crowd heads back to the monastery to watch masked performers act out ancient tales of the triumph of good over evil. Monks hand out *chapatis* that promise good luck and jesters entertain everyone by mimicking the dancers.

WHEN TO GO: The festival is held in early fall, the exact date depending on the Bhutanese calendar.

■ *Essentials:* No independent travel is allowed in Bhutan. Find a registered tour operator at tourism.gov.bt.

A monk performs purification rituals around the fires.

SILK ROAD BAZAAR

Every Sunday, jostling crowds of villagers throng the dusty streets of Kashgar, a Silk Road throwback in western China, for the Sunday Market (Yekshanba Bazaar in the local Uighur language, Xingitian Shichang in Chinese). Despite its name, the Sunday Market is open every day, but it is busiest on Sundays, when the Uighur people travel into town from miles around to sell or trade their wares and produce. They arrive before dawn.

WHAT TO EXPECT: The pungent aromas from huge sacks of cumin and saffron in the spice market, the mounds of luscious-looking green melons, and the piles of handwoven rugs and fabrics in bright reds and blues launch a full-blooded assault on the senses. It's easy to feel overwhelmed by the seemingly endless rows of stalls and the sheer quantity of goods on sale. The rule of thumb, as ever, is that the superior stalls—particularly those selling food—tend to attract more business, so follow the crowds. If you're male and in need of a haircut, you can go to the barbers' section and join the line of customers having their heads shaved with cut-throat razors.

WHAT TO BUY: Leatherware and jewelry are good value, and there is an amazing assortment of headgear—from embroidered skullcaps to warm sheepskin hats. Dried fruit and nuts are inexpensive and good quality. Bargaining is expected. You can also get a decent, probably meaty, meal for around US$1 in one of the hundreds of stalls in the market's food section.

■ *Essentials:* Sunday Market (Aizirete Lu near the East Gate, across the Tuman River, chinatravelguide.com); Livestock Market (Mal Bazaar/Dongwu Shichang)

DIGGING DEEPER

There is a livestock market in the western suburbs, about 20 minutes from the Sunday Market by cab. It is a great place to see the locals in serious sheep-trading negotiations, but keep out of the way of people test-driving donkeys and carts.

Fabric stalls do a
constant trade.
Opposite: The donkey
section of the
livestock market

Dim sum combines
elegance and flavor.

HONG KONG, CHINA
DIM SUMTUOUS

In Cantonese, *yum cha* is to drink tea, but it means to eat *dim sum* as well. And in Hong Kong absolutely everyone does it—breakfast time, lunchtime, and tea time. Dim sum are mostly bite-size snacks from south China that typically come as little parcels in bamboo steamers. They once arrived at your table in wobbling towers on the backs of hissing carts, but now these little explosions of flavor are more commonly made to order.

HOW TO ORDER: The classics are *hargow*, minced shrimp steamed in a pleated translucent wrapper, and *siumai*, dumplings made of ground pork, shrimp, and mushroom seasoned with ginger and rice wine. But dim sum is constantly evolving: The neon-yellow egg tarts come from Portugal; the beef balls with ginger need

Worcestershire sauce; the dumplings filled with piping hot soup are from Shanghai.

WHERE TO GO: For traditional Hong Kong ambience, visit Luk Yu Tea House, all ceiling fans and dark wood booths. "It can be hard to get in, but it's worth it," advises printer Stephen Wong. For the bustle of the old dim sum carts, go to the branch of Maxim's at City Hall. "There's a Maxim's in every district of Hong Kong," says Wong. "Everyone goes there. The one at City Hall is not too big, and the quality is reliable."

■ *Essentials:* Luk Yu Tea House (24 Stanley St., Central, tel 852 2523 5464); Maxim's Palace (2F, City Hall Low Block, Central, tel 852 2521 1303)

DIGGING DEEPER

The small and immensely popular backstreet Tim Ho Wan (2–20 Kwong Wah St., Mongkok, tel 852 2332 2896), with an ex-Four Seasons chef, is the world's cheapest Michelin-starred restaurant. Try the barbecued pork buns—succulent meat in a crispy pineapple bun shell.

HAPPY VALLEY RACECOURSE

More than US$10 billion is wagered at Happy Valley each year. Dating from 1846, it is one of Asia's oldest and most prestigious horseracing venues and its Jockey Club is a focus of society life. But racing in Hong Kong is popular with everyone. "Make sure you are ready to fight with local taxi drivers for the best places on the terraces," says student John Bremridge. "They mark out their spots with newspapers."

WHEN TO GO: The season runs from September to July during Hong Kong's cooler months, with meetings on Wednesday nights. Gates open at 5 p.m. with the first of 12 races at 7 p.m. The last race is around 11 p.m.

JOINING IN: Happy Valley offers the option of slumming it or going high society. General admission (HK$10) gains entry to the public enclosure and its huge betting hall, as well as egalitarian outlets such as the Beer Garden with its beer tents and barbecue stalls. Anyone with a foreign passport can purchase a tourist badge (HK$100) for the Jockey Club with its vertigo-inducing seating areas and upscale eating places. Smart casual is de rigueur at the Jockey Club, but flip-flops and shorts are fine elsewhere.

MORE: Racing Suppers

Moon Koon Watch the action and place your bets while eating really good Cantonese food—claypot dishes (*boh*) and seafood recommended—at this elegant restaurant in the Jockey Club. Tel 852 2966 7111

Stable Bend This informal open-air barbecue restaurant with buffet curves around the bend leading to the home straight. Tel 852 3690 3690

LOCAL KNOWLEDGE: "Some of the betting combinations are unfathomable, but the minimum bet is HK$10 (roughly US$1.30)," says Bembridge. "Be sure to keep back enough money for the tram ride home."

■ *Essentials:* Happy Valley Racecourse (2 Sports Rd., Happy Valley, Hong Kong Island; tel 852 2895 1523 or 2508 1817, happyvalleyracecourse.com)

Taking a bend at the Happy Valley Racecourse

798 ART DISTRICT

Beijing's Da Shanzi 798 Art District began life as a secretive warren of 1950s industrial buildings erected with East German help. In 2002 it became a refuge for artists, who sold work directly from their studios to an eager public with new-found disposable income. As the area took off, galleries opened.

WHAT TO EXPECT: There are dozens of galleries, including branches of big global names. Much of what's displayed courts instant appeal and treats the entire Western canon as an image bank. The heroism of 20th-century Communist propaganda is applied to logos of Western commerce, while mildly coded hints of political rebellion are also popular. The Terra-cotta Warriors or Mao Zedong are depicted in the style of Warhol or Mondrian.

It is thoroughly entertaining and highly photogenic. Crowds of DSLR-toting locals eye each other's cameras and pose in front of life-size dinosaurs, psychedelic dragons in Mao suits, and giant figures of glossy nakedness.

WHERE TO GO: Among the serious galleries, Bauhaus-style 798 Space is the most famous. Its vast roof lights illuminate both the art and the fading Mao-era political slogans on its walls. Neighboring galleries include Belgian-owned multi-venue Ullens Centre, Japanese-owned

Beijing Buzz

The Art District is a magnet for hip young Beijingers, who granted might be more interested in *renao* (buzzing) destinations full of color and amusement than in buying art. Fashion outlets, trendy giftshops, vast art bookshops, performance art, and cool cafés draw these young Chinese consumers.

Beijing Tokyo Art Projects, and the Beijing branch of New York's Pace Gallery. Do as the wealthy Chinese clients do and buy expensive work only from the major galleries; otherwise, "unique" works are often reproduced, "limited" series are often unlimited, and the artist's involvement may only be his signature. Cheaper prints, photographs, and arty gifts are legion.

■ *Essentials:* Da Shanzi Art District (off the Airport Expressway northeast of the city center, tel 86 (0) 10 5978 9798, 798.org, some galleries closed Mon.)

Strolling the 798 Space. Opposite: 798 exhibit

BEIJING, CHINA
TAI CHI IN THE PARK

In Zhongshan Park, just west of Beijing's Tian'anmen Gate, groups of *taijiquan* ("tai chi") practitioners move with slow-motion fluidity. These are the *laobaixing*, or "old hundred names" as ordinary Chinese call themselves.

The park is full of such Beijingers taking exercise, dancing, and simply enjoying themselves, their different sound systems often competing with each other. You'll see groups performing *yangge* folk dancing—its gentle, repetitive movements requiring less finesse than tai chi—and disco-exercisers following the moves of their instructors. In another part of the park serene couples practice their ballroom dancing.

SPECIAL ATTRACTIONS: Solo musicians play on instruments such as the *erhu*, a two-stringed bowed lute; sword enthusiasts perform routines with floppy blades; and groups of singers perform the revolutionary anthems of their childhoods, otherwise rarely heard now. Sometimes they'll lapse into Viennese opera, or "Beautiful Dreamer," sung to the accompaniment of a piano accordion.

JOINING IN: The best time to go is pre-beakfast; practitioners begin gathering at dawn. If you fancy trying some tai chi moves, add yourself to the edge of the group and copy your neighbors. Afterward, take a place under the trees and soak up the passing scene. "The park is a great place to hide from the crowds on Tian'anmen Square," says journalist Li Yuhua.

LOCAL KNOWLEDGE: On Sundays the park becomes home to a matchmaking service. Parents converge bearing photo albums and papers describing offspring too busy to find a partner for themselves.

■ *Essentials:* Zhongshan Park (W. Chang'an Ave., Dongcheng, zhongshan-park.cn)

Popping Up Tulips

Each spring, a **tulip festival** is held in Zhongshan Park. Rare Queen of the Night black tulips and delicately fringed Crystal Beauties blossom alongside more than a hundred other species. The flowers are carefully planted in blocks of color and attract legions of visitors when they bloom in their thousands between April and May.

Taijiquan is a walk in the park for regulars.

I ♥ My City

Li Yuhua
Editor, NG Traveler, China

Ilive in Tongzhou District, east of Beijing's CBD area, and I often go to the Yunhe Cultural Square Park with my daughter. It's on the Grand Canal from Beijing to Hangzhou—the longest ancient canal in the world. Everyone knows about the Great Wall, but this canal is seldom mentioned. It dates from 486 B.C. and is 1,250 miles (2,000 km) long. There are many activities going on in the park. My favorite is flying a kite. On weekends, you'll see hundreds of kites here. There is a playground with a merry-go-round and climbing wall. The elderly sing Beijing operas, dance, play cards or chess. I like the joyful atmosphere. Sometimes I have tea at the Moon River Resort five minutes' walk away. We sit by the pond, watching the swans and ducks.

Enter the New Year dragon, Macau

CHINESE NEW YEAR

Fifteen days of festivities bring parades, good luck customs, and tasty treats.

■ Dragon Dance, Macau, China

All 12 animals of the Chinese zodiac step out for the New Year parade in Macau, but the dragon has pride of place. The longer the dragon, the more luck it brings, and this spectacular beast is 820 feet (250 m) long. The dragon dances from Senado Square, accompanied by floats, bands, and fireworks.
en.macautourism.gov.mo

■ Chinese New Year, Kuala Lumpur, Malaysia

Around 40 percent of the population of the Malaysian capital is Chinese, so it's no surprise that New Year here is especially vibrant. People rush to buy new clothes beforehand, and Kuala Lumpur's malls become a part of the festive scene.
kuala-lumpur.ws/festivals

■ Chingay Parade, Singapore

Known as the Mardi Gras of the East, Singapore's Chinese New Year, or Welcoming of Spring, is a parade of dragon dancers, acrobats, and floats. It takes place in front of the Formula One Pit Building on the waterfront.
yoursingapore.com

■ Imlek, Jakarta, Indonesia

In this more somber celebration of the Chinese New Year—called Imlek in Indonesia—Buddhists converge on Vihara Dharma Bhakti, the oldest of the Chinese temples in Jakarta. Beggars come for alms, and the temple, thick with incense, swells with worshippers. Birds are released from cages for good fortune.
jakarta-tourism.go.id

■ Lion Dance, Kolkata, India

For three days in Kolkata's Tangra area, India's only Chinatown, lions, dragons, and Muppet-like monsters, accompanied by drums and firecrackers, tour the streets, going in and out of houses to bring good luck.
ctlion.webs.com

■ Lunar New Year Parade, Chicago, IL

An explosion of fireworks kicks off a procession of floats, marching bands, and a 100-foot (30 m) dragon in Chicago's Chinatown. Shops, restaurants, and community groups all take part in the festivities, and there are activities around the Chinese American Cultural Museum on 238 West 23rd Street.
ccamuseum.org

■ Chinese New Year, Toronto, Canada

Food features strongly here. All kinds of dishes and sweets—filled with meaning and portents—are on sale. In downtown Toronto, action focuses on Spadina Avenue and Dundas Street West. The Harbourfront Centre holds family activities, while concerts and other events take place at the Confucius Institute and Chinese Cultural Centre.
cccgt.org

■ Dotting the Eye Ceremony, London, U.K.

London's Chinatown and Trafalgar Square fill with music, lions, dragons, and acrobats. In the Dotting the Eye (Hoi Gong) ceremony, the mayor awakens the festive lions by painting their eyes, bringing good fortune.
chinatownlondon.org

TAIPEI, TAIWAN
SHOP INTO THE NIGHT

Markets form a big part of Taiwanese nightlife, and Taipei's great Shilin Night Market—vast, bustling with students and families, and open from late afternoon until the early hours—is the best one of them all. It centers on Wenlin Road, Dadong Road, and Danan Road in the Shilin district.

WHAT TO BUY: Stalls and shops sell anything you ever wanted—clothes, underwear, power tools, watches, bags and shoes, tables and chairs, used books, toys, pets, and more, each in their own area and all at low prices. With so many lanes and alleys, a map isn't much help, so ask people to point you in the right direction. Stop off to try your luck at karaoke or to enjoy a foot massage; or wait with locals to have your future tapped out with chopsticks in the fortune-tellers' alley. At the heart of the market, shoppers stop off to pray at the little Cicheng temple with its rows of red lanterns and carved stone dragons.

WHAT TO EAT: Shopping over, everyone heads over to the food court. The fried chicken slice—exactly that: an enormous piece of deep-fried chicken held in the hands—is as good as it looks. You'll also find dumplings, sausages, candied strawberries, and, most popular of all, oyster omelettes, tossed ten at a time in gigantic pans.

■ *Essentials:* Shilin Night Market (101 Jīhé Rd., tel 886 (0) 2 2882 0340, taipeitravel.net)

The market carries on long after midnight.

"I'm never too tired to visit the night market. It has everything I need for daily life." —LILY CHUANG, TAIPEI RESIDENT

DASHU, TAIWAN
MEDITATING WITH THE MONKS

Gilded Buddhas, pagodas, and shrines nestle among pines and swaying bamboo, and moon gates and auspicious bridges appear at every turn. Goldfish swim in lily-covered pools, cherub statues hide in flowering shrubs, and a lotus pond mirrors the Goddess of Mercy.

Fo Guang Shan Monastery lies on a hill overlooking the Kaoping River in Dashu. Combining worship, education, and charitable work, its socially engaged brand of Buddhism attracts young Taiwanese who want to develop their understanding of the religion. Often prosperous and middle class, they attend classes in Buddhist thought and meditation, come on short retreats, or learn calligraphy.

WHAT TO EXPECT: Monks head for the library or the calligraphy hall, nuns in conical hats whisper in the shade. Quiet as it seems, however, this is a busy place where everyone has a job to do: cleaning, teaching, gardening, cooking, showing visitors and pilgrims around. The complex is so vast that golf buggies are on hand to explore some of the many highlights, from the Mountain Gate (the main entrance) to the Great Wisdom Shrine or the Pilgrims' Path.

STAYING OVERNIGHT: When the scores of day visitors have left, stillness returns to the monastery. Nothing disturbs the peace but the evening chorus of frogs and birds. On the hilltop, the 118-foot-high (36 m) Buddha statue turns coppery gold in the setting sun and garlands

of fairy lights twinkle along the monastery roofs. There is time to study and meditate or reflect on the impermanence of life on Earth.

Overnight visitors stay in two large modern guesthouses—Pilgrims and Bamboo Garden. The modest rooms, with names such as Bliss or Compassion, have air-conditioning, bottled water, and tea-making facilities.

A wooden clapper sounds all over the compound at 10 p.m. to signal lights out to the monks and nuns—the monastery authorities hope that guests will follow suit.

JOINING IN: You can join in the monastery's activities, such as morning chanting (though this entails an early rise), meditation, and calligraphy lessons. Guests have dinner in their own restaurant but can request breakfast in the monks' dining room, sharing the same food and eating, as they do, in silence. Following Buddhist principles, all meals are vegetarian. The food is considered to be the best on the island by many Taiwanese. Try the lucky noodle soup or the hot pot—a bowl of fragrant broth brought to the table on a burner along with a dish of raw vegetables that you can cook yourself.

■ *Essentials:* Fo Guang Shan Monastery (No. 153 Xingtian Rd., Dashu District, tel 886 (0) 7 656 1921, fgs.org.tw)

Buddhist Eats

Called **Water Drop** like all the other restaurants in Fo Guang Shan ("one drop of kindness will be paid back in ripples"), the light and airy Buddha Memorial Center teahouse offers much more than tea. All food is cooked by the monks: After the complimentary bowl of soup, try noodles with tofu, mushroom, and spinach. Payment is by donation. fgs.org.tw

DIGGING DEEPER

In Buddhism, the practice of calligraphy is thought to have a meditative purpose, helping to purify the mind and develop character. The value is not in the end result but in the journey there.

A resident reads a sacred text. Opposite: The monastery's main shrine

FAST FASHION

Seoul may be the most technologically savvy city on the planet, but there is much more besides electronic gadgetry to buy in its vast malls and street markets. Shopping for Seoul's fashion-concious citizens is not just a favorite pastime but a way of life, fueled by abundant choice and great prices.

WHERE TO GO: Citizens of all ages converge on the vast spread of malls, stores, and street stalls that is Dongdaemun market—a repository of five shopping districts over ten blocks comprising 26 shopping centers, 30,000 specialty shops, and 50,000 manufacturers purveying every consumer item known to man; it's best for clothing (the work of young designers as well as factory-produced) and fabrics. The shops are generally open 10:30 a.m. to 5 p.m.; the crowds are intense, especially on Saturday afternoons and in the evening. Jeil Pyeonghwa mall is the best for clothes, shoes, and accessories, while the Doota mall showcases cutting-edge fashions. "Doota has the best shopping in town," says fashion student Yumi Oh. "Young, trendy locals head to its lower ground floor. I love Be—simple lines and an elegant muted color scheme at a good price."

MORE: Seoul Markets

Gyeongdong Medicine Market: Stock up on medicinal ingredients—herbs, roots, bark, and even millipedes. A whole arcade of stalls sell fresh ginseng. visitseoul.net
Janganpyeong Antiques Market: Close to the Dapsimni subway station, this is the perfect place to root about for unusual old pots, paintings, and brassware. visitseoul.net

For a change of pace, go to the Insadong district just north of downtown. Dotted among traditional houses and teahouses (*jeontong chatjip*) you'll find dozens of litte shops selling classic arts and crafts; cards, wrapping paper, and dolls made of high-quality *hanji* paper are particularly good buys.

■ *Essentials:* Dongdaemun (Euljiro 6, Jung-gu, tel 82 (0) 2 20, dongdaemun.com, closed Mon.)

Dongdaemun is famous for silks, displayed in a dazzling array of colors and patterns.

Snow, water, and steam create the perfect bath.

TSURUNOYU, JAPAN
ONSEN THERAPY

Japan's hot-spring resorts, or *onsen*, are where modern Japanese go to rediscover their traditional culture. They have a special word for the more tucked away and ancient resorts: *hito*, or hidden, hot springs.

WHAT TO EXPECT: At onsen you get into a bath that's too hot, stay in it too long, and then go walking about outside too soon, or so your mother might say. Onsen bathing is traditionally done naked and continues year-round, even in outdoor baths called *rotenburo*. "The water has different colors—red, yellow, and milky—depending on what minerals are there," says language teacher Hiromi Stewart.

WHERE TO GO: Tazawa-ko's Tsurunoyu resort in the north of Japan is as hito as they come. In winter, the walk in a thin *yukata* cotton gown from the traditional rooms to the nearly 400-year-old bamboo-screened rotenburo is grueling. But you are rewarded with complete relaxation in the embrace of creamy water. All is sensation: Water on

skin, pebbly bottom on soles of feet, the pop of bubbles rising from the sulphurous water, and birdsong. Says patent attorney Philip Yoshihito Fujii: "Afterward, I like to cool down on a tatami mat, looking at the moon and enjoying a cool breeze, while waiting for a traditional dinner of sashimi, wild vegetables, and freshwater fish."

JOINING IN: An all-over soaping and rinsing is compulsory before entering the bath. You can protect your modesty with a towel, but this must be abandoned at the water's edge—no bathing suits here. Many baths have separate entrances for men and women and a dividing screen across the water, but some are mixed. For a less exposed experience, enquire about *kashikiri*—private baths.

■ *Essentials:* Tsurunoyu Onsen (Tazawako Sendatsuzawa Kokuyurin 50, Akita, tel 81 (0) 187-46-2139, www.tsurunoyu .com)

SAPPORO, JAPAN
FROZEN FUN

Of all the world's snow festivals, the one in Sapporo, on Hokkaido Island, has the biggest piles of snow to play with. Giant snow castles, ice creatures, and other winter delights transform the city into a magical kingdom. The Yuki Matsuri, as citizens call their festival, celebrates everything about winter—snow, ice, winter sports, breath-catchingly cold air, and warming drinks.

WHERE TO GO: The main venue is Odori Park, an open space stretching for a mile (1.5 km) in downtown Sapporo, but the festival spreads across two additional sites: The nearby Susukino district holds an Ice Festival; the Tsu Dome, about 6 miles (10 km) from downtown Sapporo, has ice slides, snow-rafting, and a playground. "At night," says navy wife Beth Storz, "the sculptures are lit up and some of them have amazing light shows projected onto them."

WHAT TO WEAR: You should dress warmly, in layers, as temperatures can drop below 14°F (–10°C). Down is the insulator of choice. The streets are icy and anti-slip shoe crampons are helpful. A covered walkway provides warm access to an underground world where winter cold doesn't dampen the locals' passion for fashion shopping.

JOINING IN: Take a tip from the locals and visit Odori Park in the first day or two of the festival, while the sculptures are still clean and gleaming white. The park also hosts an ice rink and a "big air" snowboarding contest. Susukino is less crowded and everyone gravitates there at night, when the area really comes to life. Try one of the area's clubs or just admire the illuminated ice sculptures while warming up with a hot sake.

WHEN TO GO: Given how much snow falls on Hokkaido island, they have a surprisingly short winter. The Sapporo Snow Festival runs over one week in early February. The snow sculptures are only available to view during the week of the festival itself.

FARTHER AFIELD: The Sapporo Snow Festival is the tip of the iceberg of regional snow festivals; almost every town in Hokkaido celebrates the massive snowfalls in its own unique way. The nearby Otaru Snow Gleaming Path and the Sounchyo Ice Waterfall festivals are worthy destinations with their own particular charms.

■ *Essentials:* snowfes.com; Susukino (Ekimae-dori); Tsu Dome (885-1 Sakaemachi, Higashi-ku)

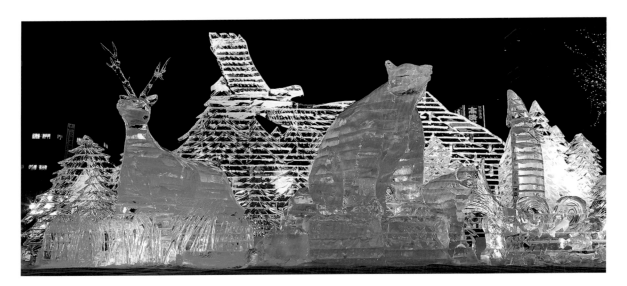

"Warm up with a steaming bowl of Sapporo's signature dish—ramen noodles. Sooo oishi (delicious)!" —Beth Storz, Navy wife stationed in Japan

Snow sculptures fill
Odori Park. Opposite:
Giant ice animals in
Susukino look especially
impressive at night.

Overgrown deities watch over you on your journey.

KUNISAKI PENINSULA, JAPAN
PEAK-TO-PEAK PILGRIMAGE

High on the spiny ridge of the Kunisaki Peninsula on the island of Kyushu hikers down from Tokyo greet white-robed monks. While the city folk are here to commune with nature, bathe in the mountain's hot springs, and stay in traditional inns or mountain cabins, the monks are practicing *mine-iri*—the monkish ritual of traversing sacred mountain paths in prayer. Says walking guide Yohei Totsuka, "Kunisaki is a place of verdant forests dotted with ancient temples linked by mountain paths that have been walked by monks for more than 1,200 years. The modern world barely seems to encroach on life in this rural haven."

JOINING IN: The original trail has virtually vanished, and what remains is a series of penetential climbs and descents. You'll need a guide to show the way. In places, the route is ancient highway with centuries-old stone paving tilted by tree roots, but more often it snakes up soft slopes ankle-deep in wildflowers and bracken, or winds through giant groves of skyrocketing bamboo. The views

MORE: Pilgrim Paths

Nakahechi route: Cross the Kii peninula in the steps of tenth-century pilgrims. tb-kumano.jp
Shikoku temple track: Seldom visited by tourists, the island of Shikoku ("the lost Japan") has 88 temples connected by leafy trails. jnto.go.jp

across the tangled green valleys of the Inland Sea are incredible while the precarious paths along the ridgetops, with sheer drops on either side, are thrilling.

LOCAL FAVORITES: At the area's chief temple, the eighth-century Futogo-ji near the mountain's base, join locals in prayer to the deity Fudo Myo-o to ensure a safe trip.

■ *Essentials:* General information: jnto.go.jp

MATSUMOTO, JAPAN
CHERRY-BLOSSOM TIME

At Matsumoto Castle, named Black Raven for its layers of darkly lacquered wood, crowds gather to see the magnificent displays of pink cherry blossom set against the curving eaves of the black-and-white tower. It is the annual Hanami, or cherry-blossom viewing, a celebration that takes place in public parks across Japan, from as early as January in subtropical Okinawa to as late as May in northwestern Hokkaido.

JOINING IN: Wander through the castle grounds and picnickers may ask you to join them for a drink. Better still, take a groundsheet, a bottle of sake, and snacks—sushi places sell special bento boxes—and invite people to join you. If they say *"Hanaga kirei desu ne?*—Aren't the blossoms beautiful?"—reply *"Mankai desu ne*—In full bloom."

Locals compete for the best spots under the blossoms, and offices send out junior workers in the mornings to find and hold a petal-shaded location for a picnic at the end of the day. "I prefer a quiet hanami," says retired patent attorney Takeo Sugiura. "I meditate on the blossoms. Sometimes there is quiet conversation and a drink of *maccha*—green tea."

MORE: Blossom Viewing

Hanami is hugely popular throughout Japan. Try:
Iwatsuki-koen Park, Saitama City: The grounds around the ruins of Iwatsuki Castle provide a perfect backdrop for the park's 700 cherry trees. jnto.go.jp
Takato Castle Ruin Park, Takato, Nagano: See the blossom of 1,500 kohigan-zakura cherry trees—smaller and redder than the typical blossom. jnto.go.jp

LOCAL KNOWLEDGE: TV weather forecasts include predictions of when blossoms will open across the country. The blossoms' peak lasts only a week, less if interrupted by heavy rain. Blossom viewing is good from mid-March to mid-April in the middle of Japan.

■ *Essentials:* General information: jnto.go.jp; japan-guide.com; Matsumoto Castle (1-4 Marunouchi, tel 81 (0) 263-32-2902)

Cherry blossoms soften the austere outlines of Matsumoto Castle.

OSAKA, JAPAN
GOURMET TO GO

T he Japanese call Osaka the *kuidaore*—eat-til-you-drop—city, as the food here is superbly delicious and the variety boundless. This is evident as soon as you step off the train, for many of the city's stations (and Japan's, for that matter) house *depachika* (department stores) with huge food courts that do a roaring trade with commuters.

LOCAL FAVORITES: A favorite among Osaka *jan* (natives) is Hanshin's depachika in the Umeda district. Located at the final stop on the Hanshin Line, which runs between Kobe and Osaka, it has every raw and prepared food item imaginable. Counter staff reel in customers with free samples and cookery demonstrations and slash prices on perishables at the end of the day.

WHAT TO ORDER: The array of food covers fresh and preserved, sweet and savory, and rare specialties. Highlights include seasonal *tsukemono* vegetable pickles and *umeboshi* plums; sea bream marinated in miso and *kasu* (sake lees); and elegant East-West fusion confectionery, including sesame and lavender macaroons. You might also encounter the curious, jelly-like deep-sea fish, *gokko*, which makes a tasty addition to soups and *nabe* (hotpots). Be sure to try the deep-fried tofu sandwich—sold at many counters—and look out for seasonal specialties. At Setsuban, marking the start of spring, in February, people buy *eho-maki*—lucky direction roll. Says local foodie Michael Baxter: "This sushi roll contains seven lucky ingredients. It is eaten without stopping or talking, and facing the direction of good fortune for the year."

■ *Essentials:* Hanshin Department Store (Umeda Main Building 1-13-13, Umeda, Kita-ku, tel 81 (0) 6 6345-1201)

MORE: Osaka Depachikas

Mitsukoshi Isetan Like Hanshin, this stylish department store is conveniently situated next to Osaka's main station. Its extensive depachika has bargains late in the day. 3-1-3, Umeda, Kita-ku, tel (0) 6 6557 1111

Takashimaya You can spend hours browsing—and sampling—your way through the halls of the depachika of this well-known department store. 1–5 Namba 5-chome, Chuo-ku, tel 81 (0) 6 6631 1101

Hanshin Department Store's underground food court is a gourmet's delight.

Songkran isn't just for kids.

CHIANG MAI, THAILAND
FESTIVE WATER FIGHT

The holiest and most festive of all Thai holidays is Songkran, a New Year celebration based on the lunar cycle that falls in mid-April, the hottest time of year, and lasting three or four days. Thais embark on a journey of ancient rituals: Clean the house, cook a feast, offer food at Buddhist temples, and pay homage to the ancestors. Before, after, and in between, they douse family, friends, neighbors, and strangers with water from buckets, bottles, hoses, and squirt guns.

WHERE TO GO: For a very local take on the festival, head for one of the smaller cities or towns, such as Chiang Mai in northern Thailand. Then look for water—the banks of the Ping River or around the Old Town moat, beginning at Tha Phae Gate. Wander the old brick streets. Even in quiet side roads well-concealed residents may drench you from upper windows with cheery calls of "*Sawasdee pee mai!*—Happy New Year!" Or visit the city's ancient *wats* (temples) full of merrymaking patrons. Say yes when friendly locals offer you sweet treats or sips of beer. "When I'm home for Songkran, I look forward to home-cooked specialties," says Tanyalux Hodson, who grew up in Chiang Mai. "I especially love *kanom tien*—sweet shredded coconut and sticky rice flour wrapped in banana leaf."

JOINING IN: Arm yourself with a water pistol or Uzi and squirt anyone in sight—except monks, the elderly, very young children, and food vendors. Have fun. Wear nothing expensive, delicate, or with dyes that run. And wrap your camera, cell phone, and any other valuables in a plastic bag.

■ *Essentials:* General information: tourismthailand.org

"When I was young, the best place for Songkran was Grandpa's. I'd hide in the truck if things got really wet." —TANYALUX HODSON, CHIANG MAI NATIVE

BANGKOK, THAILAND
TEMPLE OF MASSAGE

Lemongrass, lime, and soothing song: These are the hallmarks of a Thai spa massage. Yet traditional Thai massage is more about working the body than indulging in repose. Practitioners refer not to massage but to "Thai bodywork" to describe the 1,000-year-old practice of twisting, stretching, pressing, and maneuvering intended to heal body and mind and keep the body's energy balanced. "At the end of a long week," says Kunlawan Phitakpol, secretary at the International School Bangkok, "I enjoy the healing power of Thai massage. Although more intense, the focused attention to specific areas of my body relaxes me."

WHERE TO GO: Home to the Temple of the Reclining Buddha, Wat Pho is also Bangkok's center of traditional medicine. Massage plays an integral part: It is deployed to cure various ailments, as well as to promote well-being and relaxation. Choose 30 minutes or an hour on the mat beneath the golden temple spires, where learned masseurs work weary limbs.

MORE: Bangkok Massages

Shopper's massage: Hundreds of massage chairs line Bangkok's Old Town walking market on Sunday evenings. bangkok.com
Traveler's massage at Suvarnabhumi Airport Savvy passengers take the opportunity to have a pre-flight massage before the security gates. A little muscle work soon calms pre-flight nerves. suvarnabhumiairport.com

LOCAL KNOWLEDGE "There's no gain without pain, so if you prefer a more relaxing massage," says Phitakpol, "go for an oil massage instead."

■ *Essentials:* Wat Pho (Sanam Chai Rd., tel 66 (0) 2 225 9595, watpho.com)

Massage has been part of Thai daily life for centuries.

One of Wat Phu's Buddha statues in festival dress

CHAMPASAK, LAOS

WAT PHU FESTIVAL

For three days each February, the 1,000-year-old Khmer temple complex of Wat Phu in southern Laos teems with people making offerings at the temple's shrines and enjoying the processions, competitions, and carnival that are all part of the Wat Phu festival. Inhabitants from local villages and nearby mountain communities meet up, and are joined by families and pilgrims from all over Laos and eastern Thailand. The atmosphere is friendly and joyful, with added exuberance at night when the music gets going and the local *lao-lao* (distilled rice wine) flows.

JOINING IN: Originally a Hindu temple, Wat Phu was later converted for Buddhist worship. Follow the streams of devotees, from young to old, climbing the flights of stone steps up to the main sanctuary. Here, people leave offerings of flowers and incense, pray, or sit in contemplation. Then head for the temple grounds where, in true, easy-going Lao tradition, the crowds engage in many distinctly unspiritual diversions running in parallel with the Buddhist piety. It's

hard not to get swept up in the excitement of the elephant races and kick-boxing competitions. Or you can try your hand at darts or balloon popping. The final evening culminates in a magical candlelight procession under the light of the full moon, the parade wending its way through the lower pavilions, the air heavy with the scent of incense and frangipani.

LOCAL KNOWLEDGE: There are lots of steep, uneven steps leading up to the viewpoints above the main site, but the climb is worth the effort. At the top you'll have a panoramic view, with the cluster of temple ruins and the Mekong River laid out below you against a backdrop of craggy, forested hills.

WHEN TO GO: The Wat Phu Champasak Festival is held around the full moon of the third month of the Buddhist lunar calendar (usually in February).

■ *Essentials*: General information: tourismlaos.org; vatphou champasak.com; reservations recommended

HANOI, VIETNAM
PHO-TASTIC!

Up alleys, down lanes, beside churches, with motor-bikes buzzing by—you'll see locals consuming *pho*, Vietnam's famed rice noodle soup, at stalls and cafés all over Hanoi. A clear, aromatic broth in which fresh rice noodles mingle with meat, onions, and herbs, pho is the national dish and comfort food of the nation. Hanoians slurp it early in the morning and late at night, as a snack, a meal, or a cure for a cold, chill, or hangover.

LOCAL KNOWLEDGE: Hanoi pho houses specialize in either *pho bo* (made with beef stock) or *pho ga* (made with chicken stock). Pho bo sellers add beef brisket or tendon, or thin, raw slivers of beef that are cooked rare under a ladle of hot broth. Pho ga vendors offer heart and other organs on the side. Many locals have pho with a side order of *banh chao quay* (fried bread sticks) for dipping in the broth.

LOCAL FAVORITES: For pho ga, head for 172 Ton Duc Thang, on the outskirts of the city. The chicken is luscious and tender—some say it is the best in the city. For pho bo visit Gia Truyen in the Old City, where you'll have to join the cluster of expectant locals waiting to order. Then carry your scorching hot bowl to your seat. The pho here is made with a rich, dark beef broth. Hanoi-based writer Mark Lowerson describes it as "one of the best [stocks] I've encountered. I could almost feel it doing me good inside."

JOINING IN: There is a ritual to eating pho. Give your chopsticks a cursory clean while you wait for the broth to arrive. When it is set down, customize it with your favorite flavors— a squeeze of lime juice, hot red sauce or a few slices of fresh chili, a drop of garlic-infused vinegar, or just a shake of pepper. Then, using chopsticks and a spoon, lift and drop the noodles repeatedly to mix the flavors well.

■ *Essentials:* 172 Ton Duc Thang (Dong Da, from 6 a.m.); Gia Truyen (49 Bat Dan St., Old Quarter, 7–11 a.m.)

"I feel better when I eat pho—it's the perfect way to start the day."
—VAN CONG TU, HANOI RESIDENT

A chef at Gia Truyen prepares a bowl of pho.

KL takes street food to a new level at Jalan Alor Night Market.

KUALA LUMPUR, MALAYSIA
STREET EATS

Three major food cultures collide in Kuala Lumpur—indigenous Malay cuisine and the culinary arts of China and India, which arrived with 19th-century immigrants. Over 200 years, these cultures have blended to produce dishes unique to Malaysia. The best places to sample them are the hawker stalls and food courts around central KL. Signature dishes include *laksa* (spicy noodle soup), *ikan bakar* (grilled fish), and *satay* (barbecued meat on sticks).

WHERE TO GO: Bazaar Baru Chow Kit is the city's main vegetable and meat market, and its hawker stalls are among KL's best. "If I had to choose one thing to eat it will have to be *char koay teow*, a spicy stir-fried flat rice noodle with prawns, cockles, and bean sprouts. The very thought of it gets me drooling!" says salesman Steve Lam.

Join locals at the Jalan Alor Night Market in old Chinatown. In Little India, the Jalan Masjid India stalls offer *roti prata* (bread) and curries. Those who prefer air-conditioning should head for the Signatures Food Court at KLCC Mall.

■ *Essentials:* General information: tourism.gov.my; Bazaar Baru Chow Kit (Jalan Tuanku Abdul Rahman); Jalan Alor (Bukit Bintang, open Sat.); Jalan Masjid India (Little India); Signatures Food Court (2nd Floor, Suria KLCC Shopping Center, Jalan Ampang, tel 60 (0) 3-2382 2828)

DIGGING DEEPER

Nose-tingling aromas beckon from the small, open-air food courts that dot the streets. Stop for a laksa, a dish of spicy curry, or a bowl of *bee hoon*, Malaysia's most comforting noodle dish. Finish with a strong, sweet iced coffee for an instant pick-me-up.

KUALA LUMPUR, MALAYSIA
HAPPY FEET

When feet are tired from shopping in the malls and kiosks along KL's busiest shopping street, Jalan Bukit Bintang, local Malaysians are inclined to push on a little farther past the hawker stalls of Jalan Imbi to the quiet oasis of Reborn foot spa. The sounds of the traffic fade as soon as the door opens, and crisp air-conditioning, the sound of running water, and gentle flute music welcome the weary.

JOINING IN: A great way to begin a treatment is with a 20-minute fish spa. Take a seat on a cushioned bench and plunge your feet into the pond of tiny gray gara rufa fish. You're likely to hear squeals of amusement from your neighbors as the fish nibble away at dead skin.

WHAT TO EXPECT: After sinking into an easy chair, reflexology clients will first have their feet washed in warm water. Then comes the massage. "The masseuses at Reborn apply just the right amount of pressure and do not cause pain, as is a fear of many first-timers," says Cindy Childress, a writer living in Kuala Lumpur. "Afterward it's nice to visit the Woods Bio Marché next door to complement freshly aligned feet with a well-balanced Malaysian dish."

MORE: Relaxing Treatments

Swasana Spa, Impiana KLCC, KL: Many indulgent therapies are on offer at this award-winning spa. impiana.com

The Spa, Mandarin Oriental, KL: Locals relax with one of the spa's signature foot rituals. mandarinoriental.com

Vila Manja, KL: The masseuses here are famed among Kuala Lumpur's residents for their hot stone therapy and full body massage. vilamanja.com

WHAT TO WEAR: Wear loose clothes so you can fully enjoy the calf massage. Feel free to drop by—no appointment is necessary.

■ *Essentials:* Reborn (No. 18 Jalan Bukit Bintang, tel 60 (0) 3-2144 1288, reborn.com.my); Woods Bio Marché (Ground Fl., Wisma Bukit Bintang, Jalan Bukit Bintang, tel 60 (0) 3-2143 1636, healthyfoodmalaysia.com)

Feet are pampered at one of KL's many spas.

SINGAPORE

A GARDEN TO DELIGHT THE SENSES

Paved walkways meander through lush palms, towering heritage trees, and a misty rain forest dotted with crystalline lakes and rocky waterfalls. Singapore's locals—joggers, families, school groups, inspiration-seeking gardeners—come to this peaceful place daily, while evening concerts at the Symphony Stage draw crowds of picnickers. "The Botanical Gardens are a cool, green getaway from the heat of the city," enthuses Singapore native Janice Chua. "When I come, I drop by the Halia Restaurant for a refreshing cup of ginger tea."

WHERE TO GO: The Orchid Garden is a riot of color, showcasing 1,000 species and 2,000 hybrids. Singapore's national flower, Vanda Miss Joaquim, shades from pink blush to fuchsia and is treasured for its year-round blooms. A celebrities' corner features the Vanda William Catherine,

a purple-spotted, white–petaled hybrid named after the U.K.'s Prince William and his wife, who visited the gardens in 2012. A rare and award-winning collection of fragrant orchids, including a chocolate-scented variety, is on display at the Mist House. The Ginger Garden is home to 250 ornamental, edible, and scarce species, including the flashy Torch Ginger, believed to have medicinal benefits.

LOCAL KNOWLEDGE: A naturalist at heart, Singapore's founding father, Sir Stamford Raffles, planted a botanical garden for his new city. His vision languished after his death, but was restored in 1859 when a new 180-acre (73 ha) oasis was planted at its present location.

■ *Essentials:* Botanical Gardens (1 Cluny Rd., tel 65 (0) 6471 7138, sbg.org.sg); Halia Restaurant (tel 65 (0) 8444 1148; thehalia.com)

Concert-goers at the Garden's Symphony Stage

Grab a bay-side seat at Singapore's Esplanade outdoor theater.

PERFORMANCES UNDER THE STARS

With nature as a backdrop, open-air theaters are the perfect place to enjoy a show.

■ **Esplanade Outdoor Theatre, Singapore**
Marina Bay provides a stunning backdrop for performances under the sail-like roof. Locals come to see music, dance, and theater in this 450-seat venue as the city's lights twinkle on the water.
esplanade.com

■ **Hollywood Bowl, Los Angeles, CA**
The largest natural amphitheater in the U.S. lies in a hollow among hills and the concrete shell arch provides excellent acoustics. Join locals for a pre-concert picnic before moving to the Bowl to listen to jazz, pop, or classical music.
hollywoodbowl.com

■ **Tuacahn Amphitheater, Ivins, UT**
The 1,500-foot (455 m) red sandstone box canyon gives this non-profit arts venue dedicated to the American musical tradition the wow factor. The "Broadway in the Desert" summer season stretches into the fall, while a Live Nativity runs from Thanksgiving until Christmas.
tuacahn.org

■ **Filene Center, Fairfax County, VA**
From May to September, seating spills onto the lawn as residents from nearby Washington, D.C., enjoy a varied program of conerts and film. At the open-air Children's Theater in the Woods, morning performances attract area kids Tuesday through Saturday, late June to mid-August.
wolftrap.org

■ **Impression Lijiang, Lijiang, China**
It's hard to know which is more impressive: the snowcapped Jade Dragon Snow Mountain in the background or the 500 performers on stage. Film director Zhang Yimou, who staged the opening and closing ceremonies at the 2008 Beijing Olympics, created this spectacle celebrating the traditional music and dance of China's ethnic people.
seeyunnan.net

■ **Minack Theatre, Cornwall, U.K.**
The Atlantic views are the distraction here. Carved out of a granite cliff, this 20th-century amphitheater seems ageless. Classic plays, light operas, musicals, and children's shows are staged from May to September.
minack.com

■ **Jardins do Palácio de Cristal, Porto, Portugal**
The Crystal Palace and gardens have been here since 1862. Join Porto's residents at concerts in the open-air Concha Acústica, the delightful original bandstand.
gooporto.com

■ **Arena, Verona, Italy**
The fine acoustics in this well-preserved, 15,000-seat Roman amphitheater from A.D. 30 make this a perfect venue for opera. Verdi's *Aïda* was the first opera staged here, in 1913, and remains popular today.
arena.it

■ **Teatro Greco, Syracusa, Italy**
A perfect setting for classical drama, this 2,500-year-old Greek amphitheater carved out of the rock is Sicily's largest. Today it accommodates only half the 15,000 crowd it could once hold. The annual five-week Greek theater festival season runs from mid-May. Shows start at sunset.
indafondazione.org

DRAMA IN JAVA

For a few weeks each summer, audiences take their seats around an open-air stage at Prambanan Temple in southern Java to watch a distinctly local version of the ancient Hindu epic, *Ramayana*, told through the medium of traditional Indonesian dance accompanied by a 200-strong gamelan orchestra. Against the backdrop of the 1,000-year-old temple ruins, richly costumed warriors, princesses, demons, and monkey armies perform the story of the noble king, Rama, who saves his wife Sita from the clutches of an evil demon.

Although now predominantly Muslim, Java was ruled by Hindu kingdoms from the 8th to 15th centuries. The *Ramayana,* a version of which also appears in a series of carved panels on the temple walls, remains an important part of local Javanese culture.

WHAT TO EXPECT: There is no dialogue. Slow-motion dance and mime are at the heart of the show, accompanied by the drums, gongs, bells, and bamboo xylophones of the orchestra. Local connoisseurs in the audience call out to show their appreciation of performers' expressive mime and dance movements.

MORE: Versions of Ramayana

Ramakien, Thailand: Famously depicted in murals at Bangkok's Wat Phra Kaeo (Temple of the Emerald Buddha), the Thai version dates from the 13th century.
Ramlila, India: An adaptation of the story is performed during the north-Indian festival of Dussehra, the audience joining in the singing and narration. In Ramnagar, on the Ganges River, the action is set across the town.

WHEN TO GO: Open-air performances of the *Ramayana* take place during the dry season (May–October) on and around the full moon. The story unfolds over four nights. Many people attend just one performance, but enthusiasts follow the entire drama for four nights.

■ *Essentials:* Ramayana Open Air Theatre (Prambanan Temple, tel 62 (0) 274 496 402, borobudurpark.com)

Dancers in traditional costumes act out the *Ramayana.*

A *gunungan* in procession through Yogyakarta

YOGYAKARTA, INDONESIA
HOLY MUSIC

Indonesia's most flamboyant festival is Sekaten, a week-long celebration staged to coincide with the Prophet Mohammed's birthday, that blends solemn religious rites, sultanic pomp and circumstance, and a carnival-like atmosphere of food stalls, street performers, and thrill rides. The drama begins at 11 p.m. with a parade of sacred gamelan, the vintage instruments conveyed on bamboo poles from Yogyakarta Palace (the Kraton) to a pavilion near the Grand Mosque. There they will be played for seven days and seven nights by the royal orchestra, only stopping for prayer. On the final day, food offerings of *gunungan* (decorated rice "mountains") are delivered to the mosque. Shaped like giant beehives, they represent the ancient Javanese tree of life.

JOINING IN: Mingle with the crowds in Alun Alun Utara (North Square) waiting for the gunungan to be broken up and distributed after they have been blessed at the mosque. Pieces are much prized by the locals, who believe they bring prosperity and good health.

WHEN TO GO: Sekaten is celebrated from the fifth to the twelfth days of the month of Mulud in the Javanese calendar, which is determined by the lunar cycle. Until 2023, Sekaten will fall between October and January.

■ *Essentials:* General information: indonesia-tourism.com, yogyes.com; Yogyakarta Palace (Jl. Rotowijayan 1, tel 62 (0) 274 373 721); Grand Mosque (North Square)

"People flock to listen to the sacred gamelan because they believe that hearing them will bring good luck and health." —PING HUA, LOCAL WRITER

JAKARTA, INDONESIA
BRIDAL BATTLE

A mock wedding procession, martial arts displays, giant puppets, and hundreds of food stalls: Of all Indonesia's colorful festivals, Palang Pintu, which celebrates the city's Betawi culture, is one of the most popular with the locals. *Palang pintu* means "gate" or "door," and the two-day festival begins with a parade based on a traditional Betawi wedding procession, during which the groom and his supporters had to win a series of contests at the door of the bride's house before he could enter (see p. 269). It continues with a celebration of Betawian culinary delights, puppet theater, and music.

WHERE TO GO: The festival takes place on Kemang Raya Street, between Kober traffic lights and the Habibie Center, an upmarket area of art galleries, craft shops, boutiques, and restaurants popular with Jakartans. The street is closed to traffic for the festival.

WHAT TO EXPECT: Jakartans flock to the festival, so arrive early to get a good view of the parade. Don't be surprised when the exchange of verses between the bride's and groom's supporters grows noisy and heated. People in the crowd around you will join in and egg them on, but it's just a show. The pretend altercation is followed by *pencak silat*—an Indonesian martial arts contest—in the street.

JOINING IN: Everyone watches the parade, which includes several *ondel-ondel*, brightly colored, 8-foot-tall (2.5 m) puppets with tinsel headdresses and painted wooden face masks—red for males and white for females. Then they gather round the various stages to watch *lenong* (folk theater), *tari topeng* (a dramatic masked dance with ornate costumes), and *wayang golek* (Indonesian shadow puppet theater); or enjoy the fashion shows and pop music performances.

WHAT TO EAT: The 500 or so closely packed food stalls are laid out with local Betawi favorites. Try *kerak telor* (spicy omelet with a topping of shrimp served with fried shredded coconut), *dodol Betawi* (a sweet cake made of rice, brown sugar, coconut milk, and durian that must be cooked on a wood stove and stirred for eight hours), and *tape uli* (fermented rice and rice cake), and wash it all down with *bir pletok* (a ginger and cinnamon drink).

■ *Essentials:* General information: jakarta-tourism.go.id

An ondel-ondel puppet takes part in a procession.

I ♥ My City

Didi Kasim
*Editor, NG Traveler,
Indonesia*

The traditional Betawian wedding began with the bridegroom's procession to the bride's house. The men beat tambourines and sang hymns and the women carried gifts, including crocodile breads. At the bride's house, the Palang Pintu ritual began. Before the bridegroom was granted permission to meet the bride, the two parties were required to engage in a mock duel. First, a fighter for each side recited poetry, their voices getting louder with each verse. "Here, I give you this!" exclaimed one fighter, sending the other sprawling. "Don't make me bristle, or I'll chop you up like a pineapple!" shouted the other. The duel ended in victory for the bridegroom—as always. After this, the men in the bridegroom's party entered the house.

THE ULTIMATE DANCE-OFF

The atmosphere is electric, the chanting hypnotic, the colors vibrant. This is the Goroka sing-sing, one of the world's largest and most flamboyant festivals of indigenous music and dance. The event, which takes place in the Eastern Highlands town of Goroka, started as a way to encourage local hill tribes to stop shrinking their neighbor's heads and now attracts people from all over Papua New Guinea. "This explosion of color and sound demonstrates the warmth of the local people and their unique sense of humor," explains PNG resident, Carol Mills, who goes every year.

Upward of 100 tribes, each with its own songs, dances, and costumes, perform in different parts of the show-ground. The warriors, and in a few cases their wives and children, paint their faces in vivid colors, wear bones in their noses, or sport face masks—anything to look frightening to rival tribes. And almost all adorn themselves with the exquisite feathers of birds of paradise.

JOINING IN: Mingle with the tribes as they edge slowly backward and forward, gyrate on the spot, or run in circles. Some tribes show extraordinary precision while others

Asaro Mudmen

Twelve miles (19 km) northwest of Goroka lies the village of the **Asaro Mudmen,** who wear elaborate masks of dried mud in memory of their ancestors. Here you can watch tribal dances, try on the masks, and join a local family for a *mumu,* a feast of pork or chicken slow-cooked with yams and coconut. asaromudmen.blogspot.com

meander among themselves until the chant becomes infectious and the entire tribe is moving almost as one. Some participants brandish weapons, while others beat out rhythms on hollow logs.

WHERE TO GO: The three-day Goroka Show takes place in mid-September in Independence Park, opposite Goroka's main market.

■ *Essentials:* gorokashow.com

Huli tribesmen in traditional costume at the Goroka Show

The Beach Club bar at the Cott

PERTH, AUSTRALIA
SUNDAY SESSIONS

Hanging out with the locals in Perth couldn't be easier: Just head for the pub on a Sunday afternoon. The atmosphere is casual, many pubs have fantastic sea views, and the sun goes down over the sea to a chorus of aahs. What a way to end the weekend.

LOCAL KNOWLEDGE: Until a few years ago, shops weren't open on Sundays, making pubs and restaurants the only places to go out. Sundays are so busy that some places impose a 10 percent surcharge on food and drink.

WHERE TO GO: Gold miner and sixth-generation Perth native Brett Stralow recommends "the Cottesloe Beach Hotel and the Ocean Beach Hotel. Both are Perth institutions." At the Cott, hang out at the Beach Club bar; at the O.B.H. sit in the saloon bar and gaze out at the water. Other hot spots are the stylish riverside eatery Left Bank and, in Fremantle,

Little Creatures Brewery, based in a building that began life as a crocodile farm. Stralow says, "Go out and sit in the beer garden." You may even see a dolphin or two.

WHAT TO ORDER: Seafood: It's all fresh off the boat. Order dhufish, a super-size perch, or Western Rock Lobster, a type of crayfish. A very big crayfish. Says botanist Cassie Adam, "Half a tail is enough. They're huge." These tasty beasts can weigh in at 6 pounds (2.5 kg).

■ *Essentials:* Cottesloe Beach Hotel (104 Marine Pde., Cottesloe, tel 61 (0) 8 9383 1100, cottesloebeachhotel.com.au); Ocean Beach Hotel (140 Marine Pde., Cottesloe, tel 61 (0) 8 9384 2555, obh.com.au); Left Bank (15 Riverside Rd., E. Fremantle, 61 (0) 8 9319 1136, leftbank.com.au); Little Creatures Brewery (40 Mews Rd., Fremantle, 61 (0) 8 9430 5555, littlecreatures.com.au)

DIGGING DEEPER

Mornings are the best time to enjoy a swim, beachcomb, or sunbathe, as on most afternoons a stiff southwesterly breeze known as the Fremantle Doctor picks up, sending stinging grains of sand flying. Picturesque Cottesloe and dog-friendly Mosman are two of the best beaches.

HOBART, AUSTRALIA
STREET SHOPPING

Sandwiched between a row of old sandstone warehouses and a park facing the old port, Hobart's Salamanca Place hosts more than 300 stalls selling handmade clothes and hats, quirky jewelry and woodcraft, and local gourmet foods—all offering great value. Go early and prepare to elbow your way around—Hobartians love a bargain and turn up in droves.

WHAT TO BUY: Tasmanian timbers such as the creamy-yellow Huon pine and Blackheart Sassafras make great chopping boards, salad servers, and fruit bowls. Simon's Chopping Boards sells beautifully finished Tasmanian timber boards. Needlecraft is popular locally; look for handmade children's clothes and toys. Or hunt out unusual jewelry or robot toys made from upcycled plastics, buttons, and other non-techy materials. Fork and Spoon Jewellery sells antique teaspoon rings, fork bangles, and other eccentric adornments.

LOCAL FAVORITES: Tasmanians love to eat and drink well, as the stalls selling seasonal fruit and organic vegetables, fresh bread, local cheeses, and handmade chocolates attest. "I live about 50 km [30 miles] south of Hobart, and when I get up to town on a Saturday morning I like to check out the markets in Salamanca Place," says retired IT professional William Morris. "The main draw for me is the locally grown produce, especially the dedicated market for Asian vegetables." Or why not try some local cheeses from Bruny Island Cheese Co. or Grandvewe Cheeses washed down with a fresh, clean white wine from a Tasmanian vineyard.

■ *Essentials:* Salamanca Market (Salamanca Place, tel 61 (0) 3 6238 2711, salamanca.com.au, open Sat. until 3 p.m.)

Around the Market

Shops, galleries, and cafés border the market. They are open most days of the week. **The Salamanca Arts Building** (*77 Salamanca Pl., 61 (0) 3 6223 7228, closed Sun.*) houses Gallery 77, which sells turned wooden bowls and platters. The Ringrove Collection in the same building sells "wearable art"—knitwear made from local wool.

Salamanca Market sells food and arts and crafts from all over Tasmania.

A PASSION FOR COFFEE

Melburnians are coffee-mad. Whether you're into latte, double shot espresso, machiatto, cappucino or *affogato* (iced, or hot with a dollop of ice cream), you can grab a takeaway or sip in style for an hour or two at dozens of exceptional coffee shops.

LOCAL FAVORITES: Baker D. Chirico on St. Kilda's Fitzroy Street can be spotted by the lines outside. Says graphic designer Lee Riches, "Before work I usually order their Escargot (Danish whirl), washed down with a long black. This strong and nicely balanced coffee never fails to satisfy and kick-start the day." St. Kilda's Miss Jackson is as popular with Melburnians as the coffee is great—they make espresso on a gleaming La Marzocco machine using an Allpress Arabica blend. Seven Seeds is also authentic Melbourne. It roasts a wide range of beans, including imports from Kenya, Costa Rica, and Honduras. On Wednesdays at 9 a.m. and Saturdays at 10 a.m. they host "cupping" (tasting) sessions, where their knowledgeable staff take you through the taste and aroma of each coffee. Part of the State Library and named for the first chief librarian, Augustus Tulk, Mr. Tulk is a busy licensed

A Melbourne Favorite

A Melburnian institution, **Brunetti's** has swelled in size since it first opened its doors in 1974. Branches include 214 Flinders Lane in the CBD, but the newest is back in its original spot on Lygon St., Carlton. Classic panini and focaccia are recommended, or just munch on a cake to complement the excellent coffee. brunetti.com.au

café with tables inside and out—another great place that Melburnians love for coffee or an after-work drink.

■ *Essentials:* Baker D. Chirico (149 Fitzroy St., St. Kilda, tel 61 (3) 9534 377, bakerdchirico.com.au); Miss Jackson (2/19 Grey St., St. Kilda, enter from Jackson St., tel 61 (0) 3 9534 8415, closed Mon.); Seven Seeds (114 Berkeley St., Carlton, tel 61 (0) 3 9347 8664); Mr. Tulk (328 Swanston St., tel 61 (0) 3 8660 5700, closed Sun.)

Take a break from the Fitzroy Street crowd with coffee at Miss Jackson.

The stalls at Hokitika's wild food festival draw a crowd.

NEW ZEALAND
MAORI FOOD FESTS

Maoris celebrate their unique cuisine and their strong sense of community with a series of *kai* (food) festivals around the year, often held in spectacular locations. "Maoris love a feast," says retired schoolteacher Vivienne Paterson. "Cooking is a long, slow process. A pit [*hangi*] is dug, and a fire is lit in it and left for a few hours until only embers remain. Food wrapped in leaves is put into the pit and covered with soil, and the food cooks *slowly* for several hours."

WHAT TO EAT: On festival days, steaming hangi ovens produce huge quantities of game meat—tasty wild pork, which has rich, slightly coarse flesh—and vegetables such as *kumara* (orange sweet potato), and *pikopiko* (green fern fronds) infused with pungent *kawakawa* (bush basil) and *horopito* (bush pepper). If you can eat it, the Maori will make a fritter of it: Mussel fritters, sea snail (*paua*) fritters, and freshly caught whitebait (*inanga*) fritters. Buy from village stalls serving food in small flax baskets and eat at the big tables or in the picnic areas.

LOCAL FAVORITES: The Kãwhia Kai food festival on the North Island takes place on Omiti reserve and coincides with Waitangi Day, held in February. Tauranga Moana in the North Island's Bay of Plenty mainly celebrates seafood, but you can enjoy meat as well. At the Hokitika Food Festival on the South Island's West Coast you can try local delicacies such as *huhu* beetle grubs.

■ *Essentials:* Kãwhia Kai Festival (Omiti Park Reserve); Tauranga Moana Festival (Dive Cres., Taurang); Hokitika Food Festival (tel 64 3 756 9049)

....

"The paua fritters are to die for, but the huhu bugs require courage."
—JANE PATERSON, NEW ZEALAND NATIVE

NEW ZEALAND
AIMING FOR THE STARS

In the boiling heat of an Antipodean summer, New Year revelry in January can feel out of place. Instead, tune in to the Maori way of doing things and celebrate New Year in June. With the harvest gathered in and the light returning, Maori tribes come together to celebrate their culture with feasting, singing, and storytelling. Matariki, as the roughly month-long festival is known, is named for a constellation of stars (also known as the Pleiades or Seven Sisters) that rises above the horizon at that time of year. Says Te Rangi Huata, who organizes events in Hawkes Bay, "Matariki is becoming a little like Thanksgiving, except it's a celebration of the Maori culture here in Aotearoa [New Zealand]." Cities and local communities organize various activities, including concerts, performances, storytelling, art exhibitions, and food fairs.

WHEN TO GO: Some Maori tribes say Matariki begins as soon as the constellation appears above the horizon; others celebrate at the following full moon or new moon. Events tend to be held through June and July, focusing around the winter solstice on June 21.

WHERE TO GO: Bastion Point above Waitemata Harbour near Auckland, holds a popular kite-flying event. Hastings, a town on Hawkes Bay launches its Matariki celebrations with a large family event that includes music, a dance contest, and fireworks.

LOCAL KNOWLEDGE: Maori associate Matariki with the god Tāwhirimātea. The legend goes that Tāwhirimātea became angry when his brothers separated Ranginui, the sky father, from Papatūānuku, the earth mother. In his rage Tāwhirimātea ripped out his eyes, throwing them into the sky (Matariki means "eyes of God"). Hot-air balloons, kites, and, more recently, fireworks recall this stormy episode.

■ *Essentials:* matarikifestival.org.nz; eventfinder.co.nz

A Good View of Matariki

For the best views of the Matariki constellation, you can go stargazing at the Mount John Observatory above **Lake Tekapo.** The region has been declared a gold level International Dark Sky reserve due to the clarity of the night sky and minimal light pollution. earthandskynz.com

Enthusiasts launch giant kites at Bastion Point near Auckland as part of the city's Matariki celebrations.

MATARIKI 2010

Locals relax in the pools of thermal water on Hot Water Beach.

COROMANDEL PENINSULA, NEW ZEALAND
HOT WATER BEACH

The chance to luxuriate in a naturally heated pool draws people to a quiet, white-sand beach on the eastern shores of New Zealand's rugged Coromandel Peninsula. As the tide recedes, one corner of Hot Water Beach is soon pockmarked with dozens of shallow depressions that well up with the thermal waters from volcanic underground springs. People scoop out sand with spades and buckets in search of the optimal spot—neither too hot nor too cold. Once found, there's nothing to do but stretch out and allow the warm water to soothe and caress until the rising tide reclaims the beach, wiping away all traces of the soaking pools.

WHEN TO GO: Hot pools can be dug out of the sand for two hours on either side of low tide. Arrive early to stake out a place as the beach can get crowded, especially in summer. "The experience is just magical when low tide is at twilight," confides Auckland resident Emily Bell. "As the sun sets and the air cools, the warm water feels so good. And, by then, most people have gone home. I love the peace and quiet."

LOCAL KNOWLEDGE: Only a small area between the rocks on the southern end of the beach is thermally heated. Look for escaping steam or poke your toes in the sand until you hit a warm spot—if using your toes, do so gingerly as the sand can be hot enough to burn—and dig there. Fellow enthusiasts often chip in with advice on which spots are too hot. Or save yourself the trouble of digging and colonize an abandoned pool.

A beachside shop rents out spades, or ask to share with your neighbors on the beach. You can also pause for a drink or an ice cream at the beachside café.

■ *Essentials:* Hot Water Beach (tel 64 (0) 7866 5555, whitianga .co.nz)

> *"There's a great community spirit because everyone has just one thing on their minds—a nice, hot soak."*
> —AUCKLAND-BASED ACTOR ERYN WILSON

INDEX

ACKNOWLEDGMENTS

Contributors
Tony Allan, Ian Armitage, Jackie Attwood-Dupont, Tracy Bach, Lynn Baiori, Derek & Margaret Barton, Michael Baxter, Katie Belliel, Uri Blau, Kasia Boni, Michael Bright, Julie Brooke, Marolyn Charpentier, Cindy Childress, Bobby Clennell, Karen Coates, Celia Coyne, Sarah Deacon, Helen Douglas-Cooper, Amy Fabris-Shi, Pip Farquharson, Naresh Fernandes, Kay Fernandez, Jacob Field, Steve Fowler, Ellen Galford, Stuart Garlick, Raluca Gavris, Sari Gilbert, Art Gimbel, Conner Gorry, Jeremy Gray, Jessica Gross, Lisa Halvorsen, Solange Hando, Jeanne Horak, Karen Hursh Graber, Gul Irepoglu, Ben Jacobson, Tim Jepson, Georgette Jupe, Sam Kennedy, Kathleen Landis, Hannah Lauterback, Tom Le Bas, Jessica Lee, Sophie Lewisohn, Mark Lowerson, Glen Martin, Antony Mason, David Mendonca, Barbara A. Noe, Peter Neville-Hadley, David Nikel, Ian Robertson, Robert Sackville West, Barb Sanford, Eric Schwartz, George Semler, Michael Sommers, Barbara Somogyiova, Peter Turner, Daisuke Utagawa, Richard Whitaker, April White, Roger Williams, Joby Williams, Joe Yogerst

Toucan Books would like to thank:
Cassie Adam, the Blitz family, Susan Clarke, Linda Cognazzo and all at Rodmell Press, William Dupont and Katie Kanzler, Omri Epstein and family, Maya Feile Tomes, Marc Funde, Lori Lee, Jenny Lewisohn, Don & Vivienne Paterson, Brett Stralow, www.TLV.style.com, www.toqueandcanoe.com

Picture Credits
L = left; R = right; T = top and B = bottom.

2-3 puwanai/Shutterstock.com; 4 Franco Cogoli/SIME/4Corners Images; 6 Giovanni Simeone/SIME/4Corners Images; 8-9 Jan Greune/LOOK/Getty Images; 10-11 Audrey McAvoy/AP/Press Association Images; 12 Americanspirit/Dreamstime.com; 13 Witold Skrypczak/Lonely Planet Images/Getty Images; 14 Chris Carlsson; 15 Ron Niebrugge/Alamy; 16 Ethan Miller/Getty Images; 17 Don Ryan/AP Photo/Press Association Images; 18 Lee O'Dell/Shutterstock.com; 19 Cory Ryan Photography; 20-21 William Siegal Gallery; 22 KAZMAT/Shutterstock.com; 23 Charlie Vergos' Rendezvous; 24 David Grunfeld/McClatchy-Tribune/Getty Images; 25 Stephen Morton/AP Photos/Press Association Images; 26-27 Miami-Dade County Parks, Recreation and Open Spaces; 28 Taylor Mathis; 29 Sam Greenwood/Getty Images; 30 The Village Grille, Lauderdale-By-The-Sea; 31 West Virginia Tourism; 32 Richard Ellis/age fotostock/SuperStock; 33 Bernie Epstein/Alamy; 34-35 Donald P.Sanford; 36 John Tlumacki/The Boston Globe/Getty Images; 37 MAC Photos/Alamy; 38-39 Lijuan Guo/Shutterstock.com; 40 National Capital Commission; 41 Devonian Gardens; 42-43

WHERE THE LOCALS GO

Published by the National Geographic Society
John M. Fahey, *Chairman of the Board and Chief Executive Officer*
Declan Moore, *Executive Vice President; President, Publishing and Travel*
Melina Gerosa Bellows, *Executive Vice President; Chief Creative Officer, Books, Kids, and Family*
Lynn Cutter, *Executive Vice President, Travel*
Keith Bellows, *Senior Vice President and Editor in Chief, National Geographic Travel Media*

PREPARED BY THE BOOK DIVISION
Hector Sierra, *Senior Vice President and General Manager*
Janet Goldstein, *Senior Vice President and Editorial Director*
Jonathan Halling, *Design Director, Books and Children's Publishing*
Jerry Sealy, *Creative Director, Travel Editorial*
Marianne R. Koszorus, *Design Director, Books*
Barbara A. Noe, *Senior Editor, National Geographic Travel Books*
R. Gary Colbert, *Production Director*
Jennifer A. Thornton, *Director of Managing Editorial*
Susan S. Blair, *Director of Photography*
Meredith C. Wilcox, *Director, Administration and Rights Clearance*

STAFF FOR THIS BOOK
Larry Porges, *Editor*
Elisa Gibson, *Art Director*
Marshall Kiker, *Associate Managing Editor*
Judith Klein, *Production Editor*
Mike Horenstien, *Production Manager*
Katie Olsen, *Production Design Assistant*

PRODUCTION SERVICES
Phillip L. Schlosser, *Senior Vice President*
Chris Brown, *Vice President, NG Book Manufacturing*
George Bounelis, *Vice President, Production Services*
Nicole Elliott, *Manager*
Rachel Faulise, *Manager*
Robert L. Barr, *Manager*

CREATED BY TOUCAN BOOKS LTD
Ellen Dupont, *Editorial Director*
Helen Douglas-Cooper, *Managing Editor*
Dorothy Stannard, *Senior Editor*
John Andrews, Natasha Kahn, *Editors*
Sophie Lewisohn, *Editorial Assistant*
Thomas Keenes, *Designer*
Christine Vincent, *Picture Manager*
Sharon Southren, *Picture Researcher*
Rosalind Munro, *Proofreader*
Marie Lorimer, *Indexer*

The information in this book has been carefully checked and to the best of our knowledge is accurate. However, details are subject to change, and the National Geographic Society cannot be responsible for such changes, or for errors or omissions. Assessments of sites, hotels, and restaurants are based on the author's subjective opinions, which do not necessarily reflect the publisher's opinion.

The National Geographic Society is one of the world's largest nonprofit scientific and educational organizations. Founded in 1888 to "increase and diffuse geographic knowledge," the member-supported Society works to inspire people to care about the planet. Through its online community, members can get closer to explorers and photographers, connect with other members around the world, and help make a difference. National Geographi reflects the world through its magazines, television programs, films, music and radio, books, DVDs, maps, exhibitions, live events, school publishing programs, interactive media, and merchandise. *National Geographic* magazine, the Society's official journal, published in English and 38 local-language editions, is read by more than 60 million people each month. The National Geographic Channel reaches 440 million households in 171 countries in 38 languages. National Geographic Digital Media receives more than 25 million visitors a month. National Geographic has funded more than 10,000 scientific research, conservation, and exploration projects and supports an education program promoting geography literacy. For more information, visit www.nationalgeographic.com.

For more information, please call 1-800-NGS LINE (647-5463) or write to the following address:

National Geographic Society
1145 17th Street N.W.
Washington, D.C. 20036-4688 U.S.A.

For information about special discounts for bulk purchases, please contact National Geographic Books Special Sales: ngspecsales@ngs.org

For rights or permissions inquiries, please contact National Geographic Books Subsidiary Rights: ngbookrights@ngs.org

ISBN: 978-1-4262-1194-2

Printed in Hong Kong

13/THK/1

FIND YOURSELF THERE

Travel around the world with National Geographic
and discover more than you ever imagined.

Spanning the globe with
100 top places to go each
season, National Geographic's
expert travel writers and photographers invite you to experience the world's most tempting
locales with this lush gift book.

Filled with cool things to do,
fun facts, wacky roadside attractions, and games, all on easy-to-
read road maps, this book is sure to
keep kids engaged for hours.

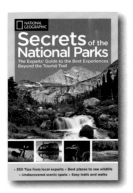

Written in collaboration with
park rangers, superintendents,
and frequent park visitors, this
guide provides the inspiration
and information you need to
plan your visit beyond the well-
trodden, touristy spots in 32
great national parks.

THE COMPLETE TRAVEL EXPERIENCE

NATIONAL GEOGRAPHIC TRAVEL

EXPEDITIONS

MAGAZINE

for iPhone®,
iPod touch®,
and iPad®

APPS

Kids who learn to travel will travel
to learn. *National Geographic
Traveler* Editor Keith Bellows sends
you and your children globetrotting
for life-changing vacations that will
expand their horizons and shape
their perspectives.

Like us on Facebook.com: Nat Geo Books

Follow us on Twitter.com: @NatGeoBooks

AVAILABLE WHEREVER BOOKS ARE SOLD
nationalgeographic.com/books